Choosing to Die

In this book, C. G. Prado addresses the difficult question of when and whether it is rational to end one's life in order to escape devastating terminal illness. He specifically considers this question in light of the impact of multiculturalism on perceptions and judgments about what is right and wrong, permissible and impermissible. Prado introduces the idea of a "coincidental culture" to clarify the variety of values and commitments that influence decisions. He also introduces the idea of a "proxy premise" to deal with reasoning issues that are raised by intractably held beliefs.

Primarily intended for medical ethicists, this book will be of interest to anyone concerned with the ability of modern medicine to keep people alive, thereby forcing people to choose between living and dying. In addition, Prado calls upon medical ethicists and practitioners to appreciate the value of a theoretical basis for their work.

C. G. Prado is Emeritus Professor of Philosophy at Queen's University in Canada. He has published many books, most recently *Searle and Foucault on Truth* and *A House Divided: Comparing Analytic and Continental Philosophy*.

Choosing to Die

Elective Death and Multiculturalism

C. G. PRADO

Emeritus, Queen's University

CAMBRIDGE
UNIVERSITY PRESS

CAMBRIDGE UNIVERSITY PRESS
Cambridge, New York, Melbourne, Madrid, Cape Town, Singapore, São Paulo, Delhi

Cambridge University Press
32 Avenue of the Americas, New York, NY 10013-2473, USA

www.cambridge.org
Information on this title: www.cambridge.org/9780521697583

First published 2008

Printed in the United States of America

A catalog record for this publication is available from the British Library.

Library of Congress Cataloging in Publication Data
Prado, C. G.
Choosing to die : elective death and multiculturalism / C. G. Prado.
p. ; cm.
Includes bibliographical references and index.
ISBN 978-0-521-87484-7 (hardback) – ISBN 978-0-521-69758-3 (pbk.)
1. Right to die.   2. Patient refusal of treatment.   3. Death – Moral and ethical
aspects – Cross-cultural studies. I. Title.
[DNLM: 1. Right to Die – ethics.   2. Attitude to Death.   3. Cross-Cultural
Comparison.   4. Cultural Diversity.   5. Ethical Relativism.   6. Euthanasia,
Active – ethics. W 85.5 P896c 2008]
R726.P733 2008
179.7–dc22   2007031648

ISBN 978-0-521-87484-7 hardback
ISBN 978-0-521-69758-3 paperback

In memory of
Nancy Sutherland and Rose Candeloro Williams,
who chose to die;
and
Larry Baker, Hugheen Ferguson, Nathan Jaganathan,
Russ Savage, Carolyn Small, George Teves, and Bill White,
who didn't

[A]ble to say a holy No when the time for Yes has passed.
Friedrich Nietzsche, *Zarathustra*

Contents

Preface

Book prefaces often are skipped. This one should be read because it is important for readers to appreciate the intent and nature of what follows and to whom it is addressed.

This book is about the rationality, and so the permissibility, of choosing to die and is addressed to medical ethicists and to those on their way to being medical ethicists. More particularly, the book is addressed to medical ethicists who deal or will deal with terminal patients. And most specifically, the book is addressed to those who deal or will deal with terminal patients considering ending their lives to escape the physical and personal devastation and torment that many terminal conditions produce.

The writing of this Preface was prompted by events at a recent conference on end-of-life issues to which I was invited. I presented some material from the first two of the following chapters, with a view to both sharing my observations with participants and seeking constructive criticism.

The conference participants were mostly clinicians, with a significant number of health-care administrators and some lawyers specializing in terminal-illness issues. I regret that the comments and questions about the material I presented made it clear that few in the audience thought what I had to say was relevant to their work. My commentator ridiculed the abstractness of my presentation and dismissed my concern with the rationality of choosing to die by saying simply that we cannot be rational in terminal suffering.

In his closing remarks, the conference organizer attempted to
remedy matters by saying a little about the importance of the questions I raised. His remarks were well intentioned, but he succeeded
only in further marginalizing my position when he said I had spoken
about a "noble death" achievable only by a very few. However, he
summed up by asking a question that has stayed with me and that I
return to in Chapter 7. The question he asked was, "After all, how
many Socrateses die?"[1]

While I was disappointed and frustrated by my commentator's and
the audience's reactions, I benefited from the experience. It brought
home to me how important it is to attempt to narrow an undeniable
communicative gulf that exists between theoreticians concerned with
end-of-life issues and clinicians and others who must deal directly
with those who are dying.

This gulf is precisely the one that medical ethicists must straddle.
The gulf has two aspects; one is perceptual. Medical ethicists are
usually perceived by theoreticians as clinicians because of their
applied work and regular contact with physicians, nurses, medical
administrators, and patients. But medical ethicists are seen as
theoreticians by clinicians and other practitioners because of their
educational backgrounds and contact with academic ethicists, epis-
temologists, psychologists, and often theologians. The second aspect
of the gulf is institutional and has to do with responsibility and
defined function. The fact is that medical ethicists are advisors; they
advise both clinicians and patients, as well as patient family members
and sometimes the clinics and hospitals in which they work. Medical
ethicists are not implementers or agents in the treatment of patients
and thus are distanced from clinicians in a manner that cannot be
changed by remedying misperceptions.

Medical ethicists, then, occupy a unique position, and in order to
function effectively they must balance theory and practice. Their
main job is to apply ethical theory to clinical situations and on that
basis to offer the best guidance they can to those who make the actual
treatment decisions. And this means that medical ethicists must
reconcile the sort of abstract considerations regarding rationality and
permissibility that this book discusses with the actualities of terminal

---

[1] My thanks to David N. Weisstub for this productively provocative question.

patients' states of mind, pressures exerted by families, and physicians' priorities, responsibilities, and liabilities. Regarding the choice to die, medical ethicists stand between those who, like me, try to formulate standards to govern the surrender of life in dire medical situations, and those whose primary mandate and fiduciary responsibility is to preserve life.

The unavoidable complication is that some terminally ill patients *do* choose to die, that some physicians *do* assist in suicide, and that a few even perform euthanasia for compassionate reasons. It is of paramount importance, therefore, that medical ethicists be provided with standards and especially a rationale on which to ground their advice when patients choose to end their lives, whether by refusing treatment or by taking more direct means. Without standards and an underlying rationale, advising clinicians, patients, and family members regarding terminal patients' choices to end their suffering can only be a more or less happenchance sequence of more and less successful instances of coping with a recurring problem.

What prompted this book, as opposed to a planned third edition of my *The Last Choice*,[2] is that provision of standards and a rationale for dealing with terminal patients have been greatly complicated by the contemporary rise of multiculturalism and especially the relativism inherent in it. The need to respect cultural values and their influences on assessment standards, and factor them into policy and particular decisions about end-of-life issues, has made dealing with those issues greatly more complex than it was when policy and decisions were made and assessed in the context of a single dominant culture.

The key question, then, is not how many Socrateses die – though I return to this question in Chapter 7. Rather the key question is, How close can we come to emulating Socrates? The criteria I offer here, and the consideration of how relativism and culture impact their formulation and application, are intended to provide medical ethicists, as well as individuals considering ending their lives, with a basis for assessing the rationality of choosing to die for medical reasons.

---

[2] Prado, C. G. 1998. *The Last Choice: Preemptive Suicide in Advanced Age*, 2nd edition. New York and Westport, Conn.: Greenwood and Praeger Presses.

1

Setting the Stage

This book is about the two most fundamental questions underlying current debate about suicide, assisted suicide, and requested euthanasia in medical contexts. Those questions are whether choosing to die rather than endure hopeless torment can be *rational*, and, if so, whether it is *morally permissible*. Only if choosing to die is rational and morally permissible can we go on to consider whether provision of assistance in suicide or of euthanasia should be legalized and allowed by codes of medical ethics.

The questions are hugely complex and cannot be asked without provision of criterial contexts within which they can be answered. If it is rational to choose to die, it is so within philosophical or conceptual parameters. If it is morally permissible to choose to die, it is so within either universal or culturally determined parameters. Moreover, because most cases of choosing to die occur in institutions like hospitals and hospices, institutional cultures – the policies, priorities, and practices of the relevant institutions – need to be considered in establishing the latter parameters.

My original concern with choosing to die or what I call elective death was purely philosophical: I focused on whether choosing to die can be *rational*; that is, whether it can accord with reason and be judged to be for the best. At the time I felt that if my work was applicable in actual dealings with individuals prepared to die rather than face personal and physical devastation, that was all to the good, but that was not my main concern. Further work and especially growing familiarity with medical ethics made me realize that I had to give a much higher priority to the applicability of my criteria for rational suicide to the cases medical ethicists and clinicians deal with in practice. Though the rationality of choosing to die remains fundamental, I now see that it is insufficient just to establish it. Criteria for rational elective termination of life must be practically applicable. My aim in this book is to provide medical ethicists both with practically applicable criteria for rational and so possibly morally permissible elective death, and with clarification of the grounds of those criteria.

*   *   *

"Rationality" is defined by the *Oxford Companion to Philosophy* as that "feature of cognitive agents that they exhibit when they adopt beliefs on the basis of appropriate reasons."[1] This definition captures that to be rational is to rely on sound reasoning and evidence in adopting beliefs and drawing conclusions. The definition, however, is incomplete because it focuses on the cognitive and is silent on the practical. *The Cambridge Dictionary of Philosophy* defines rationality as "a normative concept ... that, for any action, belief, or desire, if it is rational we ought to choose it."[2] The two definitions complement one another, and they jointly capture what is central to assessing choosing to die as rational, which is that *the decision to end life is based on sound reasoning*, and that *the act of ending life is for the best*. This is the sense of "rational" that I have used elsewhere in discussing choosing to die and that I mean in everything that follows.

The question whether it is rational to choose to die is prior to those more commonly asked about whether electing to give up life for avoidance of or relief from great suffering is morally permissible, and whether assistance in doing so should be allowed. If it is not rational to choose to die, then elective death cannot be permissible by any other standard. Only if it is first rational to choose to die do questions legitimately arise about whether it can be morally permissible and

---

[1] Honderich, Ted, ed. 1995. *The Oxford Companion to Philosophy*. Oxford: Oxford University Press, 744.

[2] Audi, Robert, ed. 1995. *The Cambridge Dictionary of Philosophy*. Cambridge: Cambridge University Press, 674.

might properly be assisted. The priority of the rationality of choosing to die is bedrock to my claims and arguments.

I have argued elsewhere that choosing to die can be rational.[3] Here I recapitulate my arguments and the resulting criteria in order to address the more familiar, and often more pressing, question whether choosing to die may be morally permissible. Doing so requires consideration of a number of issues I was earlier able to avoid, chief among them being issues about how cultural values figure in reasoning about elective death. What mainly prompted me to address the separate question of moral permissibility is the historically recent social development of widespread concern with respecting diverse cultural values in assessment of most acts and practices, including elective death.

The result of needing to deal with questions about the role of diverse cultural values in assessing decisions and their enactment is that consideration of elective death cannot remain at the abstract philosophical level of thought about the pure rationality of choosing to die. The issue of moral permissibility must be addressed. However, that issue can no longer be addressed while presupposing a universal morality. It is now necessary to factor in cultural diversity.

The way I go about determining the rationality and moral permissibility of elective death is by employing what one reviewer of this project called "reflective equilibrium." This involves venturing criteria, testing them against intuitions and critiques, and revising the criteria to achieve a final version. I employ reflective equilibrium in this and the next two chapters and again in applying the resulting criteria in later chapters. The object of the exercise is to deal as productively as possible with the complexity of the questions about the rationality and moral permissibility of choosing to die. Venturing and revising criteria shed light on the different aspects of

---

[3] Prado, C. G. 1990. *The Last Choice: Preemptive Suicide in Advanced Age*. New York and Westport, Conn.: Greenwood Group; Prado, C. G. 1998; *The Last Choice: Preemptive Suicide in Advanced Age*, 2nd edition. New York and Westport, Conn.: Greenwood and Praeger Presses; Prado, C. G. 2000a. "Ambiguity and Synergism in 'Assisted Suicide.'" In C. G. Prado, ed., 2000b. *Assisted Suicide: Canadian Perspectives*. Ottawa: University of Ottawa Press, 43–60; Prado, C. G., and S. J. Taylor. 1999. *Assisted Suicide: Theory and Practice in Elective Death*. Amherst, N.Y.: Humanity Books (Prometheus Press). See also Prado, C. G., and Lawrie McFarlane. 2002. *The Best Laid Plans: Health Care's Problems and Prospects*. Montreal: McGill-Queen's University Press.

the basic question about rationality and on application of the criteria. I proceed, then, by first applying reflective equilibrium to my own development of criteria for rational elective death, and then segueing into consideration of establishing when elective death is morally permissible. In this way, the basic conceptual issues that concern elective death are illustrated, and I can then consider the more practical issues that concern how cultural values bear on abandoning life rather than enduring the pointless torment of some terminal illnesses.

It merits mention that I realize much of what I recommend in this book is already practiced by many medical ethicists. However, as indicated in the Preface, the point of what follows is to articulate and clarify the theoretical basis of what should be and often is done. There also is the need to provide instruction on the underpinnings of present practices for those new to medical ethics generally, or to the issue of elective death in particular.

*   *   *

In 1990, when I published *The Last Choice*, my first book on suicide, choosing to die to escape intolerable terminal conditions was beginning to be accepted by medical professionals and in some cases by the public. I agreed with Margaret Battin's comment on the book's dust jacket that suicide would "replace abortion as *the* social issue" of the 1990s. However, choosing to die *in anticipation* of intolerable terminal conditions was still perceived as unacceptable and likely pathological. Contrary to that view, I believed that preemptive or anticipatory suicide is a rational option to avoid the personal and intellectual diminishment and eventual devastation that terminal conditions like Alzheimer's disease and ALS (amyotropic lateral sclerosis or Lou Gehrig's disease) inflict on those who contract them. I devised criteria for rational preemptive suicide done for medical reasons, and while I thought their provision might be a little ahead of time, I was confident they would soon be acknowledged as important and useful.

Not many agreed with me. Even so ardent a supporter of the right to die as Derek Humphry did not endorse preemptive suicide. Humphry, who at the time was head of the Hemlock Society, made it clear in his review of *The Last Choice* that his concern was limited to affording terminally ill people the opportunity to end lives that were already irredeemably ruined and increasingly unendurable.[4] His widely read and debated *Final Exit* exemplified that concern, being a manual devoted to the curtailment of the slow and agonizing process of dying from terminal illness.[5]

As matters worked out over the next eight years, Battin was proven right; suicide did become a major social issue and Humphry's endorsement of suicide as release from pointless suffering came to be shared by many, including legislators in Oregon and Australia. Professional and public debate focused on *surcease* suicide, or on choosing to die to escape present, intolerable circumstances, and especially on *assisted* surcease suicide in medical contexts. The reason for the latter focus is the problematic involvement of others, especially physicians, in the enactment of decisions to die rather than face terrible medical situations. In 1998 I published an extensively revised second edition of *The Last Choice*.[6] By that time both professionals and laypeople were more familiar with the complex issues of assisted suicide and so-called active and passive euthanasia, and I thought the time had come for preemptive suicide to be taken seriously.

That did not happen, and it took me some time to understand what should have been obvious from the start, which is that preemptive suicide simply is not a social issue – at least in small numbers. Preemptive suicide really is the concern of the individual and perhaps family and close friends. Professional involvement in preemptive suicide, where there is any, is largely limited to a physician, psychologist, or psychiatrist consulted about the likelihood that a terminal illness will develop and perhaps about the would-be suicidist's competence to make a life-and-death decision. Preemptive suicide is mainly the suicidist's own business, and so neither a social nor professional concern on the order of surcease and assisted surcease suicide considered and committed while under medical care.

---

[4] Humphry, Derek. 1992b. "The Last Choice." *Hemlock Quarterly*, October, 4.
[5] Humphry, Derek. 1992a. *Final Exit: The Practicalities of Self-Deliverance and Assisted Suicide for the Dying*. New York: Dell.
[6] Prado 1998.

Central to its low professional and public profile is that preemptive suicide does not pose questions about professional and legal conflicts, and consequently draws little media attention and is rarely publicly debated. Contrary to this, surcease and especially assisted surcease suicide pose serious professional predicaments and readily capture media and public attention: witness the extensive coverage given to cases like that of Sue Rodriguez.[7] What most captures media and public attention is that these cases involve individuals who choose to die to avoid surviving in intolerable circumstances, but who for various reasons are physically unable to take their own lives and must rely on the cooperation of their physicians or other caretakers to help them die. These cases, then, essentially are about the conflict between compassion and respect for professional ethics and the law; they are about physicians' conflicts between doing the best they can for patients who are in hopeless situations and having to adhere to legal and ethical requirements.[8]

My concern with preemptive suicide as a rational way of avoiding insupportable personal destruction has not changed. I still see it as a rational and advisable way of avoiding survival as a tormented and much lessened shadow of oneself. However, I came to appreciate that surcease suicide, assisted surcease suicide, and requested euthanasia definitely constitute the social issue meriting primary attention. In 1999 and 2000 I published work on assisted suicide, and that has been the focus of my thinking and research for the last several years.[9] I still think that consideration of the rationality of preemptive suicide is fundamental to better understanding of the rationality and moral permissibility of surcease and assisted surcease suicide and of requested euthanasia. The reason is that contemplation of preemptive suicide is conducted in the best possible circumstances: that is, when the potential suicidist is not yet affected by the pressures and

---

[7] Mullens, Anne. 1996. *Timely Death: Considering Our Last Rights*. New York: Alfred A. Knopf.

[8] Quill, Timothy. 1996. *A Midwife Through the Dying Process: Stories of Healing and Hard Choices at the End of Life*. Baltimore and London: Johns Hopkins University Press; Quill, Timothy. 2001. *Caring for Patients at the End of Life: Facing an Uncertain Future Together*. New York: Oxford University Press.

[9] Prado and Taylor 1999; Prado 2000a, 2000b.

uncertainties that inevitably accompany any terminal illness dire enough to prompt thoughts of self-destruction. I believe that keeping in mind how preemptive suicide can be a rational option for someone can help clarify much about elective death that becomes murky with the introduction of a pressing need for release from a punishing condition. Nonetheless, I recognize that surcease suicide, assisted surcease suicide, and requested euthanasia pose the pressing questions.

This new book, then, differs from my earlier ones in terms of focus. But it also differs from earlier ones in other important ways. A second way it differs is that it is written from a perspective reshaped by what I have learned and thought about since publication of *The Last Choice*. Thirdly, the book is written in light of the sea change in health-care professionals' and the public's attitude toward suicide in terminal illness. Briefly put, in the past ten years there has been remarkably quick growth of acceptance of elective death in hopeless medical situations. This growth of acceptance is surprisingly due less to greater willingness to allow avoidance of pointless suffering than to the placing of a higher value on the preservation of personal autonomy and dignity. Perhaps as a legacy of the 1960s, or simply as a result of maturing values, more and more people have come to appreciate the critical difference between living and merely surviving. The idea of preserving life at all costs has waned in importance, and there has been growing recognition that life is not of ultimate and unquestionable value. Given this appreciation, someone's choosing to die rather than bear great suffering is now seen as wise and heroic, when not long ago it was seen as cowardly and immoral, if not pathological.

A fourth, and perhaps the most noteworthy, way this book differs from my earlier efforts is in its consideration of the impact of contemporary *multiculturalism* on the moral, social, and practical permissibility of elective death. At base, multiculturalism is equitable recognition of diversity of belief and value systems and the imperative to respect and accommodate those differences in the assessment of individual acts and of practices. It is no longer possible, then, to discuss whether suicide, assisted suicide, or requested euthanasia is permissible without taking into account how assessment standards applied in particular cases of elective death are affected, if not determined, by different cultural values.

It is important to appreciate at the outset that my concern with multiculturalism is not political; it does not focus on the rights of indigenous or immigrant minorities, as does so much present-day discussion of and legislation regarding cultural diversity. Generic or specific group-directed recognition or protection of ethnic, religious, or linguistic minority rights is not what is at issue here. What is at issue is that individuals reared and enculturated in diverse cultures have diverse cultural values, and those values influence their perceptions and decisions regarding elective death – just as cultural values influence whether a promiscuous young woman is seen and treated as someone needing counseling and support or as defiled and unmarriageable.

Most important to understanding the role of diverse cultural values in deliberation and assessment of choosing to die is that the multicultural imperative to respect the diversity of cultural values is abandonment of construal of assessment standards as universal, as cross-cultural, and so by intent or by default relativization of standards to culture. In Chapter 5 I consider more carefully how multiculturalism is relativistic; here it suffices to say that preparedness to respect diverse cultural values, and all that entails regarding culture-defining beliefs and doctrines, requires that other cultures' basic beliefs not be merely tolerated as current in those various cultures. Those beliefs must be accepted as *legitimately* held in their respective cultures; that means they cannot be critically compared to beliefs held in other cultures. Multiculturalism precludes judgmental assessment of a given culture's core beliefs from the perspective of another culture. Multiculturalism is inherently relativistic: every culture's defining beliefs are as good as any other culture's defining beliefs.

This relativization poses both a philosophical issue and a practical one. The philosophical issue has to do with the acceptability and scope of the entailed relativism; the practical issue has to do with the inevitable disagreements due to different cultural beliefs and values that arise in assessment of the choice to die. In the chapters that follow it will be necessary to consider both issues to the extent that they affect judgments about the rationality of choosing to die.

It is also important to appreciate that how multiculturalism is considered and treated in what follows has little to do with established, particular, cultural suicidal practices, such as *seppuku* or

sallekhana. What concerns us is the role of cultural values in deliberating and assessing the rationality of choosing to die to avoid the
devastation of terminal illness, not specific cultural practices having
to do with forfeiture of life to avoid dishonor or demeaning capture,
or in the interests of political protest. Most identifiable and fairly
cohesive cultures have established notions of suicide, notions often
bound up with codes of honor or ritualized practices. But self-
inflicted death for honor's sake, as manifestation of loyalty, as fulfillment of obligation, as sacrifice for a greater good, and even as the
only avenue open to lovers from incompatible families or castes is not
relevant here except to the extent that these practices manifest a
culture's general attitude toward elective death.

The first point to note, and one to which I return in Chapters 4
and 5, is that cultural attitudes toward elective death are often based
on religious doctrinal beliefs. To the extent that generalizations of
this sort are viable, it can be said that in Chinese culture, for instance,
attitudes toward elective death are mainly a function of Buddhist and
Confucian beliefs. Indian culture's attitudes toward elective death are
mainly a function of beliefs rooted in Buddhism, Hinduism, and
Sikhism. Islam determines attitudes toward elective death in cultures
as different as those of Saudi Arabia and Indonesia. European, North
American, and Latin American attitudes toward elective death are
determined by Christianity, with perhaps the most negative being
those grounded in Catholicism. In these latter belief systems, life is a
gift from God and not one's own to dispose of. Christianity, like other
religions, venerates its martyrs, but martyrdom, however deliberately
entered into, is still not *self*-inflicted death. The notable exception in
European culture is, of course, the Netherlands, which has pioneered –
if that is the appropriate term – elective death for medical reasons.

In any case, our concern is not with cultural specifics or, for that
matter, with whether attitudes toward elective death are religious or
secular in origin. Our concern in what follows is not with cultural
particulars but with the *differences* that diverse cultural values produce
in judgments about the acceptability of elective death. These judgmental differences pose a complication with respect to end-of-life
issues in that they are products of the application of varying standards
to the assessment of both policy and particular decisions about elective
death. But the application of varying standards is now inescapable.

Clearly cultures do differ with respect to the acceptability of choosing to die, and assessment of terminally ill patients' choices to die now requires respect for the different cultural values held by those patients, their families, those caring for them, and those assessing the acceptability of their choices.

There are still those who see multiculturalism as a passing phenomenon, but there are many others who see recognition of and respect for different cultural perspectives as established and unavoidable in assessment of whether any act or practice is or is not permissible. In any case, as I consider in Chapter 6, the *political* reality of multiculturalism in Europe and North America is now a given and not soon to change. If only for the latter reason, it now would be intellectually disingenuous to discuss the moral, social, legal, medical, and practical permissibility of elective death in terms of criteria grounded on principles assumed to be cross-cultural in conception and application.

Lastly, the fifth factor that helped to shape this book is my recognition of a persistent problem plaguing public debate about elective death in medical contexts. The problem is the common running together of assisted surcease suicide and voluntary euthanasia as simply "assisted suicide." This is a misuse of the concept of assisted suicide, a misuse that fosters confusion about the differences between genuine assisted suicide, on the one hand, and requested, voluntary, and passive or even involuntary euthanasia. The main reason for running these forms of elective death together is that the media and, sadly, the public have little patience with distinctions between assistance in suicide and various forms of euthanasia where the patient is not the primary agent in effecting death. If a physician or other clinician is involved in a patient's death, "assisted suicide" is almost invariably the label used to describe the case, regardless of the actual nature of the action taken.

Another and somewhat darker reason for running together forms of elective death where the terminal patient or the physician is the primary agent as "assisted suicide" is that it usefully obscures just whose decision it is to end a life, thus allowing courses of action that physicians may follow in dealing with hopeless cases. These courses of action run the gamut from clear cases of euthanasia to cases that defy classification. The most common and perhaps least classifiable is simply forgoing aggressive treatment. Another is allowing pneumonia to be contracted. I have personal knowledge of a case illustrating this option. The son of a woman with Alzheimer's disease who broke her hip was told by her doctor that after surgery pneumonia would almost certainly develop. Its development was described as "a window of opportunity" regarding the release death offered. However, a caring nurse turned the woman in her bed every twenty or thirty minutes and she did not contract pneumonia; she lived another three years. There are a number of other options, such as not resuscitating a patient, whether or not there is a do-not-resuscitate order in place, or simply delaying indicated treatment. More active options include use of massive doses of painkillers or other drugs whose use is justified by one aspect of a patient's condition but counterindicated by other aspects.

Most of the decisions to follow one or another of these courses of action are not made by the patients themselves but by their attending physicians, sometimes on their own, sometimes with the agreement and support of family members or others with fiduciary responsibility for the patients. Nonetheless, problematic use of the term "assisted suicide" is often justified on the grounds that the course of action taken is what the patient would have wanted or was in the patient's best interests. But the fact remains that current use of the term blurs crucial differences between cases of elective death that are genuine assisted suicide, in the sense of being the patient's autonomous act done with enabling help, and cases where someone other than the patient makes the decisions to do or not do something that leads to death.

This book, then, is informed by a number of developments, the most salient of which is the impact of the cultural relativism inherent in multiculturalism on assessment of what is rational and morally permissible. Relativization of standards and the truth of beliefs to culture is central to what follows, and I take as a working definition of cultural relativism that it is the view "that those who belong to one culture cannot form a valid judgment of any custom, institution, belief, etc. which is part of a culture which differs significantly from their own.[10] For the cultural relativist, then, all assessment of

---

[10] Mautner, Thomas, ed. 2005. *Dictionary of Philosophy*, 2nd edition. London: Penguin Books, 132.

standards and beliefs must be *intracultural*. Contrary to this view, the book's objective is to articulate *cross*-cultural criteria to determine when suicide, surcease suicide, assisted surcease suicide, and requested euthanasia are rational, and hence possibly socially, morally, and practically permissible options, and when each is chosen on the basis of sound reasoning and acceptable motivation. Though it should go without saying, to prevent possible misunderstanding, when I use "cross-cultural" in what follows, I of course do not mean that assessment of elective death must include representatives from all or even just the dominant cultures in a multicultural society. That would be impractical if not practically impossible. What I mean is that elective-death assessment must include participants from more than elective-death deliberators' respective cultures. I am using "cross-cultural" to contrast with "intracultural," not in an inclusive sense.

*   *   *

To proceed, I need to make a few points that must be in place from the outset and kept firmly in mind as we continue. The first of these points is that it is fundamental to what follows that the proposed criteria for the rationality of elective death apply to choosing to die that is considered and done (i) *autonomously* and *knowingly*; that is done by an individual who is (ii) *competent* to decide to commit suicide or request euthanasia; and that if there is assistance in the commission of suicide it is (iii) purely of an *enabling* sort. These requirements separate out what is possibly rational and morally permissible elective death from the many other sorts of self-inflicted death, such as prompted by clinical depression, by despair due to interpersonal, financial, or legal reasons, or by one or another form of pathology.

The importance of these three requirements is evident in the difficulties posed by ambiguous use of the term "assisted suicide." Misuse of the term is seldom intentional, but, as suggested, it is undeniable that some interests are served by the misuse and resulting ambiguity. "Assisted suicide" is generally preferable to "requested euthanasia" as a descriptive term because it puts the responsibility for the actual termination of life on the persons dying rather than on those performing the life-terminating acts. This fudging of the locus of responsibility may be crucial when questions arise about professional and legal accountability. However, assisted suicide, to be that, must be autonomous, knowing, and competent *self*-killing, even if assisted in the sense of being enabled in some way. Requested euthanasia may be rational and advisable in some circumstances, but it is not suicide. For it to be suicide, the person dying must be the primary agent in the causing of death, in the sense of both deciding to act and enacting the decision. In the case of requested termination of life, autonomy, knowingness, and competency apply to the act of asking for euthanasia, not to the act of terminating life.

A second point needing to be made here concerns the distinction implicitly drawn previously between moral and ethical questions surrounding the permissibility of elective death. This is a distinction that is evident in practice but seldom articulated. To many, the terms "moral" and "ethical" are interchangeable, and at one time they were. But for three decades or more, "moral" has mainly been used to describe overriding standards governing right conduct in all activities, while "ethical" has mainly come to be used to describe principles and rules that govern right conduct in professional activities, particularly those carrying fiduciary responsibilities.

When the distinction between morality and the ethical is acknowledged, professional codes of ethics – henceforth simply "ethics" or "ethical codes" – are commonly taken to be application of broader moral standards to specific activities and responsibilities, such as working as a doctor or a lawyer. But it is a central characteristic of ethics that they do not only govern the conduct of individuals plying their special expertise with a view to ensuring the morality of their actions. Ethics also govern practitioners' conduct with a view to preventing liability. While people who behave immorally have to answer to their own consciences, sometimes to society, and occasionally to the courts, those who behave unethically in their professional capacity must also answer to their patients and clients as well as to regulatory bodies. It is integral to the intent of medical and other ethical codes that practitioners perform their duties prudently: that they fulfill their obligations without incurring legal responsibility for unfortunate results. The import of this is that on occasion prudential considerations built into ethical standards may qualify the application of moral standards.

Consider a simple example to illustrate the point: a physician and a layperson are present at the scene of an automobile accident. Both may feel a moral obligation to pull the driver out of the vehicle in case of fire, but the physician's ethics will restrain the action because medical expertise indicates that moving the driver may exacerbate possible internal injuries and incur significant liability. The layperson is not so restrained and can act on the felt moral obligation with at least a much reduced risk of incurring liability.

* * *

The distinction between moral and ethical codes or standards takes us to the first specific instance of multiculturalism's impact on choosing to die. When multiculturalism makes moral standards – and ultimately truth – relative to culture, the roles of moral and ethical standards in assessment of actions grow very much more complex than when moral standards are taken as universal and ethical standards as derived from a common morality. Relativization of moral standards precludes construing various different ethical codes as based on one common moral code. This means any particular ethical code will have to be reconciled with however many culturally diverse moral codes are held by those governed by that ethical code. In effect, then, rather than ethical codes' being derived from and so secondary to a more fundamental single moral code, it is ethical codes that become primary for members of professional groups.

The importance of this with respect to terminal patients considering suicide, surcease suicide, assisted surcease suicide, and requested euthanasia is that though they will deliberate elective death in terms of their own moral standards, their deliberations and decisions will be assessed by their physicians in terms of the physicians' ethical standards. Additionally, physicians' understanding and application of their ethical standards will be influenced by their own moral standards. The consequence is that in any given case of elective death, there will be three sets of standards invoked, and the differences among them may be considerable.

For instance, a largely incapacitated terminal patient may deliberate and choose to die in terms of his moral code, which tolerates suicide

done for good reason. The patient's physician may assess his deliberation and decision in terms of an ethical code that tolerates refusal of
nourishment or treatment by a patient, but not more positive action
such as taking a fatal drug. The physician's moral standards, however, may prohibit elective death of any sort. She therefore will
construe the applicable ethical standards as narrowly as she can and
be aggressive regarding treatment, perhaps even misleading the
patient by simply not informing him about what sort of medication
is being administered. On the other hand, should the physician's
moral standards allow and even advocate elective death for good
reason she may then help the patient by administering medication
on the "double effect" principle, for instance, administering large
doses of morphine that, while effective in making the patient more
comfortable, and thus being justified, are seriously counterindicated by another aspect of his condition and accelerate his
death. In the following I consider an actual case in which something
rather like this occurred.

We have, then, a number of factors in play the moment that a
common moral code is precluded by relativization of morality to
culture. The first is that patients all have moral codes that may
differ significantly – and this is to say nothing about others
involved on the patient side, such as family, close friends, lawyers,
and advisors. Secondly, physicians also have their own moral
codes. But thirdly, physicians are bound by their ethical codes,
and in assessing their patients' deliberations of elective death,
and the measure of their own participation in enacting patients'
decisions, physicians should give priority to their ethical codes.
This is partly because of professional obligations, partly because
of the circumstance that ethical codes have to do as much with
prudence regarding liability as with right conduct, and partly
because of the now outdated assumption that ethical codes
embody the relevant aspects of a universal morality. A common
example of this institutionalized prioritization of ethical codes is the
refusal by most hospital boards and administrators to allow clinicians routinely to avoid participating in procedures like "D & C's"
because they essentially are abortions, or to refuse administering
blood transfusions for religious reasons.

Complications begin with the interplay between patients' and physicians' moral codes. With relativization of morality to culture and abandonment of a universal or common moral code, physicians' ethical codes are distanced from both patients' and physicians' own moral codes. That is, since ethical codes can no longer be taken as based on a common moral code, they must be taken either to be independent of any given culturally determined moral code or to be based on or derived from the culturally predominant moral code. In either case, ethical codes come to have a more or less coincidental relation to particular moral codes.

The surprising point is that the cases that are of greatest concern regarding elective death are not cases where patients and physicians disagree about elective death because the patients' moral codes are at odds with physicians' ethical codes and/or physicians' own moral codes. The reason is that where there is disagreement, there is also fairly thoroughgoing assessment of patients' choice to die. The serious problem is posed by cases where patients and physicians agree that choosing to die is morally permissible on the basis of a shared moral code. In these cases, the agreement between patients and physicians may cover problems with patients' deliberations about elective death. Additionally, agreement may foster circumvention of physicians' ethical codes where the moral agreement between patients and physicians is at odds with ethical strictures.

The basic problem agreement poses regarding deliberation of elective death is that it makes it likelier that patients' interest in continued life may not be adequately weighted both in deliberation of elective death and in assessment of that deliberation. The danger is that elective death may be prompted by cultural values shared by patients and physicians, but values that unduly underrate the interest in survival and so result in a choice to die that does not meet the criteria for rationality. Accord on the moral permissibility – perhaps the moral requirement – of elective death in these cases may then result in physicians' finding ways around the prohibitions of their ethical codes and assisting their patients in suicide or even performing requested euthanasia because convinced of the moral rightness of the patients' decisions. It is cases like these that constitute the most pressing reason why criteria for rational and so possibly morally permissible elective death must deal with the consequences of the relativization of morality to culture.

*   *   *

While the idea that morality is relative is as old as Protagoras, it became a pressing social issue with the advent of multiculturalism. The heart of multiculturalism, sometimes described as "the politics of difference," is that "different people should be treated differently in accordance with their distinctive cultures."[11] The application of this idea to the issue of elective death comes to treating different people differently in accordance with their culture-determined moral codes. And the essential aspect of this different treatment is that in assessing reasoning and motivation, diverse standards and values must be respected. Terminal patients' deliberations and decisions about choosing to die, then, must be assessed in terms of their particular standards, values, and moralities. With respect to involved clinicians, their decisions and actions must be assessed in terms of their own particular standards, values, and moralities. However, clinicians are bound by ethical codes at least common to those involved with any particular terminal patient. It would appear, therefore, that their ethical codes would or should take priority over their individual moral codes. However, clinicians' interpretations and applications of their shared ethical codes are bound to be conditioned by their own moral codes.

It may appear that multiculturalism and its underlying relativism introduce hopeless complexity into the consideration of elective death and especially into assessment of that consideration. It also looks to many as if multiculturalism undermines proper consideration, assessment, and consequent action by mitigating responsibility for breaches of ethical codes in giving too much weight to individuals' purportedly diverse moral codes. It seems adherence to ethical codes is weakened when a measure of legitimacy is lent to liberal interpretation of ethical requirements on the grounds that personal moral codes must be respected.

---

[11] Barry, Brian. 2001. *Culture and Equality*. Cambridge, Mass.: Harvard University Press, 295.

Multiculturalism does complicate deliberation and assessment of elective death, and especially the question of clinicians' participation in its enactment, but there are various other areas in which it also poses problems. One often troublesome sort of case involves what clinicians having different cultural values and especially different religious commitments think is covered by confidentiality.[12] Some clinicians may be prepared to dispense information about patients that other clinicians consider private to their relationship with their patients. Another sort of case has to do with which forms of treatment clinicians are willing to employ, how aggressively they apply them, and how those clinicians respond to the views of their patients regarding treatment. Perhaps the best-known instance concerns blood transfusions. Typically, a physician will insist on the necessity of a transfusion and the patient refuses it on religious grounds. A third sort of case has to do with clinicians' willingness to participate in procedures like abortion. Still another has to do with physicians' not pursuing available diagnostic or treatment options purportedly for patients' own good. Additionally, there are many small matters that nonetheless make a difference, especially to patients. One example of this is how clinicians with certain cultural backgrounds deal with women.

One consequence of the complexity introduced by multiculturalism and underlying relativism is that physicians trying to decide what to do in treating terminal patients who are suffering greatly and want to die have to consider not only patients' beliefs and standards but also those of other participating clinicians. They have to anticipate how those other clinicians will interpret and apply their common ethical code to whatever they, as attending physicians, decide to do about treating or not treating terminal patients. However, multiculturalism only worsens matters in this respect; it does not, in fact, introduce much that is new. Even where there is a common moral code, variations in clinicians' interpretations and applications of their ethical code can pose serious conflicts. This was amply illustrated by the case of Dr. Nancy Morrison.

---

[12] Battin, Margaret Pabst. 1990. *Ethics in the Sanctuary: Examining the Practices of Organized Religion*. New Haven, Cann.: Yale University Press.

In 1997, in Halifax, Nova Scotia, Morrison was arrested on a charge of first-degree murder for injecting a patient with potassium chloride. After eight or nine operations that kept him alive, the patient was on a respirator and his situation had deteriorated further and was quite hopeless. The family and his physician decided to take him off life support and not to resuscitate him. They even had a priest at the bedside. Morrison's role was that of attending respirologist. However, when the patient's respirator was turned off, instead of dying quickly, the patient gasped for breath and was obviously in extreme distress. One nurse was quoted as saying she had never seen a patient suffering so much. Ostensibly to ease the patient's great discomfort, but essentially to hasten his death, he was injected with massive doses of morphine and other painkillers, but to no immediate effect. Finally, Morrison rather desperately administered first nitroglycerine, which also proved ineffective, and then potassium chloride, and the patient died.

The hospital's board reviewed Morrison's actions and imposed a relatively slight sanction – paid leave. That did not satisfy some of the clinicians involved in the case. Their moral compunctions and strict interpretation of their ethical code moved them to go to the police, and Morrison was rather dramatically arrested – several police officers went to the hospital to pick her up.[13]

What makes the Morrison case particularly interesting here is the interplay between the ethical code shared by her and the other participating clinicians and the varying moral perspectives of all involved. The hospital Morrison worked in was by no means a paradigm of multicultural diversity. The different perspectives on her actions were products less of diverse moral codes than of differing interpretations of essentially the same moral code. What invited the varied interpretations was that while the ethical code common to Morrison and the other participating clinicians prohibited the use of drugs like potassium chloride that have no curative or pain-relieving application in the relevant doses, the code allowed administration of massive quantities of morphine and the like: doses that, while effective in treating pain, invariably prove fatal. Double-effect thinking was

[13] Bergman, Brian. 1998. "The Final Hours: Does a Doctor Have a Right to End a Patient's Life?" *Maclean's*, March 9.

evident in the ethical code, in that death could be hastened by administration of drugs, but only as long as the drugs administered had some justifying beneficial effect, most notably alleviation of pain. The sanction imposed on, Morrison was for using drugs that had no beneficial effect. However, the hospital board's action clearly demonstrated a consensus that Morrison acted properly, though in technical violation of the ethical code. This perception turned on two facts: that the patient was in pointless agony and administration of very large doses of painkillers had been ineffective, and that the life forfeited was most likely measured in minutes.

But some clinicians saw matters quite differently. They saw Morrison's use of nitroglycerine and especially potassium chloride as wholly unacceptable despite the circumstances. The clinicians went to the police despite everyone's agreeing that the patient was suffering enormously in the irreversible but surprisingly extended process of dying. His respirator had been removed and there was no intention of restoring life support; the attending physicians and family were in agreement that no steps should be taken to keep him alive. The only question was whether to let him die in agony over a period that could possibly have stretched to hours or deliberately end his life. The use of massive doses of painkillers had been clearly intended not only to ease the patient's suffering, but to hasten his death. The complication was that they had not worked even at the dosage used. Morrison's use of potassium chloride, then, was done partly because of compassion for the patient and partly because of desperation caused by the ineffectiveness of measures already taken. There was no point in her causing the patient's death other than to prevent the hopeless suffering he was clearly undergoing in the process of dying. Nonetheless, some saw her violation of the ethical requirement that any drug administered have a beneficial effect as a crime.

In the ensuing public discussion of the case, it was evident that many felt Morrison did the morally right thing in causing the patient's death, regardless of the ethical strictures. This view was reflected in the ruling of the judge who dealt with her case. He released Morrison, arguing what was basically a technicality, namely, that the prosecution had failed to meet the evidentiary requirement to force a trial because of failure to prove that the hypodermics Morrison used actually contained nitroglycerine and potassium chloride and in the requisite concentrations. Nonetheless, some felt that Morrison had acted immorally, as well as illegally, and there was significant pressure on the prosecutors to appeal the judge's ruling or to find another way to make her stand trial.[14] Incidentally, it is worth mentioning in connection with the point made previously about misuse of the term that much media coverage of the Morrison case wrongly referred to it as one of assisted suicide.[15]

The key point in the Morrison case is that according to the ethical code that bound her, Morrison basically was free to administer however much painkiller she chose to use even if the dosage hastened death. This clearly enabled her to hasten the patient's death without violating the ethical code. But she was barred from using potassium chloride because it has no medical value as a painkiller. Her use of potassium chloride, as well as of nitroglycerine, pushed her treatment of the patient into the unethical and criminal area. As indicated, what she did was to administer a drug whose use could not be justified by the double-effect principle because it could not be argued that potassium chloride was administered to ease pain and that it killed the patient as a side effect. Administering potassium chloride was on a par with putting a bullet through the patient's heart, and that is precisely how Morrison's action was viewed by the police. In doing what she did, then, Morrison went from acting in a way that would not have prompted the hospital or other clinicians to question the patient's death – much less attract the attention of the police – to acting in a way that prompted the hospital to review her actions and some clinicians to go to the police.

It would seem that given the circumstances, there was little difference between killing the patient indirectly by administering huge doses of normally beneficial drugs, as was attempted, and killing the patient more directly by administering a lethal drug. It seems the real difference was one between strict and more liberal compliance with an ethical code that tolerates use of double effect to justify terminating patients' lives – an end that, though intended, cannot be acknowledged: euthanasia that dares not speak its name.

[14] Bergman 1998.
[15] Bergman 1998.

It is not surprising, then, that some felt then – and many feel now – that there is something a little like hypocrisy in the initial formulation of the ethical code and in its application. On this view, the reaction of some to what Morrison did was grossly out of proportion, given the number of times patients' deaths are more or less routinely hastened with large doses of some opiate. The majority of those involved in the case seem to have seen ending the patient's life as a moral imperative, regardless of ethical strictures. The description of the circumstances in which Morrison chose to resort to potassium chloride certainly inclines one to think that Morrison did the right thing, in moral terms, despite violating her ethical code. But clearly others did not see those circumstances as justifying what she did, and that they did not do so suggests a deeper issue. As reported, those who went to the police regarding Morrison's action had moral and/or religious convictions about taking life regardless of the patient's circumstances. Given the drastic nature of going to the police, it is safe to assume that those who did so not only condemned Morrison's use of potassium chloride to terminate the patient's life, but also disagreed with their ethical code allowing use of unlimited amounts of painkillers to achieve the same effect.

The core of one position, then, was that the patient's agony overrode the ethical code's strictures; the core of the opposed position was that human life cannot be terminated at will regardless of the circumstances and that that moral imperative overrode the ethical code's toleration of double-effect termination of life. As indicated earlier, these positions arose not from different moral codes, but from different interpretations of the same moral code. Nonetheless, the different interpretations of the common moral code are not simply a matter of varying inclinations or temperaments. Clearly strict or more liberal understanding of the common moral code is due in part to different cultural values in the sense of how the various individuals were reared and trained. Some would have been taught their moral code strictly, for instance, interpreting the commandment "Thou shalt not kill" literally and inflexibly. Others would have been taught their moral code more liberally, allowing exception to the rule according to circumstances.

However, it is not hard to imagine variations on these positions determined by other cultural values. For example, one religious variation might be that the patient's suffering was necessary for redemption. The religiously conditioned moral imperative here would be that ending the patient's life to save him pain would ruinously curtail a divinely willed process. Another might be that the situation should never have been allowed to progress to the point at which Morrison had to make her hard and rather momentous decision, and that the patient's respirator should have been removed long before and massive doses of painkillers administered at that time. The moral imperative in this case would be taken as being that given the patient's hopeless situation, his pointless suffering not only hurt him to no good end, but put a terrible burden on his family also to no good end.

Perhaps this is a good place to reiterate that regardless of the importance of operant moral and ethical codes dealing with the tolerability of elective death or requested euthanasia, the primary need is to show that choosing to die is *rational*. Whatever morality and ethics govern commission of suicide, assisted suicide, and requesting of euthanasia, each must be rational to be permissible. Simply put, while it is possible that we might conclude that choosing to die is sometimes rational, but never permissible, or that it is never ethical to assist in elective death, we could *not* conclude that choosing to die is sometimes permissible, or that assisting elective death is sometimes ethical, but that choosing to die is always irrational. Varying moral perspectives, and differing interpretations of ethical codes, may complicate assessment of a decision to die rather than bear great suffering, but those complications enter the picture only after choosing to die is shown to be rational.

There are two serious concerns with my point about the primacy of rationality regarding elective death. One is that many relativize not only morality but rationality itself to culture; the other is that many more fail to see how the rationality of choosing to die can be assessed separately from its moral permissibility. These are complex questions and require lengthier treatment in later chapters.

* * *

To close this first chapter, it may be prudent to echo points made in the Preface and note that debate about elective death, such as occurred in the Morrison case, is complicated by the diverse professional backgrounds of debate participants. People concerned with

elective death, whether from a theoretical, policy, or practice perspective, are grounded in a number of different disciplines, and their
approaches to the issue differ accordingly with respect to priorities
and objectives, and with respect to how various types of elective death
are delineated and construed.

At the most general level, it can be said that philosophers, psychologists, social psychologists, and sociologists, to name the theoreticians most prominently involved in the debate, all approach
elective death from somewhat different angles, differing primarily in
the degree to which their interests and concerns focus on conceptual
or empirical factors. What unites them, though, is that their
approaches to the issue of elective death basically are determined by
theoretical considerations, whether they are primarily conceptual, as
they are for philosophers, or more empirical, as they are for sociologists and psychologists. However, regardless of how diverse the
approaches of theoreticians, all of them differ significantly from the
way clinicians approach elective death, especially assisted suicide and
requested euthanasia. Again speaking generally, clinicians tend to
hold views on elective death derived from their own training and
practical experience, and from the practical experience of exemplary senior individuals who have worked with them or taught them.
One has only to look at the preponderance of case-study texts in
medical ethics and the fairly recent growth of "problem-based
learning" – which often eschews texts – to appreciate this difference.

Neither theoreticians nor clinicians like to admit that there is a
significant methodological and perhaps ideological gap between
them, but the gap is real and can pose serious problems by impeding
communication and mutual understanding. The major single obstacle
to good communication between the two groups is that theoreticians
deal with elective death mostly in the abstract, while clinicians of
course are faced with elective-death cases in an immediate way. This
difference inevitably fosters attitudes of both that sometimes prove
counterproductive. Perhaps the most obstructive effect of the difference is mutual dismissiveness: clinicians have little time for theorists'
abstractions, while theorists too often underestimate the conjectural
nature of their proposals.

The relevance of the theoretician/clinician gap to what follows is
that it must be clear from the beginning that what I offer here is

offered at a theoretical level. My intention is to provide a philosophical rationale for the permissibility of surcease suicide, assisted surcease suicide, and requested euthanasia. Nonetheless, what I offer from a philosophical perspective is intended to have practical application. In providing the rationale for the acceptability of elective death, I do so mainly by suggesting criteria that must be satisfied for elective death to be rational and so possibly morally permissible. The criteria, then, are intended to be used by terminal patients considering elective death and by clinicians involved in patients' considerations, decisions, and actions regarding choosing to die. The criteria are also intended to be used by clinicians in assessing whether they may assist terminal patients who choose to die.

Unlike many books about elective death, then, this one does not employ a case-study method; that is not the nature of the exercise. The point is not to extrapolate contextually determined guiding principles from actual cases, but to provide fundamental, conceptually derived criteria prior to actual cases. Where I do offer examples in what follows, they are fictional composites of various elements gleaned from actual cases or constructed to illustrate particular points. The next chapter begins with one such example.

In proceeding to the next chapter, I need to warn the reader that for the sake of clarity I risk tedious repetition by reiterating key points and articulating some of them in different ways. I ask the reader's indulgence; I know from experience how essential it is to emphasize and restate points that, if missed or misconstrued, skew or even preclude thorough understanding of ideas that need to be stated about a highly complex issue. In the next two chapters I list and then revise criteria for rational suicide that I developed elsewhere.[16] The point of the exercise, as noted at the beginning of this chapter, is that in the process of reviewing and revising the criteria to make them clearer, more concise, and more practically applicable, what is essential about the rationality of choosing to die emerges more sharply.

[16] Prado 1990, 1998; Prado and Taylor 1999; Prado 2000a, 2000b.

2

Criteria for Rational Suicide

Lack of examples is the bane of philosophical writing. Much too often abstract points are made without practical instances to ground them in experience. At the same time, examples should not be so specific as to draw attention away from the general point being made, and, as alluded to previously, there are times when examples, even if actual events, should not be used to attempt to derive general guiding principles. This is the bane of clinical writing. Too often reliance on case studies results in generalized conclusions and recommendations that are either nearly vacuous or too specific to be broadly applicable. To try to prevent both of these problems while still providing a useful reference point for the discussion that follows, I offer the entirely hypothetical case of Ms. A.

Ms. A is sixty-five years old. For the last year or two she has been thinking hard about what life likely holds for her. The main consideration is that both her mother and her father had severe Alzheimer's disease in their early and mid-seventies. Ms. A has given serious thought to ending her life prior to succumbing to the disease. She has taken certain steps: prepared a will, organized her papers, and liquidated her assets. Her children are grown and on their own, and her husband was killed two years earlier in an accident. There are, then, no immediate familial obligations that preclude suicide. To the best of her knowledge, Ms. A is not impaired in her thinking and she has achieved a cool reflective attitude toward her own death, though she is concerned about the method by which to end her life. She does not want to suffer needlessly but does not trust drugs available to her because she does not want to risk surviving an attempt at suicide in a condition possibly worse than what she wants to avoid.

What Ms. A is doing is contemplating *preemptive* suicide. She believes she has reason to take her own life, but the reason, while threatening, is neither actual nor imminent. This situation is what I will call *Stage One* with respect to deliberation and possible commission of suicide. It is the stage at which what is deliberated and may be committed is preemptive suicide or suicide in anticipation of an intolerable situation.

What Ms. A contemplates at Stage One is the form of suicide that initially interested me. But as mentioned in the last chapter, preemptive suicide neither garners nor perhaps merits the attention that surcease suicide and assisted suicide do. For one thing, most clinicians I have spoken with do not consider Stage One to be of professional concern to them unless they are consulted regarding the reasons for considering preemptive suicide. And that is fair enough; to clinicians, Ms. A is considering a course of action that most of them would see as ill advised but one that is her own business.

Five years pass, and Ms. A either decided against committing preemptive suicide or lacked the resolve to do so. At seventy, she does not show symptoms of Alzheimer's disease. However, rather surprisingly, given her age, she is diagnosed with amytropic lateral sclerosis (ALS), a prospect as frightful as Alzheimer's. Ms. A, when considering preemptive suicide, read about Sue Rodriguez's fight with ALS and her struggle for assistance in suicide. Ms. A was appalled at Rodriguez's suffering and frustration with the bureaucratic obstacles she faced regarding her request for assistance in suicide. Ms. A, already suffering extremely serious symptoms, now considers ending her own life while she still can release herself from present distress and avoid the drawn-out process of dying from ALS. Ms. A now has actual, immediate reason to choose to die and so contemplates committing *surcease* suicide while she is still able to do so. This situation I will call *Stage Two* with respect to deliberation and possible commission of suicide. It is the stage at which what is deliberated and may be committed is suicide as release from an existent and intolerable situation.

Ms. A again delays, and some six months later her incapacity has increased dramatically and her discomfort is only marginally controllable. As Sue Rodriguez had, she begs her doctor to help her end her life. Ms. A is still just capable of taking and swallowing pills on her own, and all she wants is to be supplied with something she can take to put her into a sleep from which she will not wake. This is a case of Ms. A's asking for *assistance in suicide*. She wants to end her life, has reason to do so, but is now unable to kill herself without help. I will call this situation *Stage Three* with respect to deliberation and possible commission of suicide. It is the stage at which what is deliberated and may be committed is suicide as release from an existent and intolerable situation, but suicide that can be accomplished only with enabling help.

A few days later Ms. A undergoes emergency surgery. She pleads with her doctor not to let her survive the surgery. At this point Ms. A is no longer able to commit suicide, even with assistance, and is dependent on the willingness of her physician to end her life. Unlike what some think, this is not a case of assisted suicide, despite Ms. A's intentions and expressed desire for death. Nor is this a case, as some might think, of Ms. A's appointing her physician as an *agent* to act for her in ending her life. Others may act for us in many respects, but no one can act for us in suicide, as no one can act for us, as our agent, when, for instance, we are being sworn in to give testimony. What Ms. A does, then, is *request euthanasia*. I will call this *Stage Four* in the deliberation of elective death. This is the stage at which we are no longer dealing with suicide but with the taking of Ms. A's life, albeit at her explicit request, to release her from an intolerable and hopeless situation.

This is the sort of case alluded to earlier, where the physician has to choose whether or not to do something that ensures Ms. A does not recover from the surgery. The physician may be prompted to make the choice by Ms. A's request, or simply by compassion. In a Stage Four case, the decision is posed by Ms. A's explicit request, though it may also be posed by events themselves. For instance, partway through the surgery it may become obvious to everyone involved that the procedure must either be abandoned or be too extensive for her to survive it. But the physician must weigh more than Ms. A's request for euthanasia and her hopeless situation; the physician must also weigh whether others involved in the surgery will agree or disagree that proceeding, which would effectively terminate her life, is the right thing to do. What matters most here, however, is that Stage

Four does not involve an action done by Ms. A beyond her earlier expressing a desire to die. Not even the most fervently expressed desire to die can constitute an act of suicide, contrary to the impression often promoted by the media.

Keeping Stages One through Four firmly in mind, I now need to describe more explicitly the kind of elective death that may occur at each stage. These descriptions are fundamental to what follows and will be mentioned often, so I will label each for easy reference. It must be kept in mind, though, that the following descriptions are limited to discussion of preemptive, surcease, and assisted surcease suicide, and requested euthanasia considered and committed or requested for reasons having to do with terminal illness. I am not here concerned with suicide relating to dishonor, avoidance of torture, humiliating bankruptcy, hopelessness in light of prosecution, or psychological pathology. Nor am I concerned with euthanasia in other than medical circumstances. Henceforth, then, reference to suicide and euthanasia at the four stages will be as follows:

1. *Preemptive* suicide considered and committed during Stage One will be referred to as *PS1*.
2. *Surcease* suicide considered and committed during Stage Two will be referred to as *SS2*.
3. *Assisted surcease suicide* considered and committed at Stage Three will be referred to as *AS3*.
4. *Requested or voluntary euthanasia* considered and requested at Stage Four will be referred to as *RE4*.

To summarize, PS1 is anticipatory or preemptive suicide deliberated and done before the onset of an unacceptable medical condition. SS2 is surcease suicide deliberated and done to escape the effects of an intolerable life-debasing medical condition. AS3 is surcease suicide deliberated and done with help when a condition advances to a point where the individual is incapacitated to a significant degree. If the condition advances beyond a point where the individual is able to act to commit suicide, even with help, elective death may be achieved only through RE4 or requested euthanasia.

* * *

I turn now to the conditions that must be satisfied for PS1, SS2, and AS3 to be rational acts and for RE4 to be a rational request. Recall that only if choosing to die is rational does the question arise as to whether it may also be morally permissible. It is always possible for an individual to conclude that while PS1, SS2, AS3, or RE4 is a rational option, moral considerations prohibit it. Exercise of the rational option of elective death may also be precluded by cultural values. But as indicated, the reverse does not hold. If PS1, SS2, AS3, or RE4 is judged morally or culturally permissible but not rational, it cannot be accepted as actually permissible. Note also that while it is necessary to distinguish moral and cultural-value considerations here, in practice they are usually run together. But whether distinguished or not, moral or cultural acceptability is second to rational acceptability.

The *Dictionary of Modern Thought* states that suicide "may be regarded as rational" if the individual committing it "prefers death to any other possible future."[1] And we can extend the statement to cover requesting euthanasia. Unfortunately, this succinct statement packs too much into "prefers death"; preferring death to any possible future is insufficient to make suicide rational if the basis for the preference is misconceived, flawed by ignorance or error in reasoning, or based on motivating values that unrealistically and illegitimately contravene the interest in continued life.[2] Battin offers a more satisfactory statement, saying that in "the absence of any compelling evidence to the contrary," we have to accept that someone may choose to die "on the basis of reasoning which is by all usual standards adequate."[3] However, here too we have a reference that now is too dense; the reference to "all usual standards" needs to be expanded and refined because multiculturalism has displaced the consensus Battin assumes in speaking of usual standards. Expansion and refinement pose a compound problem, though, because reference to adequate reasoning regarding deliberation of elective death covers both the

[1] Bullock, A., O. Stallybrass, and S. Trombley, eds. 1988. *The Fontana Dictionary of Modern Thought*. London: Fontana, 721.
[2] Prado 1998.
[3] Battin, Margaret Pabst. 1984. "The Concept of Rational Suicide." In Edwin Shneidman, ed., *Death: Current Perspectives*, 3rd edition. Mountain View, Calif.: Mayfield, 297–320, 301. (Battin's article does not appear in the 1995 4th edition.)

process of reasoning and the values that motivate the reasoning. What are needed, then, are specific criteria that determine when choosing to die is both adequately reasoned and motivated.

In my earlier efforts to articulate criteria for PS1, I derived the criteria from consideration of both the process of reasoning about suicide and the motivating values driving that reasoning. There is no point in repeating that process, but some of the considerations involved will emerge as I modify the original criteria for PS1 to apply to SS2, AS3, and RE4.

I begin with the concept of rationality. To most people rationality effectively means *reasonableness*. That is, when questions arise about rationality, most people think in terms of reasonable and unreasonable behavior. Few think first of the standards reasoning must meet. With respect to choosing to die, many who participate in debates about the rightness or wrongness of PS1, SS2, AS3, and RE4 tend to impose this common interpretation of rationality on discussion of the issue. That is, they tend to think in terms of whether someone choosing to die is, say, unreasonably concerned about something or inclined to do something unreasonable, perhaps because of depression. This is not what is in question when we consider whether choosing to die is rational or not. The contrast to elective death's being rational is not that it is unreasonable; there is a sense in which any drastic act is always unreasonable precisely in being drastic, and willing abandonment of life is certainly a drastic act. The proper contrast to choosing to die's being rational is that the act is not rational in virtue of faulty reasoning, perversity, or pathology. For choosing to die to be rational, it must satisfy strict standards for the acceptability of the process of deliberation, not just be reasonable in the ordinary sense of being a course of action that is *understandable* and would be done by most people in the same circumstances.

Questions about the process of reasoning one's way to elective death basically have two aspects: one regarding the structure of the reasoning, and one regarding its content. With respect to structure, the essentials are that the reasoning must be free of fallacies; it must be *sound* in the sense that the working premises are true and inferences drawn from those premises are valid.

To illustrate, consider a very simple logical example: if we are told that *All human beings are mortal*, and then are told that *Socrates is a human being*, we may validly infer the syllogistic conclusion that *Socrates is mortal*. This is simply a matter of being told that all members of the class "human being" are members of the class "mortal (beings)," and then being told that "Socrates" is a member of the class "human beings." It follows logically that "Socrates" is a member of the class "mortal (beings)," since all human beings are. Against this, if we are told that *All human beings are mortal* and that *Socrates is mortal*, it does not follow that *Socrates is a human being*. "Socrates" in this case may be the name of a pet turtle that is definitely mortal but just as definitely not a human being. In short, we have been told that all members of the class "human being" are members of the class "mortal (beings)," and then told that "Socrates" is a member of the class "mortal (beings)." Here it does not follow that "Socrates" is a member of the class "human beings," because the class "mortal (beings)" includes members other than humans.

Similarly, if we are told that *If p, then q*, and we have *p*, we may validly infer the conclusion *that q*. Against this, if we are told that *If p, then q*, and we have *q*, we cannot validly infer *that p*. For instance, if *p* is "If it rains," and *q* is "I'll take a taxi," it does not follow that it rains if I am feeling lazy and take a taxi anyway. These are kindergarten-level examples, no doubt tediously familiar to most readers, but they illustrate what is at issue when we raise the question of whether reasoning about committing suicide is rational in the sense of satisfying structural requirements.

Note that the foregoing examples are cases of deductive reasoning as opposed to inductive reasoning. This limitation is due to the requirement that deliberation of elective death has to be deductive because inductive reasoning has to do with drawing intrinsically tentative conclusions about unobserved cases on the basis of observed cases. This is not the sort of reasoning relevant to deciding to end one's life; what deliberation of elective death requires is the drawing of valid inferences from true premises. The proper place for induction in reasoning about elective death is that inductive conclusions may be part of some of the premises in a deductive argument. The case of Ms. A illustrates this, in that in her deductive argument she moves from a premise about her parents' contracting Alzheimer's disease to another premise about the likelihood that she will contract Alzheimer's disease. What Ms. A does is draw an inductive inference from a true premise about her parents and medical statistics to the likelihood that she, too, will contract Alzheimer's disease. The inductive conclusion about her likelihood of contracting Alzheimer's is itself a premise in Ms. A's deductive argument and is not itself sufficient to turn the argument into an inductive one.

Ms. A's reasoning has the following deductive structure:

> Premise 1: Those whose parents both contract Alzheimer's disease are likely to contract the disease.
> Premise 2: Both my parents contracted Alzheimer's.
> Subconclusion 1: I am likely to contract Alzheimer's.

Given this preliminary conclusion, another premise is introduced and a second preliminary conclusion is drawn:

> Premise 3: Alzheimer's destroys people long before they actually die.
> Subconclusion 2: I am likely to be destroyed by Alzheimer's long before I die.

At this point in Ms. A's reasoning, a value judgment is introduced that operates as her fourth premise:

> Premise 4: I prefer to die rather than be destroyed by Alzheimer's.

It is this value judgment, together with the two subconclusions, that leads to the argument's conclusion:

> Conclusion: I will commit preemptive suicide to avoid the likelihood of contracting Alzheimer's.

Aside from illustrating how her argument is deductive and not inductive, this articulation of Ms. A's suicidal deliberation shows clearly the role and importance of the inclusion of value judgments in reasoning about choosing to die. Without the fourth premise, Ms. A's deliberation would yield nothing more than a sad prediction. It is only inclusion of the fourth premise that results in a conclusion prompting an act: Ms. A's taking her own life or requesting that it be taken.

Appeal to argumentative structure will be unconvincing to those who hold the postmodern conception of rationality as itself historical and so as contextually influenced, as are values and the motives they set in motion. Ms. A's own reasoning would not itself be challenged, but on the postmodern view it would not be accepted as instantiating an ahistorical and wholly objective structure of sound argument.[4] It will be claimed that in another historical context, Ms. A's argument might not justify her choice to die. This is a difficult and often intractable position and requires more extensive treatment than is appropriate here; I consider the position in Chapter 5. For the moment I will take it that the structure of Ms. A's reasoning about elective death is ahistorical and that only its content is historical and contextually influenced.

Before proceeding, a point needs to be made about how I am here presenting the structure of Ms. A's deliberation of elective death. Essentially, the foregoing represents Ms. A's reasoning as a deductive argument. Her conclusion is that she will commit suicide. Some will feel that the reasoning should be represented as an Aristotelian practical syllogism where the conclusion is not an articulated intention prompting an act but an act itself: the act of suicide. However, we are not dealing with a practical syllogism in the case of Ms. A's deliberation. An illustration of the structure of a practical syllogism is the following:

Premise 1: Water slackens thirst.
Premise 2: I am thirsty.
Premise 3: This is a glass of water.
Conclusion: Glug glug! (The act of drinking the water)

Ms. A might well rehearse her reasoning about elective death in the last moments of life, and her act of suicide then would be the conclusion of a practical syllogism, just as is the act of drinking in the previous example. But our concern here is not with the last moments of Ms. A's life or the actual act of suicide; it is with the rationality of her deliberation of whether or not to terminate her life. What we are trying to understand is the rationality of choosing to die, and eventually the moral permissibility of doing so. That means we must focus on the reasoning, on the deliberation and motivation that lead to the decision to commit PS1, SS2, or AS3 or to request euthanasia. Additionally, only PS1 and SS2 could be committed as conclusions to a practical syllogism. AS3 requires

---

[4] Prado, C. G. 2006. *Searle and Foucault on Truth*. Cambridge: Cambridge University Press.

the participation of another person, so it could be a conclusion to a practical syllogism only if the syllogism is thought through or articulated at the last minute after the required assistance has been supplied. RE4 cannot be a conclusion to a practical syllogism thought or articulated by the person whose life is being terminated, though it might be such a conclusion done by the individual performing euthanasia.

* * *

Postmodern objections aside, it is the content of reasoning about elective death, not its structure, that most likely will be challenged in most cases. The obvious reason is that there are a number of different sorts of things that may problematize the content of reasoning about choosing to die. Most notable among these are lack of adequate information, misconstrual of available facts, overly optimistic or pessimistic prognoses and diagnoses, and incomplete or incorrect family history regarding causes of death. Moreover, as mentioned in the Preface, it also will be thought that such considerations as extreme suffering, depression, and denial simply preclude acceptable reasoning about elective death by distorting the content of the reasoning. Intense pain can obscure simple facts, depression can greatly darken an otherwise inconclusive prognosis, and denial can block out the most salient truth.

It is certainly true that in some cases, perhaps even in the majority of cases, suffering, depression, and/or denial can preclude sound reasoning, but it is not true in all cases. What is more important than numbers, though, is that the questions considerations like suffering, depression, and denial raise are not questions about reasoning itself – *pace* the postmoderns – but are questions about the ability or competence of particular terminal patients to reason acceptably. We would not consider reasoning about elective death to be acceptable if done by a patient who is, say, heavily medicated or clinically depressed, but that is not the issue. Of course, suffering, depression, and denial are present in varying degrees in any case of terminal illness, especially in the later stages, but that does not mean that no terminal patients are capable of acceptable reasoning. That view is extremely paternalistic as well as being simply false.

What is true is that it is particularly with regard to the content of reasoning about choosing to die that terminal patients are most dependent on candid input from others, especially health-care professionals. It is much too easy for someone's reasoning to be flawless but based on false premises. However difficult the matter of the content of reasoning about elective death may be in itself, it is made considerably more difficult by how that reasoning may be skewed by being misinformed or not given relevant information. This is why what is called "affective forecasting" is a concern. Affective forecasting essentially is the slanting of what patients are told because physicians, family members, and others make assumptions about patients' reactions to the information in question and factor in the consequences of their assumptions. However, the assumptions about patients' reactions have been shown in several studies to be exaggerated if not largely wrong. There seems to be consistent underestimation of patients' capacity to deal with bad news, as well as of their desire and even need to be told the truth.

An individual contemplating PS1 is faced with the need to check and recheck data relevant to its commission. The matter of content is somewhat less difficult with respect to SS2 and AS3 because in these cases there usually is little doubt about the facts of the individual's medical condition and prognosis. The chief danger regarding content in these cases is being misinformed or being given false hope for compassionate reasons. In cases of RE4, the content issue is almost always straightforward.

The real problem regarding the content of deliberation about elective death, though, is the inclusion of value judgments. Without value judgments operating as premises, reasoning about elective death, no matter how sound, would be powerless to prompt action. In the example giving the structure of Ms. A's deliberation, the fourth premise is the value judgment that she prefers to die before being destroyed by Alzheimer's disease. Without that premise, the argument is only a kind of forecast. But the fourth premise is not amenable to assessment as true or false as is, say, a premise stating that there are genetic determinants regarding the contracting of Alzheimer's. As a value judgment, it is neither true nor false but rather what Ms. A prefers. The question, then, is whether she *should* prefer dying to contracting Alzheimer's.

This is where the only recourse in assessing the rationality of reasoning about elective death is to a balanced consensus of judgment involving those who agree with Ms. A's decision and those who do not. The most crucial role of the appeal to a balanced consensus is to determine whether Ms. A is allowing her values unduly to supersede her interest in continuing to live. The reason the assessment must be balanced between those who agree and those who disagree with Ms. A's value judgment is that where the influence of cultural background looms very large, only those who are outside it can raise many of the hard questions that need to be asked. For example, it may be that Ms. A's motivation is prompted less by her own personal inclinations than by a cultural commitment, say, dread of dependency on others. In this case she needs to gain perspective on her situation, perspective achievable only with input from those whose view of her situation is not dominated by the perhaps exaggerated cultural valuation of independence. On the other hand, her decision may be prompted by something transient, such as despair, which violates important cultural commitments that have defined her life. In this latter sort of case, it is important to have input and support from those who share her cultural values.

Even if there is agreement on the acceptability of the structure of reasoning about elective death, then, there may be serious disagreement about its content when value judgments function as premises. Sound deliberation, in the sense of a conclusion validly inferred from true premises, is not enough by itself to make choosing to die rational, and the content of some of the premises may require separate assessment regarding their rationality.

It must be remembered, though, that questions about the acceptability of the content of deliberation of elective death are not yet questions about its moral permissibility. That is, we are here considering only the assessment of value judgments that function as premises in reasoning. The question of moral permissibility arises only after a verdict has been reached about the rationality of the reasoning behind choosing to die.

Progression to the issue of moral permissibility goes as follows. An individual's choice to die may be shown to be justified after establishing that it satisfies the rationality criteria. This also means that the value judgments functioning as premises in the individual's deliberation are found acceptable: that is, they are found not to contravene the interest in continued life unduly.

The issue of moral permissibility arises once the choice to die is deemed rational. It is now time to turn to the criteria for rational suicide.

*   *   *

Of the various formulations of conditions for rationally justified suicide – and, by extension, rationally justified requests for euthanasia – that I have reviewed over the years, Battin's is the most useful. She gives three "nonimpairment" conditions and two "satisfaction of interest" conditions. The former are (i) having the ability to reason, (ii) having a realistic worldview, and (iii) having adequate information pertaining to the decision to take one's own life. The latter are (iv) that suicide avoids harm in the sense that dying is less harmful to the suicidist than is continuing to live, and (v) that death is in accordance with the individual's fundamental interests.[5]

Working in some other points that Battin makes, her conditions can be fleshed out in this way: for suicide to be rational and justifiable, the decision to commit it must be made in an unimpaired way and according to acceptable standards for clear thinking; commission of suicide must better serve the individual than would continuing to live – typically by precluding pointless suffering; and suicide does not violate some personal value or objective that outweighs endurance of suffering because it gives defining meaning to the individual's life. Battin's conditions are eminently sensible and in most ways are perfectly good. However, they now raise the previously mentioned question of the scope of acceptance of what Battin describes as the usual standards for clear thinking. The growth and recognition of multiculturalism and the cultural relativism inherent in it have effectively precluded conception of standards as "usual" in the sense of commonly accepted.

In my own original criteria for PS1, I tried to spell out more extensively the sorts of considerations Battin appeals to and to mention some I felt needed specific mention. In particular, I attempted to distinguish between suicide as merely a possible option

---

[5] Battin 1984, 289.

for an individual, and suicide as posing a pressing choice for that individual. I also attempted to ensure accessibility of suicidal reasoning and motivating values to others, and to ensure that suicide is supported by the individual's values, but not to a point where those values unduly contravene interest in continued life. As should now be clear, this point has gained major importance.

I earlier also tried to say more specifically how in some cases dying does harm the individual less than does continuing to live. And because the criteria applied specifically to preemptive suicide, I tried to ensure that PS1 is considered and done at a time before suicide becomes SS2 by being driven by the need for release from an actually intolerable situation. A key aspect of this, though, was that PS1 nonetheless be done late enough to allow as much life as possible. As mentioned, the working out of these considerations is available in my earlier books so I will not repeat it here. I simply list the criteria here in order to provide a base for their revision. Note that it is the fifth criterion that makes my earlier criteria specifically about PS1.

The criteria, then, were as follows: PS1 is rational when

1. posing a real option for the agent, it results from mature and adequately detached deliberation consistent with accepted canons of discursive thought, and is unimpaired by reason errors, doxastic or psychological compulsion, false beliefs, or lack of relevant information;
2. the deliberation and operant interpretation of values are accessible to others than the suicidist;
3. suicide is consistent with the agent's well-grounded values without undue depreciation of the agent's interest in continued existence;
4. it is in the interests of the agent, not harming the agent more than continuing to live;
5. it is considered at a specific time, sufficiently prior to imminent or actual deterioration to allow an unforced forfeiture of life to avoid soundly anticipated personal diminishment.[6]

---

[6] Prado 1990, 173.

As will be obvious, the basic trouble with this formulation of the criteria is that it tried to pack in everything of relevance and the criteria ended up looking impossible to meet. Though to a lesser extent, Battin's criteria pose the same problem, but they do so less because of their inclusiveness and complexity than because of their appeal to common understanding of unimpaired reasoning and of fundamental interests. As noted, this common understanding can no longer be assumed. In any case, Battin's conditions and my criteria seem to be of questionable practical use, either because of complexity or because of changing perceptions.

With a view to making my criteria more practically applicable, I revised them in the second edition of *The Last Choice* and again in *Assisted Suicide*.[7] This last revision dropped the fifth criterion regarding timing, thereby making the criteria equally applicable to SS2, AS3, and RE4. Additionally, the simpler formulation seemed more workable. The revised criteria were articulated in this way:

Suicide – note, not only PS1 – is rational

A. when suicide is a genuine option for the agent, chosen after deliberation consistent with accepted standards of reasoning and unimpaired by error, false beliefs, or lack of relevant information;
B. *and* the agent's motivating values are cogent to others, not unduly contravening the agent's interests;
C. *and* suicide is in the agent's interests, not causing more harm than continuing to live.[8]

Criteria A through C are more readily applicable than their pre-decessors, criteria 1 through 5. However, rather like Battin's conditions, criteria A through C still appeal not only to shared understanding of standards for proper reasoning, unimpairment, and cogency, but also to shared understanding of acceptable values and interests. As indicated, the cultural relativism at the heart of multiculturalism now bars this appeal.

* * *

---

[7] Prado 1998; Prado and Taylor 1999.
[8] Prado and Taylor 1999, 39.

What is interesting about my appeal to common understanding of values and interests is that the substance and inclusion of criterion 2 in the first formulation, and criterion B in the second formulation, derived from my study of the work of Jacques Choron. The irony of this is that as early as 1972 – a decade before some of Battin's key contributions on suicide and nearly two decades before I published *The Last Choice* – Choron articulated a condition for permissible suicide premised on the role of cultural diversity.

Choron's condition was that suicide is permissible if the suicidist's motives "seem justifiable, or at least 'understandable,' by the majority of his [or her] contemporaries *in the same culture or social group*."[9] In 1990 and 1999 I used Choron's condition, but not to acknowledge culturally relative values; I used it to ensure that a suicidist's motivation was acceptable to others generally. That is, "other" is used in criterion 2 and criterion B not to refer to other members of the suicidist's cultural group, but to unspecified others who had to accept as cogent the suicidist's motives for choosing to die. The reference to others, then, implies the universality of precisely what Battin speaks of as "the usual standards." The reason for the way I intended criterion 2 and criterion B was that I was unprepared to endorse relativistic criteria for the rationality of PS1. I still am not prepared to endorse Choron's cultural relativism but now realize that it must be allowed for in formulating my revised criteria for rational elective death.

This allowance for cultural diversity means that criteria for rational and so possibly morally permissible elective death must today be framed in light of how assessment of the values motivating choosing to die has been relativized to culture in the minds of many. That is, many now reject recourse to supposedly cross-cultural or universal standards for evaluating motives. The pressing question, then, is how to formulate criteria that balance culturally determined support for choosing to die, on the one hand, and individuals' objective interest in continued life on the other. And here I use "objective" not to refer to mysterious, overarching reality, but only to the fact that culture aside, every living creature has an interest in continuing to live.

The problem about formulating criteria that maintain equilibrium between cultural values and noncultural interest in survival is posed by

---

[9] Choron, Jacques. 1972. *Suicide*. New York: Scribner's, 96–97, my emphasis.

how cultural-peer assessment of the motivation for choosing to die may be biased by shared cultural values and thereby unduly underrate the interest in survival. For example, at one time, elderly Inuit tribe members were expected to go into the wilderness to die of exposure when they could no longer support themselves and contribute to the tribe's survival. Cultural peers, then, could be expected to find elderly individuals' decisions to end their lives fitting and proper, despite the elderly individuals' interest in continuing to live. That interest would be overridden by the cultural valuation of personal independence and communal well-being. Motivation for choosing to die, therefore, would not be adequately questioned in the circumstances.

In the first edition of *The Last Choice* I considered the practice of *seppuku* or ritual atonement suicide motivated by perceived dishonor or failure. At the time I thought some cases of *seppuku* could meet the rationality criteria without relativizing the criteria to Japanese or specifically the *samurai* subculture. However, I now think I was in effect relativizing the criteria in understanding the motivation for *seppuku* too sympathetically. What I was doing is essentially what poses the problem here: once assessment of the motivation for elective death is relativized to cultural values in being circumscribed by those values, there is no external check on undue contravention of the interest in continued life.

At one stage I thought it possible to deal with the problem by appealing to the deontic moral principle of universalizability or the idea that an action is moral only if its performance can be condoned when performed by anyone in similar circumstances. At another stage I thought it better to appeal to the utilitarian moral principle or the idea that an action is moral if it contributes to the greatest happiness of the greatest number. Each of these seemed to provide an external or cross-cultural standard to apply to motivation for choosing to die. But it soon became clear that even if the deontic or the consequentialist principle was accepted as universal or cross-cultural, interpretation of its application invariably would be intracultural. It emerged, then, that instead of attempting to find a cross-cultural or universal standard, it is better to require cross-cultural participation in assessment of the motivation for choosing to die.

The criteria, then, must require that the value content of deliberation about choosing to die be assessed as understandable or otherwise, not as Choron would have it only by cultural peers, but also by members of other cultures. Essentially, involvement of members of other cultures in assessment of the motivation for choosing to die is a matter of their prompting otherwise unlikely reflection on the weighting of cultural values against the interest in survival. This is why it is not necessary that all or even the dominant cultures in a multicultural society participate in the assessment. All that is necessary is that there be *some* diversity of perspectives, values, and beliefs.

However weak the foregoing may appear, it must be made to work in the framing and application of criteria for rational elective death because the alternatives are unworkable. On the one hand, any appeal to universal value priorities that overrule cultural ones will invariably be perceived and dismissed as itself a cultural value and a misconceived one. On the other hand, adoption of Choron's view that motivation for choosing to die is acceptable if it is condoned by cultural peers leads to the insupportable situation that terminal patients would either be forced to endure avoidable agony and personal diminishment, or be too readily allowed to commit SS2 or AS3 or to be given euthanasia because of the dictates of their particular culture.

If we need an illustration of how the second of the foregoing alternatives might play out, we have only to consider Arthur Caplan's concern that it is very likely that given our aging population, "the notion will come that the older ... who are expensive should do the responsible thing."[10] Our culture is in danger of developing an ominously compelling expectation that the elderly, who are increasingly burdening the health-care system, will remove themselves as unproductive Inuit tribe members once did.[11]

* * *

[10] Caplan, Arthur. 1996. Interview on "The Kevorkian Verdict"; includes interview with Timothy Quill, courtroom coverage, and film of Kevorkian and individuals he assisted in committing suicide. *Frontline*, Public Broadcasting System (WGBH, Boston), May 14.

[11] Prado, C. G. 2003. "Foucauldian Ethics and Elective Death." *Journal of Medical Humanities*, 24(3/4): 203–211.

We can proceed by restating criteria A through C. The criteria are intended to establish when choosing to die is rational, and the sense of "rational" must be understood as indicated earlier: that PS_1, SS_2, AS_3, and RE_4 follow on sound reasoning and proper motivation. Recall that criteria A through C specify that choosing to die is rational when it is a genuine option, is chosen after proper and unimpaired deliberation, is motivated by suitable values, and is in the deliberator's interests in the sense that death is less harmful than continuing to live under shortly anticipated or already intolerable conditions.

The first criterion, A, is that choosing to die is rational when it is a genuine option for the agent, decided on after deliberation consistent with accepted standards of reasoning and unimpaired by error, false beliefs, or lack of relevant information. Mention of its being a genuine option was intended to exclude choosing to die because of social pressure of the sort Caplan fears. However, I now think this exclusion is better covered by reference to suitable motivation in the second criterion, so I am dropping the consideration from the first criterion. The rest of the criterion, as it stands, exhibits an attempt to spell out conformity with proper reasoning and absence of error. This can be more concisely put. The result is that the first criterion can be reformulated in this way:

Choosing to die is rational

A1. when the decision is a valid conclusion following from true premises that take account of facts pertinent to the decision.

The second criterion, B, had as its point establishing the acceptability of motivating values and guarding against values' being given too high a priority over interest in survival. I think this point can be better achieved with the following reworded criterion. This is also the place to introduce specific reference to cultural diversity, and to do so I borrow from Choron's condition for permissible suicide, which requires that motivation be "justifiable, or at least 'understandable,' by the majority of ... contemporaries in the same culture or social group."

Choosing to die, then, is rational when criterion A1 is satisfied and, additionally, when

B1. the motivation is justifiable to cultural peers and members of other cultures as not unduly overriding interest in continued life.

The point here is to prevent sanctioning of elective death driven by unrealistically self-sacrificing faithfulness to a value or values – for instance, an obsessive valuation of autonomy and dread of dependency.

The third criterion, C, requires that for choosing to die to be rational, it must not cause more harm than would be caused by continuing to live. This requirement now is adequately covered by the reformulated second criterion, B1. By including specific reference to motivation for elective death that does not unduly supersede interest in continued life, the criterion effectively ensures that choosing to die better serves the individual than does continuing to live.

I believe that criteria A1 and B1 strike a workable balance between absolute and relative considerations, being unstinting regarding the structural standards reasoning must meet, but more accommodating and practical regarding the acceptability of motivation. Before proceeding to clarify points and questions that inevitably arise, I want here to tweak the wording of criteria A1 and B1 to make them more intuitively clear. I also will drop the designations "A1" and "B1" and henceforth refer to the criteria more simply as "the reasoning criterion" and "the motives criterion." At this point, then, the criteria are as follows:

The reasoning criterion requires that for elective death to be rational,

Choosing to die must be based on sound reasoning in which the conclusion follows validly from true premises that include the pertinent facts.

The motives criterion requires that for elective death to be rational,

Choosing to die must be prompted by motivation that cultural peers and members of other cultures judge does not unduly override the interest in survival.

It is to be understood that both the reasoning and motives criteria must be met for choosing to die to be rational.

3

Clarifying and Revising the Criteria

The criteria articulated in the previous chapter raise a number of questions, some of which have to do with the criteria themselves, and some with broader issues. The first question that needs to be dealt with is precisely what the criteria apply *to*.

Specifically, I have been speaking of PS1, SS2, AS3, and RE4, that is, preemptive, surcease, and assisted suicide at the three stages described in Chapter 2, and requested euthanasia at the fourth stage. More generally, I have been speaking of choosing to die and elective death. To deal best with the question of exactly what the criteria apply to, I need to speak of suicide in particular, meaning PS1, SS2, and AS3, and exclude RE4 except where explicitly mentioned.

Since the criteria are offered as a way to establish when suicide is rational, it may seem odd to raise the question of the nature of the object of their application, but as mentioned before, there is currently a significant amount of confusion that glosses the differences among suicide, assisted suicide, and euthanasia. It is important, then, to make as clear as possible what it is that is to be assessed as rational or otherwise, and so as possibly morally permissible.

The *Oxford Companion to Philosophy* has it that "the most conventional definition of 'suicide' is intentionally caused self destruction."[1] Difficulties begin with how "self-destruction" is understood. Properly understood, suicide is self-*killing*, but many take a moralistic position

---

[1] Honderich 1995, 859.

and define suicide as self-*murder*, believing that taking one's own life is never justified and so is intrinsically morally wrong.[2] But to understand suicide as self-murder is preclusively to stipulate its moral status, and so to presuppose the universality of a particular moral principle. Suicide must be defined and understood here in a morally neutral way since we are concerned with the prior issue of whether suicide can be rational. Only if it can be rational, as noted several times, can suicide be moral or immoral according to one or another moral principle or code. The basic definition of suicide I will use, then, is as initially *morally neutral self-killing*. Therefore, the criteria are designed to establish whether it can be rational to kill oneself in anticipation of expected suffering and self-diminishment, to escape actual suffering and self-diminishment, or to do the latter with help. It is only after that question has been answered that the further question arises about whether killing oneself may be murdering oneself or not. By extension, the criteria may be used to establish that it is rational to request euthanasia.

However, even self-killing raises problems because it can be run together with such acts – or non-acts – as "sacrificial death, martyrdom that could have been avoided, actions that risk near-certain death, ... addiction-induced overdosing, [and] coercion to self-caused death."[3] With respect to the applicability of the criteria, the operant definition of suicide has to focus on deliberate and knowing self-killing and exclude these problematic cases as well as those where death occurs as a consequence partly of deliberate actions of an individual but also of factors not foreseen or not under that individual's control. Instances are certain high-risk acts and uninformed or even perverse refusals of treatment.

What concern us are cases of full-fledged self-killing, in the sense that the individuals choosing to die are solely responsible for their own deaths and their self-killing is done knowingly and, in legal terms, "with intent" to die. A heroic soldier charging an enemy position may be described as committing suicide, as may a two-pack-a-day smoker, but the proffered criteria do not apply to these sorts of

[2] Donnelly, John. 1978. *Language, Metaphysics, and Death*. New York: Fordham University Press, 89–95.
[3] Honderich 1995, 859.

cases. To amplify my basic definition of suicide as self-killing, and to make explicit what specific sorts of self-killing the criteria apply to, I will use Tom L. Beauchamp's definition of suicide.

Beauchamp's definition has it that an individual "commits suicide if: (1) that person intentionally brings about his or her own death; (2) others do not coerce him or her to do the action; and (3) death is caused by conditions arranged by the person for the purpose of bringing about his or her own death."[4] Note that the third condition in this definition takes care of the problematic cases of self-sacrifice, reckless behavior, martyrdom, and the like. Suicide, then, will be understood here as *intentional, uncoerced self-killing by one's own action*. That is what the criteria are designed to establish as being rational or otherwise, and so as possibly morally permissible. Failure to meet Beauchamp's definitional conditions precludes application of the criteria for rational suicide. If the action in question is not intentional, is coerced, and/or is not the individual's own action in the sense that death is even in part a consequence of conditions beyond the individual's direct volitional control, the resulting death simply is not suicide and the criteria do not apply.

One sort of question that arises with respect to this definition of suicide is about self-killing by inaction or negative action, such as intentional, informed refusal of treatment – perhaps the most common kind of case of putative suicide in medical contexts. A comparable case is self-killing by refusal to take nourishment. In these cases, an individual does not act positively once to end life, but rather acts negatively numerous times by declining medication or food or by reiterating rejection of necessary surgery or a blood transfusion. Even totally failing to act can be self-killing, as in the case of not moving when in the path of an oncoming train. It may seem odd or even counterintuitive, but inaction can be suicidal, so long as the individual is fully aware of the consequences of inaction and is perfectly able to act to prevent death. Inaction of this sort certainly seems to satisfy Beauchamp's condition that death results from "conditions arranged by the person for the purpose of bringing about his or her own death."

---

[4] Beauchamp, Tom L. 1980. "Suicide." In Tom Regan, ed., *Matters of Life and Death*. Philadelphia: Temple University Press, 77.

The crux of possible questions about these cases is the absence of a decisive act by the agent, such as swallowing pills. What seems most problematic about categorizing inaction or negative action as suicidal where there is no decisive act, especially when the onset of death takes some time as in refusing nourishment, is the possibility of intermittent indecisiveness and/or subtle coercion. In the absence of a decisive act, doubts may arise about the autonomy of a putative suicide. For example, in the case of not taking nourishment, false pride in the original decision may compel an individual to persist in not eating or rejecting intravenous feeding despite wavering intentions. On the other hand, family and friends may weaken resolve with constant appeals to abandon the original intention. However, there is little to say about these cases at a general level; they clearly call for individual consideration. What needs to be done is to assess whether specific cases meet Beauchamp's conditions; if they do, they are cases of suicide and the criteria apply with respect to assessing whether they are or are not rational. We cannot restrict suicide to acts such as putting a bullet through one's own head. The time factor may complicate matters, in that the suicidist's resolve may vary over the weeks or even months it may take to die, and there is danger of coercive influences, but be that as it may, there are no grounds on which to rule out cases of fatal negative action or inaction as not being suicide in a way that precludes application of the rationality criteria to those cases.

Given the foregoing clarification of what the reasoning and motives criteria apply to, it should be clear that the act to which they apply is intentional, knowing self-killing. But once this is clear, a different question arises, which is whether it is actually coherent to choose intentionally and knowingly to die. The question of coherency is essentially whether one can fully understand that death is personal annihilation in choosing to die. Battin acknowledges that "a great many suicides do not accurately foresee" that death is personal annihilation, adding that "Freud claims that this is true of all people, insofar as the human unconsciousness 'believes itself immortal.' "[5]

In Battin's view, this issue is a psychological one to be considered with respect to particular individuals and not a conceptual bar to rational suicide. I think Battin is correct. The coherency question

---

[5] Battin 1984, 299.

derives its force from our inability to *imagine* ourselves dead or anni-
hilated, something no one can accomplish. But that is not the same as
an inability to understand, to conceive of, ourselves as ceasing to exist.

The coherency question may appear to be complicated by religious belief because most religious individuals see death as a transition to another state of being. However, in contemplating suicide,
any rational individual, regardless of how convinced of the promise
of an afterlife, must consider that it is at least possible that death is, in
fact, annihilation. Admittedly, some believers may not be able to
entertain this possibility, or may not be willing to do so, but that is,
again, a matter of particular cases; commission of suicide is not ruled
out by incoherency in any holistic way.

It might still be argued that unconscious or subconscious beliefs
held by all human beings may render contemplation and commission
of suicide incoherent. This basically is the claim that if we are, in fact,
incapable of believing in our own annihilation as Freud claims, then
preferring to die cannot be coherent because the preference is never
really for death but rather for some unconsciously anticipated state of
posthumous existence and that this is so regardless of what we seem
to understand at the conscious level. However, the existence of
possibly distorting unconscious beliefs is not by itself sufficient to
preclude the rationality of suicide. Whatever may be the case at the
unconscious level, it suffices that potential suicidists accept the
finality of death at the conscious level. Otherwise we would have to
accept that the possible presence of distorting unconscious beliefs
renders all reasoning problematic. The real question here is not
whether self-serving illusions lurk in dark corners of our minds, as is
almost certainly the case, but whether it is conceptually possible to
consider death as self-annihilation, and there is no logical bar to such
consideration. It may be difficult to appreciate that committing suicide is to annihilate ourselves, but it must be conceptually possible to
do so; that is, there is no logical contradiction in thinking that death
is annihilation. If we allow elusive subconscious or unconscious
beliefs to preclude the coherency of death as annihilation, we would
have to abandon what then would be the sheer conceit that we are
rational creatures. I will need to return to this point in Chapter 7.

* * *

Important as they are, the foregoing definitional and coherency issues tend to look straightforward in comparison to the thornier issue of the interest in survival, which is the focus of the motives criterion. Battin sums up her own consideration of suicide and interests in this way: "We typically speak of a decision as 'rational' . . . if it satisfies [the agent's] interests."[6] She is, of course, quite right, but her treatment of interests tends to blur the distinction between interests and values. Doing so is unremarkable because for many there is little or no difference between personal interests and deeply held values. There are pressing questions, then, about just how interests are to be determined and especially how they are to be weighted when they conflict with values.

The motives criterion requires that a suicidist's motivation be justifiable to cultural peers and members of other cultures. The inclusion of the latter is designed to provide a check against the suicidist's motivation unduly overriding interest in continued life by giving priority to one or another value because of cultural beliefs or traditions. The concern is that if only cultural peers assess the sui-cidist's motivation, they will likely find that motivation acceptable according to their shared beliefs although the motivation unduly prioritizes values over the interest in survival. If there can no longer be recourse to universal or cross-cultural standards in assessing sui-cidal motivation, the only option is to include members of other cultures in the assessment in order to raise questions about too-ready acceptance of that motivation because of shared cultural values.

There are some infamous cases where suicidal motivation looks acceptable and proper to cultural peers and unacceptable and improper to members of other cultures. One instance was what happened with the appearance of the Hale-Bopp comet in March 1979. The comet's appearance was taken as a sign by members of the "Heaven's Gate" group that they had to kill themselves to be rid of their physical bodies in order to be taken to heaven in the comet.[7] At the time there was outrage at the needless death of the members of the group; most people saw their reasoning as absurd and the

[6] Battin, 1984, 289.
[7] Purdum, Todd, 1997, "Tapes Left by 39 in Cult Suicide Suggest Comet Was Sign to Die," *New York Times*, March 28.

sacrifice of their lives as a tragic waste driven by a bizarre motive. However, clearly the Heaven's Gate members saw their motive and their deaths very differently. Other, more generic, cases that come immediately to mind are the old Indian Subcontinent practice of wives' throwing themselves on their husbands' funeral pyres and the contemporary phenomenon of politically motivated suicide bombers. But the cases most relevant here are less notorious.

Individuals may deliberate suicide and decide on its commission when diagnosed with a disease that in their culture is perceived as both morally disgraceful and physically loathsome, such as leprosy. However, many diseases like leprosy are now treatable and not perceived in the wider world as bearing the stigma they once did. There is no longer any reason, assuming there ever was, for someone who contracts leprosy to commit suicide purely for motives having to do with how the disease is perceived. A more common sort of case is the refusal of blood transfusions for religious reasons. In these cases individuals' deliberations and decisions are not considered to be straightforwardly suicidal, but that is in effect what they often are, despite appearing to be only compliance with doctrine. To people who do not share the relevant beliefs and values, refusal of a necessary blood transfusion will appear unjustified. Many of these cases can be dramatic and usually receive cross-cultural consideration whether sought or not, but there are more mundane cases where matters are less clear. Many older individuals diagnosed with terminal illness may contemplate suicide simply because they do not want to be financial and practical burdens to their families. Their suicidal deliberations and decisions may appear sound to those who share their views, but often there is exaggeration of the burdensomeness of the anticipated dependency. At the very least, it may look to those not sharing the particular values that the decisions to commit suicide are simply made too soon, that a measure of dependency is tolerable in order to give the individuals in question precious months of continued bearable life.

Cultural values and the traditions they engender and support, then, may overshadow basic interests in various circumstances. But as noted, in the absence of recourse to standards that supersede cultural ones, all that can be done is to require that members of other cultures play a role in assessing suicidal motivation. This is to prevent shared commitments to cultural values from being unchallenged when they override an individual's interest in continuing to live. This requirement may look weak in contrast to the reasoning criterion, but given the imperative to respect cultural differences and abandonment of cross-cultural standards, there seems little else to be done. However, even this weak requirement has a complication.

The complication is the heart of the point made earlier that values and interests are not always readily separable. The trouble is that for human beings, interests are largely determined by values. Therefore, the interest in continued life may in fact be properly superseded by values regardless of how they are viewed by those not sharing the values in question. Though intracultural assessments and decisions may be questioned, then, that questioning may be unproductive. That is, the group members may concede that suicidal decisions give priority to value judgments over practical judgments regarding the interest in continued life but maintain that they do so quite legitimately on the grounds that individuals' continued lives would be intolerable if they chose life over the values in question. In the case of *seppuku*, for instance, it would be argued that continuing to live in shame and dishonor would be intolerable for the individuals, and that their lives would properly be sacrificed for the sake of the posthumous honor and respect gained by atonement.

The reasoning criterion offers some additional protection against values' unduly superseding interests by requiring that suicidal deliberation be sound. The significance of this requirement is that operant premises be true. This may be quite important if, for instance, the degree of dependency of terminal illness is being overstated in suicidal deliberation or if more particularly it is wrongly believed a disease such as leprosy is untreatable or is caused by immorality. The trouble is that while the truth or falsity of factual premises may be establishable, the difficulty here precisely is that some of potential suicidists' values function as premises, and values do not admit of positive or negative demonstration.

What is required to deal with problematic values is the more complicated business of showing that values that unduly override interests are ill-founded or exaggerated in application or obsessively held. But here again we end up with a weak solution. Taking this approach to religious beliefs, for instance, is unlikely to be effective in most cases. However, there is nothing else that can be done. The crucial point, then, is that assessment of suicidal motivation involve as clear an assessment of the relevant facts as possible, and that in the assessment there be dialogue with more distanced individuals who are not members of the suicidist's cultural group. With respect to such dialogue, it can at least be argued that if multiculturalism is to be genuine, rather than only camouflage for self-justification, there must be sincere efforts by all concerned to take seriously other cultural views in assessment of suicidal motivation.

* * *

At this point application of the criteria for rational suicide may begin to look most unpromising, but this is not the case. The first point to remember is that the focus here is on suicide in medical contexts; that is, the focus is assessment of the rationality of PS1, SS2, and AS3 as ways to obviate the bearing of intolerable medical afflictions that are incurable, greatly debilitating, and debasing. Consideration of the rationality of suicide deliberated for other cultural reasons, be they religious, political, or social, is not our primary concern. We must focus on the way the cultural element typically affects deliberation of PS1, SS2, and AS3 when an affliction is misrepresented by cultural values as worse than it is, as when leprosy was perceived not only as a devastating and demeaning affliction, but as carrying highly negative moral implications about those who contracted it. Alternatively, the misrepresentation may be of the dependency and/or perceived diminishment the affliction entails. This sort of misrepresentation can be best dealt with by having dialogic input from individuals who do not share the cultural values operant in problematic deliberations of elective death.

A somewhat different issue regarding the balance of motivating values and interest in survival has to do with what is, in the end, a subjective estimation of the advisability of harming oneself in committing suicide to prevent personal diminishment. Here again Battin provides a useful proposal to deal with the issue by arguing that in assessing whether one harms oneself more by committing suicide to avoid bearing something than by bearing it, the key question is "the amount of other experience permitted ... and whether this other experience is of intrinsic value." In other words, assessment of whether suicide is or is not in one's best interests must focus on deciding whether the pain and diminishment risked or borne by continuing to live is outweighed by "important experience" available if one does continue to live.[8]

The sort of case that is relevant here is where individuals considering commission of SS2 or AS3 weigh the value of the escape suicide offers against something they want still to achieve or to continue enjoying despite the pain or diminishment of the affliction prompting suicide. For instance, an individual prompted to escape debilitating pain may be willing to bear it in order to live long enough for the birth of a grandchild. Again, an author may be willing to bear great suffering in order to complete a book that is the culmination of a writing career. Both of these are in line with Battin's view that "important experience" may justify postponing or perhaps even forgoing the release provided by suicide. There are, of course, more commonplace examples of individuals willing to bear a great deal to continue their rewarding contact with friends or simply to relish pleasures still available to them. The particulars are not important; what is important is that when consideration of SS2 or AS3 becomes a reality in someone's life, the interest in continuing to live usually narrows to weighing the value of ending suffering against the value of something that life still offers. Though probably not necessary, it may merit mention that PS1 is not relevant here because in the case of PS1, what a potential preemptive suicidist may choose to do for some countervailing value is risk the onset of a dreaded condition, not bear the suffering of an existent one. Also, in the case of RE4 developments will have progressed too far for the balance issue to arise.

In connection with Battin's point about what important experience may still be possible, it is important to keep in mind that human beings are surprisingly adaptable. Consideration of suicide, especially PS1, at a given time may be premature in light of what the potential suicidist may be able to cope with later. Most able-bodied people dread physical dependency, for instance, and some might consider PS1 or SS2 as preferable to being physically impeded in some serious way. However, those same individuals may adapt

---

[8] Battin 1984, 312.

reasonably well to the feared condition. What this point introduces is that individuals contemplating suicide cannot be certain that they will in fact find the anticipated condition intolerable. This is not the case with respect to afflictions like Alzheimer's disease because, as I have argued before, the diminishment Alzheimer's and other forms of dementia cause actually destroy the persons they afflict long before these afflictions destroy those persons' bodies.[9] Moreover, dementia rules out SS2, AS3, and RE4. But as far as PS1 is concerned, even dread of intellectual diminishment could be problematic if it has more to do with too-demanding self-expectations than with actual competence.[10]

There are conditions that do not destroy the person though they severely handicap and punish the body – one need only think of Stephen Hawking and how productive his life has been despite his nearly total physical incapacity. The weighing of the benefit of avoidance of suffering by committing suicide against the personal cost of continuing to live, therefore, is complicated by the fact that most individuals really do not know how they will respond to being in the situations they dread, and, however difficult, this is a factor that must be taken into account in applying the criteria for rational suicide. Again as in the case of cultural values, the only recourse here is to dialogue, to discussion repeated over time and with various concerned persons as a check against underestimating one's ability to cope with adversity. Dialogue is also necessary to guard against rashness, misinformation, unrealistic fears, obsessiveness, and all the other factors that can cloud an individual's self-destructive decisions. Given the priority of personal autonomy in making the decision, it is somewhat paradoxical that the intensely personal matter of choosing to die should not be a solitary decision.

* * *

The need for dialogue in implementing the criteria for rational suicide is particularly evident with respect to certain preclusive perceptions many have. An especially difficult instance is how, for some,

---

[9] Prado 1990, 1998.
[10] Prado 1990, 40–44.

balancing suicidal motivation and interest in continued life is an incomprehensible exercise because they see life as having incomparable and inviolable value and so as generating an interest in survival that overrides any contrary values and precludes suicidal motivation's ever being acceptable. This view is common enough that it engenders a pronounced counterproductive tendency of some clinicians and many members of the public to discount individuals' values heavily when those values prompt abandonment of life. Individuals' conclusions that dying is in their interests because it accords with their highest values is seen by those holding this view as confused or more likely as caused by transient depression or desperation, or as just pathological. When the interest in survival conflicts with values, these same individuals take it that the conflict is due to misguided favoring of those other values because they find it unfathomable that dying could possibly be in anyone's interest. This perception is waning in importance, but it still poses an obstacle to acceptance of SS2 and much more to PS1; more importantly, it poses a preclusive obstacle to legalization of assistance in commission of AS3 and, of course, to provision of such assistance.

This perception of life as having inviolable value is not just a mistake; the misconception is more complicated. To think life as such has inviolable value is to think confusedly of life as having value per se rather than as being the most basic condition of achieving value. A little reflection should reveal that sheer survival has quite problematic worth if its conditions preclude attainment of any other value. Human beings are capable of enduring great suffering to comply with a moral code or religious creed that prohibits suicide or to achieve goals that have great meaning for them. But when they do so, they do not endure suffering for the sake of merely surviving; they do so for the sake of the value they place on their goals or their moral, social, religious, or personal commitments. This is what Richard Rorty has in mind when he defines being rational as in part being able to "establish an evaluative hierarchy" and so to "set goals other than mere survival."[11]

[11] Rorty, Richard. 1992. "A Pragmatist View of Rationality and Cultural Difference."
      Philosophy East and West, 42(4): 581–596, 581.

Choosing to survive for the sake of values, when choosing to die would better serve one's interests, is rational, and it is the other side of the coin of allowing values to override the interest in survival. But admirable though this capacity may be, it should not be overrated. In cases where individuals would be better served by SS2 or AS3 but insist on bearing great suffering for the sake of values, dialogue is as necessary as in contrary cases where values unduly override the interest in survival. There should be dialogic assessment of the values individuals are trying to serve. In some cases, there may be as much misperception of values preventing suicide as there can be when values unduly prompt suicide. Nonetheless, it must be noted that the criteria for rational suicide establish necessary conditions; they do not yield sufficient conditions for elective death. Elective death remains just that: elective, at one's choice. The point of the criteria is to assess whether the choice is soundly made. Even if the criteria are met in every respect, their satisfaction does not make suicide rationally compulsory. The criteria establish only what reason allows may be done, not what reason requires be done. If individuals choose to forgo rational SS2 or AS3, which may be strongly advisable, for the sake of values they seek to serve, that is their option.

As alluded to previously, it may look questionable to rely on dialogue in cases where the motives/interests balance in suicidal deliberation is problematic. The thinking likely will be that choosing to die should be a wholly autonomous, uninfluenced decision and act. But the hard fact is that our capacity for autonomous decision making is limited by our humanity. Application of the criteria for rational suicide cannot be contingent on an unrealistic and unachievable level of capacity to deliberate and make decisions in a wholly autonomous and purely rational way. We are, after all, human; few if any of us can deliberate and make decisions that are uninfluenced and unimpaired. As Battin puts it, "perhaps none of our acts are ever *wholly* rational," since human actions "are never wholly free from emotion, training, circumstantial coercion, or other arational components."[12] This is why dialogue is crucial. There is need for the shaping of a

---

[12] Battin, Margaret Pabst. 1982. *Ethical Issues in Suicide*. Englewood Cliffs, N.J.: Prentice-Hall, 297.

reflective consensus as to whether suicidal decisions are soundly reasoned and properly motivated.

Even if multiculturalism did not pose the challenge it does to the use of criteria for determining the rationality of suicide, it would be true that successful application of the criteria is inherently dialogical. The moment values enter the equation, either as premises in deliberation or as motives for choosing to die, it becomes necessary to engage in exchanges of views to achieve the most realistic assessment of individuals' reasons for ending their lives. The criteria are not a kind of calculator that accepts premises, values, and conclusions as input and produces positive or negative appraisals as output.

*   *   *

Another clarification that needs to be made before moving on to the next chapter was anticipated in discussion of questions raised by suicide where there is no decisive fatal act but only refusal of nourishment or treatment. I agree with Dan Brock, who maintains that the judgment or decision to die made by suicidists who end their lives by killing themselves with drugs or a bullet is the very same judgment or decision made by individuals who in effect kill themselves by refusing nourishment or necessary treatment.[13] But this view is not universally shared. The very fact that I needed to add "in effect" in the previous sentence is indicative of the problem. Many see refusal of treatment, and even refusal of nourishment, as "letting nature take its course." The judgment or decision to forgo nourishment or treatment is not seen as suicidal because it is an indirect measure. This difference is significant where there are moral or religious prohibitions against suicide. Catholics, for instance, may not actively take their lives, but there is no religious requirement that they accept treatment without which they will die.

The other side of the nature-taking-its-course view has to do with terminal patients who are entirely incapacitated, want to die, but are unable to get assistance in suicide or euthanasia. They may request cessation of intravenous nourishment or other life-sustaining

---

[13] Brock, Dan. 1989. "Death and Dying." In *Life and Death: Philosophical Essays in Biomedical Ethics*. Cambridge: Cambridge University Press, 144–183.

treatment, and with few exceptions, usually religiously motivated ones, attending clinicians do not consider themselves to be assisting in suicide by complying with those requests. It is highly relevant to this view that while assisted suicide is illegal in most jurisdictions, refusal of treatment or of nourishment is seen as a patient's right and clinicians not only are not required by law to feed or treat patients forcefully, they are prohibited from doing so.

The question that arises now is just how the criteria for rational suicide apply to cases where a decision is made to die by refusing nourishment or life-sustaining treatment. The question is posed by how the absence of a decisive lethal act implementing the decision results in a problematic temporal element. If the decision to die is made but negatively implemented by forgoing nourishment or treatment, it seems the decision must be remade at every subsequent opportunity to accept nourishment or treatment. And the time between the initial decision and death allows for changes in the reasoning and motivation behind the choice to die, and there is no guarantee that the reasoning and motivation that satisfy the criteria at one point will continue to satisfy the criteria throughout the drawn-out process of dying. It is not at all difficult to imagine how the initial reasoning or motivation could be invalidated over time. For instance, an increase in depression may distort the suicidal reasoning if it is periodically rehearsed when facing the repeated difficulty of refusing nourishment or treatment, or that same difficulty may turn the original resolve into prideful obstinacy. Can it suffice, then, that the criteria for rational suicide be applied and met at the time of the initial decision? Or must the criteria be reapplied on every occasion when nourishment or treatment is available?

Despite my agreement with Brock that the decision to die is the same whether followed by a decisive lethal act or the delayed effects of forgoing nourishment or treatment, I think that the criteria for rational suicide cannot be applied only to the initial decision in cases where the person choosing to die does not perform a decisive lethal act but chooses to die by refusing nourishment or treatment. But to reformulate the criteria in a way that would deal with even most of the questions raised by the temporal factor in choosing to die by refusal of nourishment or treatment would result in precisely the counterproductive complexity I rejected earlier and am trying to avoid. On the other hand, it seems hopeless to attempt to apply the criteria on every occasion when nourishment or treatment is offered or might be taken. The only solution appears to be that the criteria should be reapplied, not at every instance, but periodically: that is, often enough to ensure that the original sound reasoning and proper motivation for choosing to die remain operant and are undistorted.

*   *   *

Given the foregoing clarifications regarding the reasoning and motives criteria, it is evident that their formulation requires fine-tuning. At the end of the last chapter, the reasoning and motives criteria stated that for suicide to be rational, choosing to die must be based on sound reasoning in which a conclusion follows validly from true premises that include pertinent facts, and choosing to die must be prompted by motives that are judged by cultural peers and members of other cultures as not unduly overriding the interest in survival. While this formulation has the advantage of avoiding the complex inclusiveness and explicitness of criteria 1 through 5 and A through C, as set out in Chapter 2, it clearly takes too much for granted. The question now is whether the reasoning and motives criteria can be made sufficiently more explicit without undermining their clarity and practical applicability. The way to proceed is first to recap the foregoing clarifications to establish what most needs to be made explicit in the criteria.

The first clarification had to do with what the criteria actually apply to, and that is "intentional, uncoerced self-killing by one's own action." The second clarification had to do with the coherency of choosing to die, but what was concluded earlier about that need not figure in the wording of the criteria. The third clarification had to do with the balance of values and interests, but that is already adequately dealt with in the motives criterion, though it might be better stated. The next clarification had to do with the importance of dialogue in assessment of suicidal motivation. This is a crucial matter and is at present only implied in the motives criterion's requirement that both cultural peers and members of other cultures participate in the assessment of motivation. Restatement of the motives criterion, then, could include explicit reference to dialogue. Finally, there was the clarification calling for repeated or periodic assessment of suicidal reasoning and motivation when the choice to die is implemented by forgoing nourishment or treatment. This, again, may be dealt with by restating the motives criterion.

In light of the first clarification, I believe that both the reasoning and motives criteria need to be more explicit regarding what they apply to. It would be better, then, to replace the phrase "choosing to die" with explicit reference to suicide. However, "intentional, unco-erced self-killing by one's own action" is clumsy and simply using the word "suicide" runs the risk of misinterpretation. Not only is suicide taken to be self-murder by some, but as noted, there currently is a marked inclination to confuse cases of SS2, AS3, and RE4. I think the phrase "autonomous self-killing" is a good compromise. "Autono-mous" covers the need for the act to be intentional, knowing, and uncoerced, and "self-killing" is explicit and unambiguous. The one problem is that by using "self-killing" the criteria appear to be effec-tively limited to PS1, SS2, and AS3 and to exclude RE4 or requested euthanasia. However, the exclusion is only apparent. The key point is that in the case of euthanasia, the criteria apply to the reasoning and motivation leading to the act of *requesting* euthanasia.

A preliminary restatement of the criteria, then, would look like this. The first would read, "Autonomous self-killing must be based on sound reasoning in which a conclusion follows validly from true premises that include pertinent facts." The second would read, "Autonomous self-killing must be prompted by motives that are judged by cultural peers and members of other cultures to not unduly override the interest in survival."

The next point is that as noted more than once, it is important that what the criteria address is the rationality of suicide in medical contexts. That is, the criteria are about assessing the rationality of preemptive avoidance of or release from intolerable conditions attendant on terminal illness, whether those conditions are the intellectual destruction of the person or the physical devastation wreaked by great pain and incapacity. As mentioned earlier, there are other reasons for considering suicide, but the criteria I am pro-posing here cannot cover the range of reasons people have for choosing to die. The point is to produce criteria for rational suicide that can be usefully applied in medical contexts. They must, there-fore, be focused in order to be as effective as possible.

The question, then, is how best to refer to the range of catastrophic afflictions that either destroy individuals intellectually before destroying them physically, like Alzheimer's, or devastate individuals physically, causing massive suffering, dependency, and consequent psychological damage, before killing them, like ALS. A phrase like "catastrophic affliction," though, invites too much interpretation so it is best to use "terminal illness" as the least ambiguous term. Including reference to terminal illness in the statement of the criteria affords the opportunity to include reference to dialogue. As well, the reasoning criterion can be rephrased to remove its slight redundancy. Finally, to obviate the need to leave implicit the requirement that both criteria must be satisfied for choosing to die to be rational, the criteria can be recast as clauses of a single criterion. The new – penultimate – version, then, reads as follows:

> Autonomous self-killing as release from terminal illness is rational if the decision follows validly from true premises that include the pertinent facts and enacting it is judged in cross-cultural dialogue not to override interest in survival unduly.

This is what will serve in the chapters that follow as the criterion for rational suicide and, by extension, requesting of euthanasia. In stating the criterion as I have, I am using the term "release" broadly to include anticipatory avoidance of terminal illness. This is necessary in order for the criterion to cover PS1 or preemptive suicide. Second, I decided not to risk referring simply to "sound reasoning" in the reasoning clause because the technical use of "sound" may not be clear to some. Instead, I spell out that the decision to die, as a reasoned conclusion, must follow validly from true premises.

* * *

The point of this and most of the previous two chapters has been to use the stating and revising of my original criteria for rational suicide to explore the main considerations involved in assessing how suicide can be rational. In the next chapter I proceed to consider the sorts of problems that arise regarding application of the reformulated criterion for rationally choosing to die. It is also in the next chapter that I begin to consider the moral permissibility of elective death.

4

Application Issues

The impact of multiculturalism and relativism on assessment of the rationality of choosing to die has to do with the fundamental imperative to respect culturally diverse values. Doing so means that assessment of deliberation of elective death must accommodate culturally determined values that influence deliberation of preemptive suicide, surcease suicide, assisted suicide, and requested euthanasia – PS1, SS2, AS3, and RE4. The concern is that values may influence deliberation in problematic ways. The motives clause of the rationality criterion requires that for it to be rational, choosing to die must be "judged in cross-cultural dialogue not to override interest in survival unduly." The clause's point is to guard against undue depreciation of interest in survival by cultural values shared by those choosing to die and those assessing their elective-death deliberations and decisions.

It will look to many as if the problem posed by the need to respect diverse cultural values in assessing elective-death decisions is not so much cultural values' unduly overriding interest in survival as those values' precluding elective death even when it best serves terminal patients. This is no doubt a serious problem and clearly poses difficulties for some terminal patients suffering greatly and wanting to die. However, in dealing with life and death issues, the priority must be the possible violation of the interest in survival rather than proscription of elective death. Even if instances of cultural values' unduly overriding the interest in survival are few in number, in assessing elective-death decisions they are the ones that matter. The criterion developed in the last three chapters has to do with testing the rationality of choosing to die, not the rationality of being required to live.

There are moral, religious, and what I will call broadly aesthetic cultural values that may prompt individuals to choose to die without giving due weight to their interest in continuing to live. In my experience and in the experience of practicing medical ethicists I have consulted, despite their diversity cultural values influence terminal patients' elective-death decisions in relatively few and repeatedly encountered ways. The following are expressions of motivation for choosing to die that typify the ways moral, religious, and broadly aesthetic cultural values influence elective-death decisions made by terminal patients:

1. I choose to die so as not to burden my family.
2. I choose to die because merciful God does not want me to suffer needlessly.
3. I choose to die to rejoin my (deceased) partner.
4. I choose to die rather than lose my autonomy.

The motivation at work in these examples arises from moral convictions, metaphysical beliefs, and broadly aesthetic estimation of personal qualities and may seriously underweight and so unduly override patients' interests in continuing to live. With respect to the first, the underweighting of the interest in survival may be due to terminal patients' overestimation of the burden they pose for their families and underestimation of the willingness and readiness of families to care for them. With respect to the second, the existence, nature, and will of God are taken as evident although all three are problematic. The third motivating reason is similar to the second in that it presupposes a problematic metaphysical reality. With respect to the fourth, terminal patients may again be overestimating the consequences of their illness and underestimating their adaptability and resilience.

All of these value-influenced motives call for the cross-cultural dialogue required by the motives clause of the rationality criterion because all of them call for inducing those choosing to die to reflect critically on their motives for dying. However, two of the motives are easier dealt with than the other two.

Motives illustrated by the first and fourth of the preceding examples – choosing to die to prevent being a burden or to prevent loss of autonomy – call for clarification of the levels of dependency and personal diminishment that individuals actually face. The dialogue the motives clause requires would, for instance, involve discussions with others who have the same terminal illnesses and with those experienced in caring for such patients. It would also involve discussion with others who are not cultural peers of those choosing to die, since overestimation of the burden they pose may be due to low cultural tolerance of dependency. For instance, dependence may be seen as not only inordinately burdensome to others but as dishonorable. The aim of cross-cultural dialogue in these cases is to persuade those choosing to die to understand that they may be seriously overestimating both the character and the scale of their dependency, as well as the degree to which they will be incapacitated.

Motivation illustrated by the second and third examples – choosing to die because God wills it or there is promise of an afterlife – is considerably more difficult to deal with. What is required is appreciation by those deliberating elective death that it is decidedly possible that what they unquestioningly believe to be true may not be true: God may not exist and there may be no afterlife. However, given the likely depth of these beliefs cross-cultural dialogue may well prove insufficient to prompt adequate critical reflection on them. But it is the fact that they *are* beliefs that makes assessment of this motivation more complicated.

The complication is that the expressions of motivation illustrated in the second and third examples are not expressions of straightforward value-based choices as are those in the first and fourth examples. The reason is that in choosing to die because of what God wills or the wish to be with a dead partner, the choices presuppose beliefs that function as suppressed or tacit premises in the deliberation of elective death. That means the beliefs must be assessed by application of the reasoning clause. Application and possible satisfaction of the motives clause are insufficient in these cases.

Consider the second example:

I choose to die because merciful God does not want me to suffer needlessly.

This statement, as the conclusion of deliberation of elective death, presupposes no fewer than four tacit premises:

1. There is a God.
2. God is merciful.
3. (Because God is merciful) God does not want anyone to suffer needlessly.
4. God does not want me to suffer needlessly.

The problem posed by these tacit premises is that in order to establish that the reasoning about elective death is sound and not merely valid, the premises have to be shown to be true. But because of their metaphysical nature, the premises cannot be shown to be true – or false, for that matter. Therefore, the presence of the premises, even though tacit, precludes satisfaction of the reasoning clause and hence of the rationality criterion.

It merits mention that it is possible for the motives clause of the rationality criterion to be deemed satisfied even if motivation entails problematic beliefs, and this need not happen only in intracultural assessment of motivation. The reality is that belief in God, and in an afterlife, is very widespread across all cultures, so individuals' choices to die may "seem justifiable, or at least 'understandable' " even in the cross-cultural dialogic assessment of them required by the motives clause.[1] If this is the case, the clause will be satisfied. However, satisfaction of the motives clause by itself is insufficient to satisfy the rationality criterion.

The ubiquity of belief in God also poses a problem to the extent that most religions prohibit suicide and euthanasia, usually on the principle that God-given life is not ours to take at will. Religious cultural values, then, may preclude PS1, SS2, AS3, and RE4 and prevent some who want to die from doing so. Moreover, because of the prevalence of belief in God, religious cultural values may influence cross-cultural assessment of elective-death deliberation so that it goes against terminal patients' choices to die even when doing so is in their best interests.

---

[1] Choron 1972, 96–97.

What emerges, then, is that cross-cultural assessment is an uncertain means of assessing elective-death motivation. However, given the greater risks attendant on intracultural assessment, cross-cultural assessment is preferable. Moreover, we have to keep in mind the essential point behind Choron's contention that a decision is acceptable if it seems justifiable to those assessing it. We also have to remember Battin's point that a decision is deemed rational if it meets "the usual standards."[2] If we understand "the usual standards" not as implicitly universal, but as those normally appealed to in intra- and cross-cultural assessment, then her point has the same force as Choron's. That force simply is that in any given assessment situation, it is the judgment of the majority of those involved in the assessment and the standards that majority normally uses that decide the issue, whether or not that decision accords with more objective or broader-based standards than those used in the assessment. This is, in essence, the heart of the view that assessment standards are historical or contextual. As we will see in the next chapter, while this idea is tolerable enough and basically inescapable with respect to assessment of motivation, it is unacceptable when it concerns soundness of reasoning.

In any case, as noted, our concern is with values' unduly inclining individuals toward choosing to die. We may well have doubts about cross-cultural assessment of elective-death decisions that bar PS1, SS2, AS3, or RE4 for religious reasons, but this is generally in line with the main purpose of the rationality criterion. That is, the rationality criterion's main role is protective of the interest in continued life. The point of applying the criterion is to ensure that deliberation leading to the choice to die is argumentatively sound and that motivation is acceptable. At present, doubts about preclusive cross-cultural assessment of elective-death motivation amount to erring on the safe side. So long as this is so, cross-cultural assessment is acceptable. The danger is that attitudes toward the elderly and the sick will change and that preclusive religious influences notwithstanding, cross-cultural assessment of elective-death motivation will err on the side of too readily accepting that motivation. This is the sort of possibility that Caplan worries about: that eventually the majority of people will come to feel that the old and infirm "should do the responsible thing."[3]

*   *   *

Cultural values and the beliefs they generate, then, may function as questionable premises, as motives, or as both in deliberation of elective death. And they may work to lessen unduly the importance of continued survival. There may, for instance, be too high an estimation of what I am calling broadly aesthetic values such as personal autonomy or honor; religious doctrines may be either too literally or too fervently interpreted; obligations to others may be exaggerated. Any of these may compel individuals ruinously to underestimate their interest in continued life.

What is called for when application of the rationality criterion identifies undue value-driven diminishment of the interest in survival is what the motives clause requires: cross-cultural dialogue about the problematic motivation. As I have described, the aim of dialogue is to prompt those choosing to die to reflect judiciously on their motivation in light of input from both their cultural peers, who share their values, and others who do not share those values or share them but interpret them differently.

When metaphysical beliefs function as supposedly factual premises, the same sort of cross-cultural dialogue is required, but its objective is more difficult to achieve. That objective is to oblige those deliberating elective death to take seriously the possibility that the relevant beliefs may not be true, and so to cease using them as tacit factual premises in reasoning about choosing to die. In other words, the objective is to induce the person deliberating elective death to recognize that since beliefs in God, an afterlife, reincarnation, or the like cannot be demonstrated to be true, they must be understood as actually *choices*. That is, those who choose to die partly on the basis of metaphysical beliefs must recognize that what underlie their decisions are not objective truths but their choices to take something as being true. This recognition then enables them to assess the beliefs as choices by application of the motives clause, thereby resolving the problem posed by the

[3] Caplan 1996.

unmeetable requirement that the beliefs be established as true in order to show elective-death reasoning is sound.

Broadly speaking, there are five possible outcomes to engaging in cross-cultural dialogue about either or both reasoning and motivation in elective-death decisions: First, dialogue may persuade assessors that those choosing to die have satisfied both clauses of the rationality criterion. Second, dialogue may prompt adequate reflection on questionable motives by those choosing to die and dissuade them. Third, dialogue may prompt adequate reflection by those choosing to die but not dissuade them. In this case, the motives clause might still be satisfied if an expanded or rethought explanation of the motivation is acceptable to cross-cultural assessors. Fourth, those choosing to die may fail or refuse to recognize that metaphysical beliefs functioning as tacit factual premises do not admit of proof and must be acknowledged as choices. This would preclude satisfaction of the reasoning clause. Fifth, dialogue may fail to prompt those choosing to die to reflect on questionable reasoning, motivation, or both. In this case the assessors will need to consider deliberators' states of mind and competence to commit PS1, SS2, or AS3 or to ask for RE4.

With respect to the third outcome, where reflection fails to dissuade, what ultimately are at issue are deliberators' choices. The import of this is that if individuals facing serious threats to their well-being or already afflicted choose to commit PS1 or SS2, but the motives clause of the rationality criterion is not satisfied, their choice to die may have to be accepted. Intervention is justified in these cases only if the reasoning clause is also not satisfied. Regardless of how determinate the choice, personal autonomy does not trump faulty or error-based reasoning for choosing to die. Faulty or error-based reasoning is as much a basis for intervention as is evidence of clinical depression or pathology. The rationality criterion's two clauses, then, are not of equal weight; the reasoning clause has priority.

Matters are different with respect to AS3 and RE4, because both AS3 and RE4 involve the participation of others who have fiduciary and legal obligations and liabilities. Even putting aside questions about legality, if those choosing to die are not dissuaded after being prompted to reflect on questionable motives by assessors, they may not be given the assistance they need to commit AS3 or be given RE4.

And since AS3 and RE4 presuppose that those choosing to die cannot take their own lives because of physical incapacity, elective death is effectively precluded for them.

Lack of satisfaction of the reasoning clause is at once more preclusive of elective death and almost certainly more contentious. The reason it will be contentious is that in the vast majority of cases the beliefs jeopardizing elective-death reasoning will be beliefs in God and in an afterlife. These are beliefs held by most members of all cultures. Therefore, assessors who share a culture with elective-death deliberators, as well as assessors who do not share their culture, in all probability will hold the same beliefs true. The majority of assessors, then, will not see the tacit-premise roles of belief in God and in an afterlife as preventing satisfaction of the reasoning criterion.

The differences in the strictness of the satisfaction requirements of the reasoning and motives clauses center on the priority of autonomous choice and on how assessment of motivation is unavoidably less clear-cut than assessment of reasoning soundness. The main problem posed by dialogic ineffectiveness, then, is posed by values or value-determined beliefs operating as factual premises. If dialogue fails to produce recognition of these as basically choices, the reasoning clause cannot be satisfied. In the following I offer what may serve as a solution to this problem, but before outlining my suggestion, I need to make a rather different point about how cultural values may affect deliberation of elective death.

*   *   *

Dialogic efforts to have elective-death deliberators recognize that metaphysical beliefs operating as tacit premises are really choices by them to hold something true are not efforts directed at having deliberators abandon, deny, or even suspend their beliefs in deliberating PS1, SS2, AS3, or RE4. The aim is only to elicit from them recognition that what they are treating as facts actually are not facts. The point is to prompt deliberators to see that they cannot deliberate ending their lives on the basis of beliefs that cannot be established as true. In short, the point is for deliberators to recognize that their beliefs *are* beliefs rather than knowledge.

Achieving the required recognition will be most difficult in the case of deeply held religious beliefs because the response is certain to be that revelation, miracles, and sacred texts do prove the beliefs to be true. However, deliberators of elective death must be made to see that this likely response is circular thinking. It is circular to argue that revelations, miracles, and sacred texts prove the existence of God, since it is precisely the God whose existence they supposedly prove that makes something a revelation, a miracle, or a sacred text.

With respect to moral and broadly aesthetic motives, the sought-for recognition is quite different than with respect to metaphysical beliefs. Basically it amounts to inducing individuals deliberating elective death to understand that practical application of moral and aesthetic principles invariably calls for a measure of moderation. The point is to prompt consideration that moral or aesthetic principles are being too strictly understood and that what they disallow – dependency, diminishment, and the like – may in actual cases be of an order that does not warrant dying to avoid them, Crucially, though, moral and aesthetic values rarely figure as putatively factual premises in reasoning about elective death and usually are adequately dealt with by the motives clause of the rationality criterion.

It is religious beliefs that present the greatest difficulty for application of the rationality criterion. To illustrate, recall the case of Ms. A. Initially she considered PS1 because of the threat of Alzheimer's and later considered SS2 (or still later AS3) on being diagnosed with ALS. Her deliberation regarding PS1 included Premise 4: "I prefer to die rather than be destroyed by Alzheimer's." This premise is a value judgment and is clearly presented as a choice in Ms. A's deliberation. As a choice, the premise is not appraised for truth or falsity because it does not play a part in the conclusion's soundness; it is a motivational, not factual, element in Ms. A's deliberation and its assessment involves the cross-cultural dialogue required by the motives clause of the criterion. But if we change this one premise to a religious one functioning as factual, we come up with the following line of reasoning:

Premise 1: Those whose parents both contract Alzheimer's disease are likely to contract the disease.
Premise 2: Both my parents contracted Alzheimer's.

Subconclusion 1: I am likely to contract Alzheimer's.

Premise 3: Alzheimer's destroys people long before they actually die.

Subconclusion 2: I am likely to be destroyed by Alzheimer's long before I die.

Premise 4: Merciful God does not want me to be destroyed by Alzheimer's.

Conclusion: I will commit preemptive suicide to avoid the likelihood of contracting Alzheimer's.

This argument may be structurally valid, but it is unsound because Premise 4 cannot be established as true. Note that Premise 1 has not been established as true, but it is possible eventually to establish it as at least statistically true or false. However, unlike Premise 4 in the original argument, which articulated Ms. A's preference regarding dying before contracting Alzheimer's, in the new argument Premise 4 presupposes three points that are taken as matters of fact but that are not factual in the sense of being establishable as true or false. The first is that God exists; the second is that God is merciful; the third is that God does not want Ms. A to be personally destroyed by Alzheimer's.

If those assessing Ms. A's reasoning share her beliefs, they will likely accept the premise, as discussed earlier. However, there is another likely possibility arising from the multiculturalist imperative to respect individuals' cultural values and beliefs. Given this imperative, the likelihood is that even assessors who do not share Ms. A's beliefs will take it that the problematic premise is "true for" Ms. A. If this occurs, the rationality criterion will be construed as satisfied. However, the criterion will not be satisfied so long as Premise 4 remains operant as a factual one because Premise 4 cannot be demonstrated to be true or false, and so soundness of reasoning cannot be established. To accept that the premise is "true for" Ms. A essentially is to take her reasoning at face value and to accept it as we might have to accept someone's autonomous choice in application of the motivation clause.

If Premise 4 is accepted as "true for" Ms. A and her reasoning as sound in this way, we end up with a worse situation than the motives clause is designed to exclude, which is likely pro forma intracultural application of the rationality criterion. This is because here truth, and so reasoning soundness, is relativized to *individuals* on the pretext of respecting diverse cultural values.

Relativization of truth and reasoning soundness has major philosophical implications, but the implication that most immediately concerns us is actually a practical one. If truth and soundness are relativized because of the multicultural imperative to respect diversity, we end up with the paradoxical consequence that assessment of elective-death deliberation in a multicultural society is effectively always intracultural, whether the culture in question is that of a group or an individual.

Most of the trouble here is related to the way multiculturalism is popularly misconceived. Too many see a multicultural society as just a *collection* of diverse cultures. But if a multicultural society is to be a *society*, as opposed to just so many different cultures coexisting, members of the diverse cultures have to interact meaningfully. This means that while they all must respect each others' cultural values, they must also acknowledge what is common to them, and some of the most basic things common to them are standards for truth and sound reasoning. What usually obscures these commonalities is that multiculturalism's imperative to respect diversity is usually invoked to protect the cultural values of minorities. There is a tendency, then, to overlook what is common to all cultures and to focus on what is special and, in being special, most problematic regarding the respect of others.

However, a truly multicultural society is not one where minorities' cultural differences are merely tolerated by a majority and/or where cultural groups are tolerant of but basically indifferent to other cultural groups' values and practices. Unfortunately, recent immigration into Europe and North America has tended to support this misconceived idea of multiculturalism because of newer immigrants' unpreparedness to assimilate themselves into the culture of their adopted countries. The result is that "multiculturalism" is widely understood as applying to societies constituted of numerous cultural groups that coexist but otherwise have little to do with one another. This is nowhere more evident than in the adjustments that have been made in North America and Europe regarding language and education. It is striking to see legislators wrestle with the question of a nation's "official" language or languages, to have automatic teller machines require selection of one of four or six languages, and for primary and secondary schools to encompass cultural "streams" in subject matter and teaching methods.

Multiculturalism is not simply a matter of tolerating a number of values and practices; it requires acknowledgement of fundamental commonalities, some of the most basic of which are abstract standards for truth and reasoning soundness. What is reasoned about may vary by culture, and the priority of various truths may vary by culture, but the standards for reasoning soundness and for establishment of truth cannot be relativized to culture. As abstract standards independent of content, these must be recognized as universal, as cross-cultural. I return to this point in Chapter 5.

* * *

To proceed, then, is there a workable way to deal with culturally influenced premises that function in reasoning as factual but are actually articles of faith? Differently put, is there a way to open such problematic premises to productive assessment short of engaging in inconclusive philosophical or theological argument and speculation? To clarify my suggestion, consider again the case of Ms. A.

In the original case presented earlier, Ms. A considers committing PS1 because of the threat of Alzheimer's. However, she does not commit PS1 and is later diagnosed with ALS. She is still able to deliberate committing SS2, but unless she acts fairly quickly, Ms. A will be able to deliberate only AS3 or RE4. Regardless of whether it is SS2, AS3, or RE4, though, the premise that posed problems in the reasoning about Alzheimer's has a parallel in the new reasoning about ALS. Ms. A's new reasoning has the following structure:

> Premise 1: ALS is a terminal condition in which death is preceded by dreadful debilitation.
> Premise 2: I have been diagnosed with ALS.
> Premise 3: Merciful God does not want me to bear the dreadful debilitation caused by ALS.
> Conclusion: I will commit SS2/AS3 to avoid the dreadful debilitation.

In this new argument, it is Premise 3 that poses problems by implying the existence of God, stating that God is merciful, and further stating that it is God's will Ms. A not bear the pointless pain and diminishment of her condition. The difficulty is, as noted, that Premise 3 operates as a factual premise in the reasoning but is an article of faith.

How, then, might Premise 3 be dealt with effectively? What I want to suggest is that the best way to deal with such premises is not to question the problematic premises but to consider whether they can be replaced in the reasoning with what I will call *proxy premises*. To illustrate what I mean, consider the problematic premise in the foregoing argument:

Merciful God does not want me to bear the dreadful debilitation caused by ALS,

Assessors of Ms. A's reasoning could raise questions about whether God exists, or they could use dialogue to attempt to induce Ms. A to acknowledge that her premise is not factual but rather a choice she makes to accept as true her beliefs about God's existence, nature, and will. However, application of the reasoning clause of the rationality criterion might better proceed by determining whether a *proxy* for the problematic premise – one that allows the original conclusion to follow validly – is acceptable to Ms. A.

The following proxy premise should meet both requirements:

I *choose* not to bear the dreadful debilitation of ALS because I *believe* merciful God does not want me to.

The key aspect of this proxy premise is that reference to a merciful God is not an essential element of the premise. What the proxy articulates is not putative facts about God's existence, nature, and will, but a *choice* with an attached reason. And the attached reason explicitly states the reference to a merciful God's intentions as a compound *belief*. The proxy, then, turns the original problematically factual premise into a composite volitional one that has as its central element the expression of a choice, and only as a secondary element the reason for that choice.

What use of the suggested proxy achieves regarding assessment of the deliberation of elective death is that the problematically factual premise is made an expression of a choice, and so the need to establish its truth evaporates. The proxy premise then becomes the subject of the motives clause of the criterion, rather than of the stricter reasoning clause.

Of course, the original problematic content of the premise – the existence, mercifulness, and will of God – is only shifted to a subsidiary role and remains problematic as a reason for the choice. But what is gained is that Ms. A's beliefs cease to operate as purportedly factual but unconfirmable premises and thereby to preclude satisfaction of the reasoning clause of the rationality criterion.

The foregoing example involves religious beliefs functioning as premises; this is the most difficult sort of case. In the case of moral or broadly aesthetic values functioning as premises in deliberation of elective death, we usually are able to proceed with assessment without using proxy premises. For example, a premise might go as follows:

It is wrong to burden my family with my protracted suffering and dependency.

Or it might say:

Dying is better than letting demoralizing dependency lessen me as a person.

Both of these are clearly value decisions or choices and do not pose the problems caused by religious beliefs operating as implicit or explicit premises and entailing unconfirmable existential claims. The premises would need to be replaced by proxies only if they entailed that moral precepts or aesthetic principles are objective in some Platonic sense. If that were the case, then each of the premises would require replacement with a proxy that separates the choice aspect from the claimed objective existence of the precept or principle.

To reiterate, what proxy premises do in the case of religious premises is make explicitly motivational what is presented in the original premise as factual. In doing so, the proxy premises effectively remove the obstruction to assessment of the soundness of the reasoning caused by the impossibility of establishing the truth of metaphysical beliefs. More positively, the proxy premises oblige elective-death deliberators to take responsibility for their choices and motives for those choices rather than present them jointly as matters of fact.

Admittedly, there are a number of problems in using proxy premises. The most obvious is that deliberators may not accept them. Moreover, the deliberators' cultural peers may not accept them. If either happens, all that can be done is to press the question of whether deliberators are choosing to die for religious, moral, or broadly aesthetic reasons, or take themselves to be compelled to commit PS1, SS2, AS3, or to ask for RE4.

Compulsion regarding elective death unfortunately is not as rare as one might think. For instance, it may be believed by some that they have no option but to end their lives because God requires sacrifice of life as an act of faith to avoid personal dishonor. However, this and others like it are extreme positions and it is still only a smallish number of deliberators and cultural peers that believe there are such requirements. If they do, there is no option but to refrain from applying the rationality criterion, since the result of its intracultural application in these cases would be a foregone conclusion because soundness of reasoning would always be trumped by doctrine and the extremeness of the position would preclude effective cross-cultural dialogue.

The basic difficulty here is that if the existence of God and God's commands or requirements is uncompromisingly taken by deliberators of elective death and their cultural peers as unquestionably true rather than as conceivably fallible articles of faith, application of the rationality criterion's reasoning clause is pointless. While application of the criterion's reasoning clause might expose other flaws in reasoning or establish the soundness of premises and subconclusions not influenced by religious doctrines, such partial success would be insufficient to establish the rationality of choosing to die. So long as one or more unconfirmable value-determined beliefs function as factual premises, the soundness of reasoning about elective death remains unsettled, at best, and conclusions about commission of PS1, SS2, or AS3 or requesting of RE4 remain problematic regarding their rationality.

*   *   *

The burden of much of the foregoing in this chapter is that in a multicultural society, we cannot allow matters of life and death to be decided purely intraculturally. To do so is to relativize truth, reasoning soundness, and acceptability of fatal motivation. It also is to negate the very idea of a multicultural society by construing it as merely a collection of coexistent, disparate cultural groups. This will be surprising to many because the common view is that multiculturalism enables assessment of actions or practices to be intracultural precisely by respecting cultural diversity. However, this is a misperception, one likely fostered by how appeals to multiculturalism are usually prompted by concern that the cultural values of minorities be respected.

Considering life-and-death issues and multiculturalism reveals that so far little attention has been paid to reciprocity. The result is that in most cases what sought-for respect for diverse cultural values amounts to is only increased tolerance for minority values. However, for multiculturalism to be coherent as a concept and productive as a social reality tolerance is not enough; there must be respect and respect must be reciprocal. Minorities, especially tightly cohesive immigrant groups, must respect the values and practices of the majority as well as those of other minorities. Unfortunately, resentment of historical intolerance and political considerations often impede this reciprocity. As a result, multiculturalism simply has not been achieved.

In nations or even national regions where a particular culture is powerfully dominant, it may well be that assessment of the rationality of elective death must proceed intraculturally. This is not because that is desirable, but because there is little option. But in a multicultural society, assessment cannot be entirely intracultural, at least not in the case of life and death issues. A multicultural society existing in one nation, if it truly is to be a society and a nation, cannot allow matters of life and death to be decided by the values and practices of the individual cultural groups that compose it. To do so is to dissolve itself into its cultural components and to make a sham of its nationhood.

No society or culture is indifferent to the lives of its members, regardless of how low the value put on some of those lives. There is always governance of the termination of life. No society can afford to allow the termination of life without regulation. Even in societies that enslave people and devalue their lives, while the life of the humblest slave might hang on the master's whim, it does not hang on just anyone's whim. It is no different with individuals who take their own lives. Though few Western countries still criminalize suicide, there is still governance of self-killing if only to the extent that assisting it is now illegal in almost all jurisdictions, and intervention is expected, if not required, where there is any suggestion of pathological or irrational motivation.

As members of a multicultural society, we are willing to let some people live and suffer more than they should to keep faith with their core values. But we cannot allow some people to die at will for the same reason. We cannot allow assessment of elective-death deliberation to be intracultural any more than we can allow application of the criminal code to be intracultural. To be a *society*, a nation must have principles and laws that apply equally to all its members, however culturally diverse those members may be. Principles dealing with life and death – prohibition of murder, of kidnapping, of rape – must be as cross-cultural as those defining citizenship or ownership. With respect to PS1, SS2, AS3, and RE4, the fact is that cultural values may disproportionately promote elective death, and that is what compels formulation of the motives clause and its requirement for cross-cultural assessment of elective death.

Some will think that assessment of deliberation of elective death does not require cross-cultural input because even if cultural values are shared by deliberators and assessors, those assessors will not necessarily find the rationality criterion satisfied. But what poses the problem with intracultural assessment of elective-death reasoning and motivation is the *likelihood* that they will. Requirement of cross-cultural dialogue in assessment is made necessary, not by inevitability of problematic intracultural unanimity, but by its probability.

The problem posed by possible cultural unanimity in assessment of elective-death deliberation is, ironically enough, a direct consequence of precisely what multiculturalism demands be recognized and accepted, namely, that cultures differ in terms of the core values that define the social selves of their members. Given these differences, it is no surprise that the same motivation for elective death that is acceptable and even admired in one culture may not be acceptable and may be deplored in another. But while multiculturalism demands that we accept and respect this diversity, so long as we are all human beings and death likely is personal annihilation, a cross-cultural perspective on elective death is as indispensable as on murder, kidnapping, and rape.

A consideration that merits mention here is the temporal one. For instance, a given culture may have values that too readily prompt suicide in cases where dependency is seen as jeopardizing personal and family honor. But much has changed since most cultures arose and their core values were developed, and some cultural values may prompt action that is now out of line with present circumstances. Certainly North American society now can and does bear a higher degree of dependency among its members than it could or did bear three hundred years ago, and dependency no longer has the stigma that earlier periods attached to it. Moreover, not only can greater dependency now be accommodated in social and economic terms, but technology has provided means by which it can be significantly ameliorated in many cases. Suicidal deliberation undertaken in 2008, then, should not weight dependency in terminal illness as negatively as would have been appropriate in 1708 or even in 1908.

The need for cross-cultural dialogue in the assessment of elective-death deliberation arises from the possibility that there may be a culturally determined but questionable acceptance of the deliberation. If there is no such unanimity, intracultural application of the rationality criterion may be sufficient, but if appraisal by members of other cultures identifies problematic values unduly overriding the interest in survival, the conclusion that must be reached by all concerned is that cross-cultural dialogue is required to properly assess motivation for choosing to die.

*   *   *

The motives clause's requirement for cross-cultural dialogue raises the practical issue of *timing*, an issue that I touched on earlier in connection with choosing to die by refusing treatment or nourishment. Here, the issue is broader and has to do with the timing of elective death by any means when the choice is made to die rather than bear the ravages of terminal illness. As described, the cross-cultural dialogue required by the motives clause will clearly involve significant periods. For one thing, as was mentioned, it is important that those choosing to die discuss their motivation with others a number of times to establish that theirs is not a transient decision made in a moment of despair or desperation. The more obvious consideration is that cross-cultural assessment of motivation will involve several people and will take time because the more people are involved, the longer it takes to get them together to engage in the required dialogue. All of this means that there is some pressure on those deliberating elective death and those assessing their deliberations with respect to the timing of PS1, SS2, and AS3. As will emerge, RE4 does not pose a significant timing problem.

I outlined in Chapter 2 how my original criteria for PS1 included consideration of the timing of elective death. The point about timing with respect to preemptive suicide is that for PS1 to be a rational act, it must be committed when one surrenders the least amount of worthwhile life that is practically possible but still dies before the onslaught of the dreaded illness. As reproduced in Chapter 2, the criterial reference to timing regarding PS1 was that preemptive suicide is rational if the first four criteria are satisfied and PS1 is committed at a time that is

> sufficiently prior to imminent or actual deterioration to allow an unforced forfeiture of life to avoid soundly anticipated personal diminishment.

The importance of timing for PS1 is special because the potential suicidist only *anticipates* a debilitating and diminishing disease. The importance of timing is rather different in the case of SS2 and AS3. Choosing to die necessarily involves choosing *when* to die, but in SS2 that choice is dictated in large part by the potential suicidist's physical condition and the progression of the relevant terminal illness. In AS3, timing must involve the availability of those willing to provide the necessary assistance.

More specifically, individuals deliberating SS2 do so because their lives are already blighted by a terminal condition. The key difference with PS1 is that if the feared condition is already present, thereby precluding PS1 and requiring SS2, then there are known factors that affect timing directly. For instance, in Ms. A's original situation, when she considered PS1, the crucial question about timing was how long she might wait to end her life while still free of Alzheimer's. However, after she is diagnosed with ALS, the timing question is much more straightforward and centers on capacity. Ms. A, familiar with Sue Rodriguez's plight, needs to commit SS2 as late as she can, but soon enough not to risk being unable to commit surcease suicide and then finding she is not able to persuade someone to help her commit AS3.

If Ms. A passes the point at which she can commit SS2, she and those assessing her deliberation have to consider what she is willing to bear and when assistance in commission of AS3 might be available to her – putting aside the matter of the legality of assistance. In cases of RE4, the timing question is resolved by the individual's physical condition, and given the legal aspect and other considerations, RE4's timing will almost invariably coincide with some treatment situation, most likely surgery. Unlike PS1, then, the timing of SS2, AS3, and certainly RE4 is progressively dictated by the point to which the relevant disease has progressed and what the person afflicted is willing to bear.

There are psychological complications regarding the timing of SS2 and AS3. Consider yet again the case of Ms. A. Once diagnosed with ALS, and late enough that she is already significantly incapacitated, she decides to end her life rather than endure what the disease still holds for her. Assessors find that her reasoning and motivation satisfy the two clauses of the rationality criterion. Ms. A, then, is at a point where the decision as to when to commit SS2 – which she is still able to do – is her own. But those experienced with terminal illness and consideration of elective death know that there is a marked tendency for terminal patients who decide on SS2 to put off its commission once they actually have the means to end their lives and are able to do so at their option. In interviews with terminal patients one hears that when termination of life became a real option for them, the pressure to commit SS2 abated. If Ms. A delays for this somewhat elusive psychological reason, she will soon find herself unable to commit SS2 and dependent on assistance to commit AS3.

A different but related complication is that when the SS2 option becomes a real one for her, Ms. A may find she is psychologically incapable of taking her own life. But if she does not commit SS2 fairly promptly, she may find she is no longer physically able to do so. It may seem that her next option is AS3, assuming assistance is attainable, but this option still requires Ms. A to perform the crucial act of ending her life, regardless of the assistance provided, and if she was unable to commit SS2, she may not be able to perform the minimal act involved in committing AS3.

Another complication is that even if Ms. A is capable of committing SS2 and prepared to do so, she may be loath to take her own life with the means most readily available to her, such as slashing her wrists or asphyxiating herself. But acquiring the appropriate drugs may well affect timing and cause Ms. A's resolve to weaken or possibly prompt desperation that affects the rationality of her decision.

Still another complication that arises with respect to the timing of SS2 is that individuals intent on its commission almost certainly will be encouraged by those caring for them to hold out as long as possible, perhaps even until AS3 is required. This well-intentioned advice would have as its point enabling terminal patients to live as long as possible, given their conditions and decisions, but it may seriously alter the situation. If Ms. A follows such advice, she very likely will end up dependent on assistance to commit AS3 rather than being able to commit SS2, and then find that illegality bars her receiving the necessary assistance.

These comments do little more than sketch some problems regarding the timing of elective death, but the point is not to attempt detailed consideration of timing questions; it is only to indicate the kinds of difficulties that arise. Our focus in this chapter is on issues to do with application of the rationality criterion, and timing problems certainly merit mention. However, their importance here lies not in their details; it lies in the fact that application of the rationality criterion proceeds in situations having many ramifications, one of which is timing. Clearly, we cannot pack into the criterion all the considerations and requirements to deal with these many ramifications. The point regarding timing, then, is that those assessing the reasoning and motivation of terminal patients deliberating elective death must be constantly aware that assessments of those patients' positive decisions have a temporal dimension.

We saw in considering choosing to die by refusing treatment or nourishment that reasoning and motivation cannot be continuously assessed over the time it takes for individuals to die for lack of nourishment or treatment. What needs to be done is to review or even repeat the assessment periodically. In a similar way, even when active commission of SS2 or AS3 is planned, positive assessments of reasoning and motivation for elective death have temporal limits and may need to be reviewed or repeated if there are significant delays.

* * *

To close this chapter, I need to touch on a common perception that affects deliberation of elective death and assessment of that deliberation. Brief consideration of this perception is important in its own right, but it also serves as a bridge to the next chapter by shifting our focus from application issues and motivation to soundness of reasoning about elective death.

Media coverage of assisted suicide and euthanasia in particular and of multicultural issues in general conveys the strong impression that being on one or the other side of an issue about core values is determined by personal background influences rather than by reasoning about the issues. I believe that as is often the case, the media here are not imposing an idea on the public but reflecting what many think. It does seem to be widely thought that being for or against abortion, assisted suicide, or capital punishment is a matter of *having* a position as opposed to *taking* a position in the sense of reasoning one's way to it. Pro or con positions on such issues, like the values that underlie them, are perceived as products of rearing, education, and enculturation rather than as deliberate espousals based on reasoned consideration.

As a consequence of this perception, it is assumed that with respect to issues like legalization of assisted suicide, all that can be done is to wait and see which group prevails in the courts. What is crucial here is that it is presupposed that individuals' views on these issues are not amenable to change through reasoned argument because those views are not the products of reasoning in the first place.

There is, of course, little question that as we are reared, educated, and enculturated we internalize values that determine the cast and much of the content of our attitudes and beliefs. It is also clearly the case that the majority of people never reflect seriously on these inculcated values as adults. The most common sort of case where reflection – and often rejection – does occur is with respect to religious affiliations. Often such reflection is spurred by clashes in close relationships or, as we have seen of late, scandal in one or another organized religion. Less often there is reflection on – and again often rejection of – other values, beliefs, and attitudes, as when children raised in a racist environment reject racism after being prompted to consider it critically by events in their own lives or the lives of others. And unfortunately, perception of the inculcated character of values and the positions they generate is repeatedly reinforced when people argue about moral, social, and political issues. It invariably appears to those on each side of arguments as if those on the other side are unwilling or unable to think through the implications of their positions or really appreciate the nature of whatever claim or event prompted the argument.

If core values and the beliefs and attitudes they support are perceived as unchangeable, as the fixed effects of rearing, education, and enculturation, the impact on deliberation of elective death is that positive or negative decisions are taken as predetermined and assessment of them as pointless. Worse still, individuals' responsibility for their decisions is drastically reduced or is eliminated altogether. The criterion for assessing the rationality of choosing to die, then, becomes a useless abstraction and its application a sham or rationalization. Cross-cultural dialogue about elective-death deliberation is rendered ineffectual because, based as it is on different inculcated values, it can only clash with the decisions made, or, if it does concur with them, it does so only coincidentally.

However, unless our conception of ourselves as *homines sapientes* is a delusion, we must understand that reason can prevail over the deepest internalized values and that a sufficient measure of objectivity can be achieved in deliberation of elective death and assessment of that deliberation. With this point in mind, we need now to turn to another challenge to reasoning about elective death: the historicization of reason and rationality.

5

What Standards?

There is little question that assessing motivation for elective death across different cultures poses serious difficulties. But however difficult assessment of motivation might be, it at least is open to the cross-cultural dialogue required by the motives clause of the rationality criterion. If nothing else, the value of human life affords a shared basis for discussion of its deliberate abandonment. Moreover, however difficult the application problems considered in Chapter 4 might be, they also are open to cross-cultural dialogue. In short, motivational assessment is amenable to the most intuitive treatment: we can *talk* about it. We can also talk about the application issues it raises. What we need to discuss in this chapter is still more difficult. Assessment of elective-death reasoning is harder than of motivation because the problems it poses are partly about the very standards used in the assessment. And the standards at issue are fundamental: they are what determine whether a claim or belief or premise is true and whether reasoning is sound. The greater difficulty, then, is due to the need first to find common ground to discuss differences about what standards are appropriate to use in the assessment of elective-death reasoning.

As noted earlier, there is a significant contemporary relativistic inclination to consider reason and rationality historical in nature, and if reason and rationality are deemed historical, the standards for sound reasoning and the truth of beliefs or premises are in effect relativized to culture by being made historically contextual. This is because culture is one of the most important determinants of historical contexts. The import of contemporary historicist relativism – usually glossed as "postmodernism" – for what concerns us is that just as some believe that motivation for choosing to die must be intraculturally assessed, some also believe that elective-death reasoning must be intraculturally assessed. The idea is that individuals' reasoning about choosing to die must be assessed by their own culturally determined standards for reasoning soundness and for truth. This is essentially Choron's view of elective death as acceptable if an individual's choice to die is understandable to cultural peers.

The main difficulty cultural relativization of standards causes for us is that if intracultural assessment of the motivation for elective death poses problems regarding undue depreciation of the interest in survival, then intracultural assessment of reasoning soundness clearly poses similar problems that are at least as serious.

Attempting to deal with cultural relativization of standards regarding sound reasoning and the truth of belief begins with trying to understand precisely what the content is of the claim that such standards are relative to culture. For instance, taking perhaps the most obvious case in point, it is difficult to see how *validity* could vary from culture to culture. For a logical argument to be thought valid in one culture and invalid in another culture seems intelligible only if what vary are interpretations of premises and conclusions rather than the logical rules governing the drawing of conclusions from premises.

If it is claimed that it is the rules of logic themselves that vary, that is like claiming that addition varies from culture to culture and that adding 5 and 7 equals 12 in one culture but equals 57 in another culture. What one wants to say in response to this claim is that there is misunderstanding of what *addition* is. In like manner, the only response to the claim that validity varies by culture seems to be that there is a misunderstanding of what validity is.

Unfortunately, we cannot attempt to answer the question about what it means to relativize standards to culture by articulating relativistic philosophical positions. It will not be enough to have recourse to a good encyclopedia of philosophy or to a book like Michael Kraus's on relativism.[1] The trouble is that we are not here dealing

---

[1] Krausz, Michael. 1989. *Relativism: Interpretation and Confrontation*. Notre Dame, Ind.: Notre Dame University Press

with familiar philosophical relativism. The relativism that concerns us certainly is in the tradition of Pythagoras's contention that we are the measure of all things, of Nietzsche's pronouncement that there are only perspectives, and of Foucault's understanding of forms of rationality as endlessly created.[2] But the relativism that concerns us differs from traditional relativism in that it does not only construe standards as relative; the relativism that concerns us is different and perhaps novel in having a *deontological* basis. That is to say, the position basically is that we are morally obliged to hold standards relative.

The relativism that bears on questions about cultural diversity and elective death has a deontological basis in the sense that unlike traditional relativism, it does not arise primarily from epistemological acceptance of the purported unattainability of objectivity. The relativism that concerns us does arise partly from claimed recognition of the hopelessness of achieving objective knowledge but primarily arises from misconceived extension of the ethical imperative to respect persons as ends in themselves.

Traditional relativism's source, as illustrated by everyone from Pythagoras and Sextus Empiricus to Descartes and Hume, is the alleged epistemological impossibility of establishing observation-based or empirical beliefs as being objectively true and hence constituting *knowledge*. Traditional relativism's thrust is that beliefs cannot achieve the status of knowledge because they cannot be demonstrated to be objectively true, and the conclusion reached is that therefore their truth must be held relative to individual or to group perspectives.

The relativism that bears directly on assessment of elective-death reasoning has a different focus than beliefs about the world. The relativism at issue is in a sense second-order because its focus is judgments about individuals' beliefs. Differently put, this form of relativism is about the legitimacy or propriety of individuals' believing what they do, rather than about the correctness of the content of what

[2] Nietzsche, Friedrich Wilhelm. 1968. *The Will to Power*. Ed. Walter Kaufman and trans. W. Kaufman and R. J. Hollingdale. New York: Vintage Books, 267; Foucault, Michel. 1988. "Critical Theory/Intellectual History." In Lawrence D. Kritzman, ed., *Michel Foucault: Politics, Philosophy, Culture: Interviews and Other Writings 1977–1984*. New York and London: Routledge, 17–46, 35.

they believe. The classic basis for relativism – renunciation of the possibility of epistemological certainty regarding empirical matters – is certainly shared. However, the emphasis is not put on forgoing the archetypal standard for the truth of beliefs – conformity to objective reality – because of the impossibility of establishing that the standard is met. That much is taken as given. The emphasis is rather on the impropriety of judging beliefs false *because they are held by persons who must be respected*. Since no beliefs can be demonstrated to be objectively true or false, they must be judged true for those individuals holding them in virtue of their being held by those individuals.

For the sake of distinguishing it from traditional relativism, I will call the position that concerns us *cognitive libertarianism*: "cognitive" because the position is about *beliefs* and their truth or falsity, and "libertarian" because it is essentially a broadly permissive moral position. Cognitive libertarianism, then, is the view that respect for persons necessitates holding their beliefs "true for them."

The underlying thinking goes something like this: in the absence of objective standards that can be met and be known to be met, respect for persons requires that what they believe is true *be* true for them. What is seen as justification for this is that in the absence of objective standards, the only opposition to particular individuals' beliefs being deemed true is contrary beliefs held by *other* individuals, but respect for persons bars giving preference to the beliefs of any one individual or group of individuals. Beliefs, then, do not derive their truth from conformity to external or objective realities but from the very fact that they are held by persons.

The key idea that underlies the foregoing thinking, and so cognitive libertarianism, is that in being held, beliefs are partly constitutive of individuals as the persons they are, and that the moral imperative to respect persons therefore puts their beliefs beyond the judgment of others because that imperative entails acceptance of those beliefs as constituents of the persons that must be respected.

This conception of beliefs as constitutive of persons connects cognitive libertarianism and multiculturalism because the constitutive beliefs that partly define persons are taken to be the direct or indirect products of enculturation. If there were only one global culture, individuals' beliefs would be largely similar and so in being held true for them those beliefs would be held true for most people. But there are many cultures, and each fosters its own beliefs, so there is great variety in the beliefs that are deemed true for the individuals holding them. However, one culture or many, individuals' beliefs, as well as their standards and values, are culture-determined constitutive elements of who they are as persons and so demand respect as parts of persons demanding respect. Given that individuals' standards, values, beliefs, attitudes, opinions, desires, and inclinations are the results of rearing and training rather than of individual choice or inquiry, the imperative to respect individuals as persons entails the obligation to accept what they believe as "true for them" because what persons hold true is largely what they have been made to hold true. The parallel is with accepting individuals' racial characteristics as part of who they are.

*   *   *

Though it is not presented as such, the most succinct statement of the thinking underlying cognitive libertarianism that I have found is an argument formulated by Roger Paden and discussed by James Rhem in connection with consideration of relativism among university students.[3] That they use the argument to consider students' views does not qualify or weaken its usefulness here because regardless of Rhem and Paden's own focus and objectives, the argument nicely captures the essence of the view I am calling cognitive libertarianism.

The argument, of course, is not one that Rhem or Paden – or I – think sound; nor is Paden's formulation of it intended to portray the argument as sound. The argument is intended only to reflect what relativistic students think, and dubious though the argument's soundness may be, it does encapsulate that thinking. However, it is important for my purposes to appreciate that the thinking the argument captures goes well beyond university students. Though Rhem and Paden focus on what they see as a troublesome and wrong-headed view held by students, one that obstructs productive education, the view in question is now quite widespread. Paden's argument,

---

[3] Rhem, James. 2006. "Responding to 'Student Relativism.'" *The National Teaching and Learning Forum*, 15 (May 4): 1, 2, 4.

then, does not just capture a line of thought students take up; it captures thinking that I believe is of a piece with conception and endorsement of contemporary multiculturalism and thinking that seems to be gaining dominance in our society. Rhem makes clear that he also believes this form of relativism is not limited to students when he remarks that students fall into it because of "the thoughtless cultural pressure for relativism we all experience."[4]

Paden's argument is as follows:

1. Respect for persons requires that everyone has a right to his or her own opinion.
2. Therefore, it is wrong (i.e., impermissible) to try to force anyone to change his or her opinion.
3. Arguments can force someone to change his or her opinion.
4. Therefore, it is not morally possible (i.e., is impermissible) to argue against someone's opinion.
5. If it is not possible to argue against an opinion, it must be true.
6. Therefore, if someone holds some belief, then due respect for that person compels us to say that belief is true for that person (even though it is not true for me).[5]

The fifth premise is the argument's worst element but can be made more plausible, if not viable, by inserting "morally," "accepted as," and "for whoever holds it." The insertions also clarify why Paden introduces truth into the argument in the fifth premise. The altered premise would read as follows:

5a. If it is not *morally* possible to argue against an opinion, it must be *accepted as* true *for whoever holds it*.

As will emerge later, the addition of "accepted as" actually will not work beyond the argument because it would be rejected by cognitive libertarianists, who insist that beliefs *are* true for those who hold them, not that they only must be accepted *as* true. I return to the point; what is important here is that Paden's argument captures how

[4] Rhem 2006, 4.
[5] Rhem 2006, 4.

respect for persons is seen as requiring holding their beliefs true for them as an integral part of respecting them as persons. Slightly differently put, beliefs held by individuals must be respected as true for those individuals on the basis of the moral imperative to respect those individuals as persons. This latter statement is what I will use to express the essence of cognitive libertarianism.

With the basic idea of cognitive libertarianism in hand, I now need to say something about how – somewhat paradoxically – cognitive libertarianism is a position espoused by *supporters* of multiculturalism, but a position only rarely espoused by *members* of the cultures multi-culturalism embraces.

*   *   *

What supporters of multiculturalism add to cognitive libertarianism, which is essentially individualistic rather than communitarian, is that respecting persons and their beliefs also requires respecting their collective cultural standards, beliefs, and values along with their individual ones. The key idea, referred to earlier, is that as usually endorsed, multiculturalism demands that persons be respected as individuals, but as individuals who not only are representative mem-bers of cultural groups but most importantly are the persons they are because of how they were enculturated. This key idea is quite distant from the liberal individualism so long dominant in North America, which determines cognitive libertarianism's focus on individ-uals' beliefs. The idea is the communitarian one that persons are who they are and have the rights that they have as members of communities, and hence as members of cultures, not simply as individuals.

We come, then, to the problem alluded to previously, a problem with two complicated aspects: one generated by the nature of the relativism inherent in multiculturalism, and the other by the character of the many cultures multiculturalism attempts to embrace. Briefly put, the first aspect has to do with the difference between *individual* relativism and *cultural* relativism; the second aspect has to do with the fact that most cultures are not themselves relativistic. The complication, therefore, is that while support for multiculturalism is invariably cul-turally relativistic in conception and impetus, few of the cultures mul-ticulturalism tries to embrace are relativistic in tradition or allegiance.

Historically, philosophers have distinguished between cultural relativism, as defined in Chapter 1, and individual relativism; the distinction is basically in terms of how, in the former, standards – particularly truth – are relativized to groups' shared perspectives, while in the latter they are relativized to individuals' own personal perspectives. It merits mention that some argue that cultural relativism is unstable because once truth is relativized, there is no effective way to prevent its ultimate relativization to individuals' own perspectives. It also merits mention that individual relativism, however initially qualified or nuanced, can also collapse into what Michael Krausz calls "extreme relativism" or the view that "all claims involving truth ... are on a par."[6] However, what is most relevant in the present context is cultural relativism because it is what underlies multiculturalism. Recall the definition of cultural relativism given in Chapter 1 as holding that members of one culture cannot form valid judgments about the beliefs or practices of other cultures that differ from their own and so that all such assessment must be intracultural.[7]

In cultural relativism, because truth and other standards are relative to the perspective of the cultural group, individual members of the group must accept their culture's defining beliefs as true and endorse their culture's values. In individual relativism, truth is determined by individuals' own judgments, so standards and beliefs in effect are identified and beliefs and values held are products of individuals' particular experience and inclinations. Beliefs and values, then, are held and applied as individuals judge appropriate at particular times and in particular contexts.

As noted, cognitive libertarianism – exemplified by the student relativism Rhem and Paden worry about – is individual relativism. What must be respected are individuals' own beliefs; it is individuals' own beliefs that are true for them. Requiring individuals to accept group standards and beliefs would be seen by cognitive libertarians as unwarrantedly authoritarian and unconscionably disrespectful of persons; it would be seen as violating individuals' rights by attempting to force on them beliefs claimed to be universal truths despite the impossibility of establishing them as such.

---

[6] Krausz 1989, 1.
[7] Mautner 2005, 132.

As now conceived, multiculturalism seems to preclude individual relativism for two reasons. First, the basic idea is, of course, that standards and beliefs are relative to culture, and so they are what the community holds as opposed to what given individuals hold or may hold. Second, and somewhat less obvious, is that from the multiculturalist perception the beliefs given individuals hold are products of those individuals' enculturation and group membership. Therefore, what the individual members of a given culture hold should be the same set of standards and the same basic beliefs. If particular individuals reject some standards or beliefs held by their cultural community, it is either because they have embraced a heresy of one or another sort or because something went wrong with their enculturation. This is especially true of what concern us most, which are fundamental standards and core or doctrinal beliefs. There may be room for disagreement among cultural peers about some standards and beliefs, but supposedly not about those that define their culture. Religious beliefs provide a model: dietary rules may be open to dispute in a religious culture, but not God's existence or nature.

What I believe emerges here is that multiculturalism is and can only be an *external* relativistic perspective. This is because as indicated earlier, the essence of multiculturalism is relativization of standards and beliefs to culture, and all cultures are held as equally deserving of respect, but the various cultures that multiculturalism embraces mostly are not themselves relativistic. Most cultures deem their own standards, beliefs, and values to be objective and in principle universal, if not in practice because of ignorance or prejudice. In fact, it is precisely because most cultures are objectivistic that so many see multiculturalism as necessary. If the world's cultures were mostly relativistic, multiculturalism would be the default reality; there would be no need to advocate it in order to win tolerance for diverse cultures because cultures would already accept other cultures' standards, beliefs, and values as "true for them" and hence pay them the basic respect of recognition.

What I am arguing can be clarified by revising the first premise and conclusion of Paden's argument to bring out more sharply the connection to multiculturalism. Recall that the original first premise and conclusion were

1. Respect for persons requires that everyone has a right to his or her own opinion.
6. Therefore, if someone holds some belief, then due respect for that person compels us to say that belief is true for that person (even though it is not true for me).[8]

Restated in multiculturalist mode, the premise and conclusion read

1a. Respect for cultures requires that each has a right to its opinions [beliefs].
6a. Therefore, if a belief is held in a culture, then due respect for that culture compels us to say that belief is true in that culture (even though it is not true in ours).

As should be clear, the restated conclusion, 6a, is one that can be properly asserted only from a relativistic position: from the meta-cultural relativistic perspective, from the perspective of a particular relativistic culture, or from the perspective of individual relativism. To assert 6a from the perspective of an objectivist culture would be either to attempt to relativize truth in that culture or tacitly to change the sense of "true in that culture" to something like "is accepted as true in that culture." Assuming the first option is not at issue for a member of an objectivist culture, it looks as if the second option is the only one open. But this is only apparently so, as was alluded to earlier. The reason is that implicitly or explicitly to change "are true" to "are *accepted* as true" in referring to a culture's beliefs is unacceptable to the cognitive libertarian supporter of multiculturalism. This is because saying, even tacitly, that the beliefs are *accepted* as true in the particular culture is to contrast those beliefs by implication with beliefs that *are* true. That is, to say the beliefs are accepted as true is tantamount to saying that they are taken to be true the way other beliefs are in fact true. That is why adding "accepted as" to Paden's fifth premise ultimately does not work, as mentioned earlier.

The point here is that cognitive libertarianism holds that persons' beliefs *are* true for them, not that they are thought true by the persons in question and accepted by others as thought true by those persons.

---

[8] Rhem 2006, 4.

Accepting that a belief is thought true by some, and accepted by others as thought true by those who hold it, entails the possibility that the belief may *not* be true even though thought to be so. This possibility is due to the way describing a belief as thought to be true or as accepted as true implies a contrast with beliefs that are in fact true. Cognitive libertarianism precludes this implicit contrast because allowing it would not be relativistic, since allowing it means that at least some beliefs are objectively true and thus contrast with beliefs that are only thought true. Whether or not the idea is coherent in the final analysis, the central idea is that individuals' – and by extension cultures' – beliefs *are true* for them.

The consequence of all this is that whereas multiculturalists, being largely cultural relativists, accept diverse cultures' beliefs as true for those holding them, most cultures are objectivistic and unprepared to accept other cultures' beliefs as true for those holding them. Objectivistic cultures are unprepared to relativize truth, so they are willing only to allow that members of other cultures think their beliefs true. And, of course, tolerance of this sort usually means the beliefs at issue are taken as at best seriously distorted and at worst false.

*   *   *

Of greatest interest to us is that the normally objectivist nature of most cultures has serious implications for how members of different cultures participate in assessment of elective-death reasoning and in the cross-cultural dialogue required by the motives clause of the rationality criterion. Members of relativistic cultures do not pose a problem with respect to disputes about the soundness of elective-death reasoning. The problem they pose is quite different; it is that their participation is likely to play too minor a role in the assessment, since they will too readily accept deliberators' premises and conclusions. Their role, then, goes little or no way to making assessment of elective-death reasoning *cross*-cultural and contributes more to making it effectively *intra*cultural. Against this most members of objectivist cultures will inevitably assess the reasoning of someone choosing to die from their own perspective and impose their own standards on that reasoning.

As a consequence of the involvement of members of objectivist cultures in assessment of elective-death reasoning, one possible problematic outcome is that the differences among assessors from different cultures will involve polar-opposite positions on standards and/or their application. Perhaps the most common kinds of radical differences regarding standards involve uncompromising religious doctrines and demanding codes of honor. In these extreme cases, some assessors will see elective death as required while other assessors will see it as precluded by the relevant code or doctrine. Differences of this order inevitably lead to intractable impasses regarding the soundness of the reasoning being assessed. A different kind of extreme case, but one just as bound to produce intractable impasses, is where the radical differences center on claims about the historic or ahistoric nature of rationality and its attendant standards for validity and soundness. In this sort of case, some assessors will find the reasoning in question sound while others will reject it as unsound because of their willingness or unwillingness to accept an inferential move as logically sanctioned. Unfortunately, I do not see what can be done in cases like these except to engage in the kind of dialogue required, not by the reasoning clause but by the motives clause of the criterion, in the hope that consideration of different perspectives will resolve the disagreements.

Another kind of difference that may lead to intractable impasses is one that centers on abstraction. There are many who strongly resist giving a decisive role to abstract logical requirements in assessing elective-death reasoning. As I mention in the Preface, I have encountered impatience and even dismissal of considerations having to do with abstract rationality and logical validity and soundness when discussing elective death. Nurses, physicians, and others who work closely with the terminally ill resist assessment of individuals' elective-death reasoning in terms of general and abstract requirements regarding valid inferences and the truth of factual premises. They do so because of their personal experience and sympathies with the particulars of the elective-death deliberators' circumstances, fears, and prospects. Moreover, this resistance is often reinforced by cultural influences.

I think it noteworthy that in my experience resistance to abstract considerations in dealing with elective death tends to be gender related, as women are to some extent more inclined to give priority to individuals' particular circumstances over abstract logical requirements. In any case, resistance to abstract considerations need not be

particularly dogged or obvious. More often than not it will be a
matter of the degree to which one or another abstract requirement is
pressed in applying a standard to the elective-death reasoning being
assessed. Nonetheless, this resistance may result in impasses as
unyielding as those produced by any of the foregoing differences of
opinion.

A second possible problematic outcome of cultural differences'
influencing assessment of elective-death reasoning is one where
differences arise among assessors but are due less to opposed positions on standards and their application than to what I will call the
salience of reasoning elements. The point here is that differences
among assessors may not involve contrary conceptions of the nature
and/or applicability of standards but rather center on what elements
in the reason they see as most prominent and important. For
instance, assessors with some cultural backgrounds may feel strongly
that diagnostic or prognostic factual premises of themselves fail to
establish that dire enough circumstances obtain or will obtain soon to
justify surrender of life because of impending distress. Assessors with
another cultural background may place a high value on independence and mobility and give premises establishing or strongly pre-
dicting physical incapacity considerably more weight than those who
tolerate higher measures of dependency on others for the sake of
continued life. Still other assessors whose culture gives priority to
family may discount diagnostic or prognostic factual premises, taking
the risk and even actuality of great suffering as a fair price to pay, less
for continued life itself than for maintaining contact with family as
long as possible, surviving to witness the birth of a grandchild,
or serving as a model of courage and determination to younger
relatives.

Variances on salience or weighting of reasoning factors are perhaps best illustrated by considering diagnostic test results regarding
feared medical conditions. For example, an individual may greatly
fear contracting ALS and resolve to commit PS_1 or SS_2 rather than
suffer the ravages of the disease. If this individual is diagnosed with
ALS while still presenting only the mildest of symptoms and chooses
to die rather than bear the inevitable devastation ALS will produce,
assessors of his or her elective-death reasoning likely will be divided
on the weight to be given the test results. Some will find most salient

that the individual choosing to die is as yet free of serious symptoms and may continue to be so for some time; they will see choosing to die on the basis of the test results and very mild symptoms as precipitous and unjustified. However, others will find most salient what threatens the individual in the unpredictably near future and will give greater weight to the present symptoms; additionally, they also will give greater weight to the individual's preparedness to die while still free of complicating symptoms. These others, then, will see choosing to die on the basis of the test results and initial symptoms as justified.

Generally speaking, then, cross-cultural assessment of elective-death reasoning will most likely produce one of two main kinds of results: First, the reasoning may be found sound by all or most assessors; again, the reasoning may be found unsound by all or most assessors for straightforward reasons like the reasoning's being factually defective because the individuals deliberating elective death are misinformed or have drawn erroneous conclusions from their diagnoses or prognoses. Of course, elective-death reasoning may also be unanimously rejected because the individual deliberating elective death manifests psychological confusion or pathology of some sort, but that eventuality is not of primary relevance in the present discussion. Second, assessment of elective-death reasoning may reach an impasse for one of a number of reasons: because of differences about the nature or formulation of standards applied, because of differences about the applicability of particular standards, because of resistance to the use or prioritizing of abstract standards, because of differences regarding the salience or importance of certain considerations, and because of the weight given various factual elements such as diagnostic or prognostic premises. When an impasse is reached for one or more of these reasons, the main danger is that cross-cultural assessment of elective-death reasoning will collapse into intracultural assessment because of the inability of assessors from different cultures to find common ground for assessment.

The point that emerges here is that the problems posed by obdurate differences regarding standards, salience, or weighting of reasoning elements reveal assessment of elective-death *reasoning* to be more like assessment of elective-death *motivation* than one might expect. The reason is that assessing elective-death reasoning for soundness is not a cut-and-dried matter of establishing that the conclusions in the reasoning follow from true premises according to clear and clearly applicable standards regarding truth and validity. The impasse-producing differences that arise have to do with individuals' diverse culturally influenced perspectives on standards, salience, and weighting. From one perspective on someone's elective-death reasoning, issues of validity will appear trivial, the subject's suffering or resolve will seem crucial, and the pertinent medical prognosis will be taken as decisive. From another perspective inclusion of a religious premise in the reasoning will preclude its soundness, the subject's suffering will appear bearable, the subject's resolve will seem obsessive, and the pertinent medical prognosis will look like merely an educated guess.

The result is that resolving perspectival differences, at least enough to enable decisions to be made about the soundness of the reasoning being assessed, requires dialogic identification and review of the several perspectives of the assessors and the elective-death deliberators whose reasoning is being assessed. Once the points at issue are as plain as possible, there has to be discussion facilitating better understanding of contrary perspectives by all concerned. This sort of productive, open discussion of perceptions and priorities is just what the cross-cultural dialogue required by the motives clause seeks to achieve. There is, of course, no guarantee of eventual consensus, but the very process of trying to reach a consensus will serve to clarify the elective-death reasoning for both deliberators and assessors. Such clarification should enable assessors either to sharpen their objections or to find the reasoning sound enough *given certain presuppositions*. This latter outcome, though perhaps the best that can be hoped for, has both positive and negative aspects. The positive aspect is that opposed assessors will better appreciate deliberators' reasons for choosing to die; the negative aspect is that the consensus reached may be tantamount to intracultural assessment. This is, however, unavoidable and all that can be done is to strive to make the acceptance of crucial presuppositions by assessors from other cultures as balanced and reasonable as possible so that the acceptance does not reduce to withdrawal of opposition in favor of deliberators' values.

The presuppositions that may have to be accepted by some assessors also take us back to motivation, for it is most likely that they will have to do with religious beliefs and basic cultural values. In the case of religious beliefs, my proposal about proxy premises should suffice to enable nonreligious assessors to deal with religious beliefs operating as premises in elective-death reasoning. Basic cultural values are another story. An assessor may simply be unable to accept that, say, a culturally determined code of honor requires commission of suicide to preclude the dependency that terminal illness imposes. Proxy premises are of no help in such cases, and it is in such cases that there is the greatest danger that assessors who are not cultural peers of those choosing to die will, in accepting the decisiveness of the relevant cultural values, in effect nullify their cross-cultural contribution to the assessment of elective-death reasoning. Here again, as in the case of assessment of motivation, the hope is that reservations expressed by assessors from other cultures will make some difference to deliberators' and supportive assessors' understanding of the role and significance of operant cultural values and culturally determined imperatives.

It merits mention at this point that the closeness between what is required to assess elective-death reasoning cross-culturally effectively and to assess elective-death motivation cross-culturally shows why the rationality criterion is more correctly formulated and applied as a single criterion with two clauses than as two or more separate criteria.

* * *

Our concern with the impact of multiculturalism on assessment of elective-death reasoning and motivation centers on how human life is valued in various cultures and what sorts of circumstances are deemed to take priority over its continuation. Cultures differ and affect elective-death issues in too many ways to catalog here, especially when we factor in intracultural differences due to individuals' personal experiences and interpretive inclinations. Cultural values most crucially affect elective death when they foster the sacrifice of life. In this respect, the major cultural-value influences that affect elective-death reasoning and motivation are those that promote or require abandonment of life in certain circumstances. In the present context, the pertinent circumstances have to do with terminal illness

and debilitating incapacity and may involve the threat of either as
well as their actuality.

The examples that come to mind most readily are those where
sacrifice of life is pressed when terminally ill or seriously incapacitated individuals become burdens to their families, friends, and
societies. Examples that run a close second are those where life is
considered forfeit because of the dishonor of extensive dependency
or personal deterioration. The operant cultural values may be religious or secular or a combination of both, but what matters is that
there are cultural-value influences that promote abandonment of
life. So-called Western culture has been largely free of cultural values
that endorse abandonment of life because of serious or terminal illness and extensive incapacity, but if Caplan is right, and I believe he
is, that is changing. There is a sense in which the change seems
inevitable, that cultures will become more inclined to promote
abandonment of life in hopeless situations as the world's population
grows. Fewer and fewer societies can afford to care for their terminally ill and wholly incapacitated members as their numbers swell
and doing so puts the young at ever greater risk because of the limits
on health-care institutions' and families' abilities to deal with the
personal and financial costs.

The risk, then, is that the rationality of choosing to die will be
eroded in particular cases because of shifting cultural values and
attitudes. In particular, what is of the greatest relevance in this
chapter is that the rationality of choosing to die will be eroded by
growing intolerance of the need to establish the soundness of elective-death reasoning. This is the reason why I found the response I
describe in the Preface so disturbing.

Impatience with abstract standards for reasoning soundness usually
is clothed in concern for suffering individuals. The typical claim is
that we cannot stand on logical principle when a person is enduring
hopeless suffering. This is a very dangerous position to take. It is
comparable to saying that we cannot stand on legal principle regarding evidence when we know someone is guilty of a crime. It is, in short,
to step onto the slippery slope of allowing emotions, impulses, and
other arational and irrational factors to determine the acceptability of
choosing to die. It may well be that, in the end, it is elective-death
motivation that plays the decisive role and that is taken most seriously

by the family and caretakers of individuals choosing to die. It is clear, for instance, that Choron's view that elective death is acceptable if the motives for it appear justifiable or are "understandable" to intended suicidists' peers is shared by many. But the shift from elective-death motivation's being *justifiable* to its being *understandable* is highly significant. For example, it may be understandable why a terminally ill or grossly handicapped individual wants to die, but that is insufficient to sanction PS1, SS2, or AS3 – though it may be sufficient to sanction requesting RE4. Assessment of elective-death reasoning is crucial, because finding that reasoning sound is the necessary complement to understanding and acceptance of the motivation for choosing to die.

In the next section I have to consider a different issue, so to proceed it will be useful to recapitulate the main points made so far in this chapter. Our concern here is assessment of elective-death reasoning. Basically, assessing elective-death reasoning for soundness means testing that the subconclusions and conclusion reached in that reasoning follow validly from true premises. Doing that involves relying on standards by which premises are judged true, by which the formal structure of reasoning is tested for validity and judged sound, by which more informal inferences are judged reasonable, and by which decisions are judged to be supported by the overall reasoning. Unfortunately, difficulties arise with respect to the nature of the relied-on standards, their applicability, and the relative weighting of various reasoning elements. For instance, there may be disagreement on whether standards for truth are ahistoric or historical: whether they are – properly – influenced by historical context and all that entails. There may be disagreement on whether one or another standard applies in a particular case. For example, regarding validity and the truth of premises, it may be argued that a religious premise in the reasoning should be accepted as true even though it cannot be established to be true. And there may be disagreement about the importance or decisiveness of some reasoning elements. As considered earlier, the results of a diagnostic test, present as a factual premise, may be seen as critical or largely immaterial to choosing to die.

Difficult though variances on the nature and applicability of standards may prove, they at least are usually fairly clear. Much less clear are differences on what is most salient, what takes priority in the reasoning. Prioritization is not part of assessment of the formal validity and soundness of elective-death reasoning, since salience or weighting of premises is not a factor in establishing the formal requirement that conclusions follow validly from true premises. What prioritization does, therefore, is in effect to push assessment of elective-death reasoning closer to how elective-death motivation is assessed.

How cultural values work into prioritization is elusive because it is not enough to be aware of the relevant values. Assessors also have to be aware of deliberators' and their own interpretive inclinations and how their respective life experience has shaped their understanding and application of the relevant values. There may be important differences even between members of the same culture: between individuals who are ethnic peers, share a language, even a religion, and who have had very similar upbringings. For instance, returning to Ms. A's case: she lacks extensive experience with the terminally ill. Even her experience with her Alzheimer's-stricken parents may have been limited by their being institutionalized fairly early. Against this, her physician has a great deal of experience with terminal illness of various sorts. The physician has witnessed great suffering but also has witnessed patients who achieved what Battin describes as "experience ... of intrinsic value" that outweighs the preventative benefit of elective death.[9] Their respective views on Ms. A's choice to die, then, may be quite opposed. Ms. A's physician sees her choice to die as precipitous; she sees it as timely. Her physician believes she is underestimating her own resilience and the intrinsic value of what life still offers her; she fears personal dissolution, suffering, and ruinous incapacity and cannot imagine what life could still hold that would compensate for that. And of course, others assessing Ms. A's elective-death reasoning likely will divide along the same lines.

In discussions about what elements in elective-death reasoning are or should be given priority, I have often had the example of Stephen Hawking used to show what bravery and resolve may achieve despite significant distress and appalling physical limitations. Hawking's is a highly relevant case because it illustrates well Battin's point about greater value overriding the reasonableness of elective death,

[9] Battin 1982, 312.

namely, that PS1, SS2, AS3, and some instances of RE4 are not indicated where continuing to live allows achievement of experience of intrinsic value. Given his capacity for innovative abstract thought, there are few who would think Hawking foolish to eschew elective death and bear the ruination of his body for the sake of what he has achieved and may still achieve. Hawking's case is also relevant in illustrating that technology is beginning to make more means available to cope with otherwise devastating physical incapacity. When Hawking's case is appealed to, there is usually a more or less explicit implication that elective death is, in fact, cowardly. This is a very old view and is perhaps itself the best single illustration of the influence of cultural values, given that there are cultures where elective death in the face of dishonor or personal devastation is thought heroic. What is of interest to us is that those holding to either perception of elective death seem reluctant or perhaps unable to see or admit that the difference in perception is cultural. The tendency is to generalize either perception cross-culturally and to dismiss or ignore counterindications. This takes me to the way some think that assessment of elective-death reasoning or motivation is ultimately personal.

* * *

It is, of course, the case that the obstructive differences that arise in assessment of elective-death reasoning are most immediately the products of elective-death deliberators' conflicting personal feelings and assessors' conflicting personal feelings and projections of themselves into deliberators' situations. That this is at least initially so, however, does not mean that there are no mediate cultural determinants of those feelings and projections because deliberators' feelings and assessors' feelings and projections are grounded in their enculturated values. Many, though, focus on the immediate determinants and consider the choice to die and assessment of that choice as purely "personal." This individualistic view of choosing to die and of assessment of the choice has been in the background of the foregoing discussion all along and bears directly on assessment of elective-death reasoning, but I am only now ready to consider it explicitly.

The individualistic conception of elective-death decisions and assessments is of a piece with the relativism at the heart of the view or position I am calling cognitive libertarianism. The essential idea is that the immediate determinants of decisions and assessments regarding elective death are jointly the present reality of the beliefs, attitudes, perspectives, feelings, and inclinations that define deliberators and assessors as persons, and that there is little or no reason to consider the mediate determinants of those beliefs, attitudes, perspectives, feelings, and inclinations. This is the gist of the view that elective-death decisions and assessments are personal choices to be respected, as beliefs held must be respected.

There obviously are many influences on elective-death deliberators and assessors – personal history, family relations, social factors, rearing and enculturation – all of these make a difference to how the choice to die is seen or assessed. It is very odd, then, to insist that the choice to die and assessment of that choice are personal matters in the sense that they must simply be accepted as what the involved individuals feel or believe. But what needs to be appreciated is that the philosophical position that elective-death decisions and assessments are personal givens to be taken as they are is not a position contrary to one holding that deliberators' and assessors' beliefs are the products of various influences on deliberators and assessors. Rather, the position is the cognitive libertarian one that dismisses as irrelevant the *causes* of beliefs held by individuals, construing those beliefs simply as part of the makeup of persons requiring respect. The cognitive libertarian is not interested in whether an individual's beliefs about elective death are the results of enculturation, of personal experience, or of other influences. All that interests the cognitive libertarian is *that individuals believe what they do*, that they make the decisions and assessments that they do.

The basic problem with the cognitive libertarian conception of decisions and assessments regarding elective death is that as we saw in Paden's argument in the case of other beliefs, it precludes attempting to *change* individuals' beliefs and hence their decisions and assessments. That means that cross-cultural and even intra-cultural dialogue about elective-death reasoning – or elective-death motivation – cannot be *critical*; at best it can be only generally supportive.

The view, then, is that choosing to die is a purely personal matter and that if there is to be any consideration of the choice by others, those considering it can only be asked to voice their own personal takes on the decision. Given our focus in this chapter, assessment of reasoning soundness, it is clear that this view effectively blocks that sort of assessment. If this radically individualistic view prevails, it would seem that it is not only the case that there would be no way to prevent irrational sacrifice of life in the circumstances that concern us here: commission of PS1, SS2, AS3, and requesting of RE4 in terminal illness. It also seems there would be no way to counter gradual negative changes in cultural values such as the one Caplan fears: the increasing tendency for people to think that survival into advanced age is too socially costly and that the old and sick should "do the responsible thing" and end their socially burdensome lives.[10]

Contrary to what many may think, we cannot rely on recognition of the value of human life to safeguard against individual and social excesses regarding elective death. Culturally determined valuation of human life may vary widely despite intuitive and professed values. Two cultures, whether similar or different, may profess to value human life equally but differ in what *counts* as viable human life. One culture may put an unconditional value on human life and preclude not only elective death but capital punishment and offensive – and perhaps even defensive – warring. Another culture may qualify the value of particular lives in various ways, as in the case of individuals guilty of heinous crimes or whose lives are blighted by dishonor, severe disability, or simply infirm old age. Members of cultures that qualify the value of human life will hold beliefs that sanction and even prompt choices to die that members of other cultures would see as irrational.

The bottom line, then, is that relativism in effect eviscerates assessment of the rationality of elective-death reasoning. The basic problem posed is illustrated by cognitive libertarianist conceptions of the choice to die, and assessments of that choice, as personal preferences flowing from essentially inviolate beliefs constitutive of the persons holding them. The basic problem, then, is the implied preclusion of the possibility that individuals choosing to die might

---

[10] Caplan 1996.

be *wrong* to so choose. If personal preferences override other considerations, how might the cognitive libertarian stop short of accepting choices to die made by depressed teenagers or demented individuals?

The question we face here is the most abstractly philosophical of those to be considered in this book. It is about the relativism that underlies cognitive libertarianism in particular and multiculturalism in general, and that poses one of the most worrying challenges to assessment of reasoning soundness in attempting to establish the rationality of choosing to die. In light of the considerations that prompted the writing of the Preface, I apologize to those readers who may find the discussion of relativism too academic but trust they will recognize its necessity.

6

Relativism and Cross-Cultural Assessment

For a proper historical review of truth's relativization, we should begin with Protagoras, but for our purposes it suffices to begin with Kant and Nietzsche as the thinkers who most directly influenced the development of contemporary relativism. The combination of Kant's and Nietzsche's ideas conceptually enabled a paradigm shift in philosophical thinking about truth, a shift that turned Pilate's question, "What is truth?" from a rhetorical evasion to a philosophical problem. Protagoras's old claim that we are the measure of what there is gained new depth as language became our Newtonian universe and Derrida's "axial" proposition, "There is nothing outside of the text," became conceivable.[1]

Contemporary relativism was inadvertently conceptually enabled by Kant when he recognized that trying to establish the truth of our beliefs about the world leads us to realize that as Bernard Williams puts it, "We cannot step entirely outside our ... conceptions and theories so as to compare them with a world that is not conceptualized at all, a bare 'whatever there is.' "[2] In other words, given the inescapability of conceptualization, of our organizing the contents of awareness in particular ways by applying concepts, it follows inexorably that the

[1] Derrida, Jacques. 1976. *Of Grammatology*. Trans. G. C. Spivak. Baltimore: Johns Hopkins University Press, 159.
[2] Williams, Bernard. 1998. "The End of Explanation." Review of Thomas Nagel, 1997, *The Last Word*, New York: Oxford University Press. *The New York Review of Books*, 45(18): 40–44, 40.

world is knowable to us only from one or another conceptually determined perspective. The immediate consequence of this is that our beliefs cannot be established as true by straightforward comparison with reality as it is in itself. We cannot access reality from a conceptually neutral point of view. It follows further that in attempting to confirm our beliefs about how things are in the world, our perception of how things are not only is always conditioned by how we organize our experience and believe things to be, but may also be conditioned to some extent by precisely the beliefs we are trying to establish as true. Many then conclude that truth is relative to conceptual perspective.

But however momentous it may have been, the Kantian realization about the unavoidable role of conceptualization might not have been sufficient to prompt widespread and cross-disciplinary acceptance of relativism. Relativism might have remained a fairly arcane philosophical position had not Nietzsche taken matters further by raising the question of why we should think we must strive for neutral awareness of the world from no particular point of view in the first place, why we should seek to attain a single, uniquely correct description of the world or any of its aspects. Nietzsche's question about why we value supposedly objective truth contributes powerfully to raising the issue of whether it makes any sense to think the world is any determinate way at all independently of how we represent and describe it if we can never know it wholly objectively.

Once the idea is entertained that it may not make any sense to try to think of reality extraconceptually, to think of it independently of how we construe it, some go on to make an illegitimate move, which is to raise doubts about the existence of a "bare 'whatever there is.'" This step is illegitimate because, *ex hypothesi*, we have no direct evidence to say that there either is or is not a reality that is as it is in itself. Problematic denial or skepticism regarding objective reality is a dubious move from the justifiable *epistemological* admission that we are limited to perceiving the world through our conceptual frameworks, to the unjustifiable *ontological* claim that the contents of those conceptual frameworks exhaust what there is.

Given his realist inclinations, Kant would have none of this ontological relativism; it is not altogether clear that he considered it a serious position. However, given his own epistemological position, his only ontological option regarding objective reality was less than satisfactory. Kant proposed that objective reality is "noumenal." That is, he maintained that reality *is* a bare "whatever there is," and that as such it is unknowable other than indirectly through its conceptualized effects on sentient creatures. Conceptualization's mediating role forever separates us as knowing entities from the bare "whatever there is" that is objective or noumenal reality.

For his part, Nietzsche would have none of Kant's somewhat desperate ontological position and argued forcefully that "the antithesis 'thing-in-itself' and 'appearance' is untenable."[3] In other words, we cannot draw the Kantian distinction between a bare "whatever there is" noumenal reality and how that reality presents itself to us through conceptualization. Nietzsche maintained that Kant's directly unknowable reality "is not a fact but a fable" and that there are "*only interpretations.*"[4] There are only the perspectives we have. But Nietzschean perspectivism does not necessarily entail that what exists is exhausted by the conceptualized contents of consciousness. Essentially, Nietzschean perspectivism is the position that there can be no holistic description within which diverse perspectives could be reconciled as so many true but incomplete points of view on the same objective reality. Nietzschean perspectivism does not assert the subjective nature of what there is; rather it denies that "there could ever be a complete theory or interpretation of anything, a view that accounts for 'all' the facts."[5]

The upshot of the foregoing with respect to our particular concerns is that once diversity of conceptualization is recognized, and since we have no way to establish which of the many conceptualized realities individuals inhabit best corresponds to how things really are in themselves, we have no choice but to accommodate a diversity of perceived realities.

As we saw in the last chapter, accommodation is insufficient for cognitive libertarians. They go further than accommodating conceptual diversity by holding that we are ethically obligated to accept different conceptualizations of reality as true for those who hold

[3] Nietzsche 1968, 267.
[4] Nietzsche 1968, 330; 267, my emphasis.
[5] Nehamas, Alexander. 1985. *Nietzsche: Life as Literature*. Cambridge, Mass.: Harvard University Press, 64.

them, not just as what they believe – and hence could be wrong to believe. Only respecting diverse conceptualizations retains the possibility that they are wrong in believing what they do. Cognitive libertarians reject this as failing to recognize the supposedly fundamental nature of particular conceptualizations; they insist that the beliefs comprising diverse conceptualizations must be accepted as true for those whose conceptualizations they are. The problem this poses regarding elective-death reasoning and motivation is that, as anticipated in the last chapter, cross-cultural assessment of such reasoning and motivation may be obstructed by irreconcilable differences that we are precluded from trying to resolve by attempting to change or correct individuals' perceptions of elective-death deliberations and the circumstances of those considering PS1, SS2, AS3, or RE4.

Though the matter is more complicated from a purely philosophical point of view, for our limited purposes the conclusion to be drawn at this point is that it is not relativism per se that poses a major problem for us, but rather the brand of relativism I dubbed "cognitive libertarianism" in the last chapter. The major cause of difficulties regarding cross-cultural conceptual diversity of perceptions of elective-death reasoning and motivation is the imperative to accept those diverse conceptualizations at face value – as uncontestable. This imperative rules out attempting to change individuals' perceptions of some part or the whole of the reasoning or motivation being assessed on the grounds that we have to accept their beliefs as true for them. As a result, conflicts are irresolvable and as mentioned before, cross-cultural assessment collapses into intracultural assessment. Our most pressing need, then, is to deal with cognitive libertarianism in order to allow cross-cultural assessment of elective-death reasoning and motivation a measure of theoretical and practical possibility.

As I have stressed, what prompts relativism and conceptually enables cognitive libertarianism is that once the epistemological impossibility of direct confirmatory access to objective reality is accepted, we seem to be left only with what lies at the heart of Nietzsche's perspectivism and is inadvertently implicit in Kant's recognition of the role of conceptualization. That is the realization that conceptualizations of experience may vary among individuals and that we have no access to a decisive external criterion to resolve conflicts. However, not everyone accepts the apparent epistemological impossibility of direct access to how things are. John Searle, whose work I discuss later, is an influential philosopher who rejects interpretation of conceptualization as obscuring objective reality and offers strong arguments against relativism.

* * *

Kant avoided the slide into relativism because he believed that we all conceptualize noumenal reality according to fixed rules that define the workings of the human mind, so he precluded the conceptual diversity among individuals that opens the door to relativism. But Hegel and Nietzsche saw the implications in Kant's treatment of conceptualization more clearly: in sum, conceptualization of experience may differ among individuals and even in the same individual over time. If there is such variation, our most basic idea of how the truth of beliefs is established is seriously challenged and either we have to be able to show how we can establish that one conceptual perspective gets things right or we have to abandon the traditional idea that our beliefs about the world are true when they faithfully replicate a checkable objective reality. Without neutral access to reality, if we always wear conceptualizing glasses, we arguably cannot select among competing conceptual perspectives as to which accurately captures how things are. And if we cannot pick out the correct conceptualization from others, we are bound to consider all perspectives in principle legitimate, even if in practice we reject some because they are grossly at odds with our own perspectives and those of our peers.

Searle's unrelenting opposition to relativism is of special interest to us because his unqualified commitment to direct access to objective reality and his rejection of conceptual incommensurability as a reason for relativization of truth may provide us with grounds for at least qualifying relativism enough to exorcize cognitive libertarianism. To describe the aspects of Searle's position most relevant to our concerns I must begin by saying a little regarding his views on truth.

The fundamental problem with the traditional conception of truth as "correspondence to reality" is the lack of an adequate account of correspondence. This problem is less about our access to reality than it is about how correspondence is established and just what it is that beliefs and sentences correspond *to*. The problem has led many philosophers, including nonrelativists, to conclude that the notion of correspondence to reality is not viable because we cannot spell out just how we actually establish the correspondence of beliefs and sentences to states of affairs, or, for that matter, how we delineate the states of affairs to which the beliefs and sentences correspond. Searle rejects the traditional notion of correspondence, arguing that it is absurd to think we can compare beliefs or sentences to states of affairs as we compare swatches of cloth for sameness of color.[6]

What is special about Searle's position is that though he rejects the traditional notion of correspondence, he is firmly committed to its being states of affairs that make beliefs and sentences true in virtue of beliefs and sentences accurately describing those states of affairs: "Statements are made true by how things are in the world that is independent of the statement[s]."[7] The import of this most relevant to our concerns is that if statements and beliefs are true in virtue of how things are in an accessible reality, then diversity of conceptualization is ultimately resolvable and there is no relativism-prompting conceptual incommensurability.

Searle rejects a number of challenges to "the Enlightenment vision," the most relevant to our interests being that "there is no universally valid rationality [and] that different cultures have different rationalities."[8] In arguing against this claim Searle offers a number of propositions he holds true and that he calls "default positions" because he thinks most people hold them true whether or not they have reflected on them. The two propositions that interest us are:

  (ii) We have direct perceptual access to [the] world.
  (iv) Our statements are typically true or false depending on whether they correspond to how things are, that is, to the facts in the world. [9]

In Searle's view, these propositions taken together preclude relativization of truth by making truth representation of an accessible

[6] Searle, John. 1995. *The Construction of Social Reality*. New York: The Free Press, 207.
[7] Searle 1995, 219; Prado 2006.
[8] Searle, John. 1999. *Mind, Language and Society*. London: Phoenix, 4.
[9] Searle 1999, 10.

objective reality that always serves as the available external standard for assessing the truth of beliefs and claims. And the way the two propositions also preclude relativization of rationality is that being rational centers on believing and acting on the basis of what is *true*. If what is true is not relative, then rationality is not relative. There may be some variation in what is deemed rational in one or another cultural context, but ultimately, accessible objective reality determines what is true and in doing so also determines what is and is not rational by determining what is and is not to be believed and acted on.

In brief, if objective reality is accessible, relativism cannot be justified by the allegedly epistemologically insulating role of conceptualization because access to the real world enables us either to reconcile diverse conceptualizations or to show some of them misconceived. Similarly, if there is variation in conceptions of rationality, access to the real world enables us either to reconcile those conceptions or to show some of them mistaken. These are extremely important points regarding the need to restrict relativism, but unfortunately they are not unassailable, and to clarify their limitations I need to say more about Searle and conceptualization.

* * *

Despite his rejection of conceptual incommensurability, Searle acknowledges that our concepts "are made by us" and that "there is nothing inevitable about the concepts we have for describing reality."[10] Searle admits that experience always has *"aspectual shape"* and maintains that "all (normal) perceiving is *perceiving as*, and ... all consciousness is *consciousness of something as such and such.*"[11] But Searle believes that while there may be conceptual diversity, it does not entail that we are locked within our conceptual structures in a way that denies us access to objective reality. We therefore need not and should not countenance relativism.

The key point here is that awareness's being always shaped by conceptualization does not mean that we cannot have knowledge of

---

[10] Searle 1999, 22; Searle, John. 1992. *The Rediscovery of the Mind*. Cambridge, Mass.: A Bradford Book, MIT Press, 131.

[11] Searle 1992, 131, 155, 133.

the objective world as it is independent of our conceptualizations of it. Searle attempts to make this out by using a number of examples directed against what he calls "conceptual relativism." One of these is an example about different ways of counting the things in a room. According to the example, in one "conceptual scheme" – his phrase – the furniture in a room is counted as a number of individual pieces, while in another conceptual scheme the furniture is counted as one set.[12] Searle's use of the phrase "conceptual scheme" is significant because it indicates that he considers the two ways of counting the furniture as different conceptualizations in the sense relevant to the allowing of relativism. The importance of this is that many would not consider the two described ways of counting the furniture in a room as being the right sort of difference to prompt adoption of relativism because of variation in conceptualization. This point emerges more clearly in Searle's use of an example about weight.

Referring to the furniture example, Searle maintains that with respect to conceptual conflict "the appearance of a problem derives entirely from the apparent inconsistency in saying there is only one object and yet there are [several] objects" – one set or several pieces of furniture. He maintains that "once you understand the nature of the claims, there is no inconsistency whatever" and that both descriptions are "consistent, and indeed, both are true." Searle then adds that there are "many such examples in daily life" and offers an example about weight: "I weigh 160 in pounds and 72 in kilograms. So what do I weigh really? The answer is, both 160 and 72 are true depending on which system of measurement we are using." Searle's conclusion is that "there is really no problem or inconsistency whatever" in conceptual diversity.[13]

Supposedly, then, whether we conceptualize the furniture in a room as one set or as a number of pieces, or someone's weight as 160 pounds or 72 kilograms, the content of each of these conceptualizations is compatible with that of other correct conceptualizations, and all are true of how things are in the objective world. On Searle's view, if there is conflict over differing conceptualizations, either we are dealing with resolvable cases of unlike

[12] Searle 1999, 23.
[13] Searle 1999, 23.

measurement systems or inclusion criteria, or there is error of some sort in one or more of the conflicting conceptualizations. There is, therefore, no reason to embrace relativism and hold conflicting conceptualizations as equally legitimate because of an imagined inability to establish them as correct or incorrect.

If we could accept Searle's contentions, conflicts in assessment of elective-death reasoning and motivation – where they concern conceptualization of factual elements – would be resolvable by establishing the correctness of some of the conflicting judgments and the wrongness of others. However, even if Searle's position were free of difficulties qualifying its application, culturally determined assessment conflicts regarding elective-death reasoning and motivation seldom turn on straightforward matters of fact. As we have considered, most often the conflicts have to do with the weight or importance given largely uncontested matters of fact. But a more immediate problem is that Searle's position is not as solid as he believes it is. The main difficulty is that Searle is presuming precisely what the relativist is contesting: access to reality. It is his assumption of access that enables Searle to characterize conceptual diversity in a way that simply excludes the possibility of genuine conceptual incommensurability: conceptual conflict not due to demonstrable error. Searle's assumption is evident in his examples; the examples are supposed to establish that conceptual diversity does not rule out universally true descriptions of how things are, but the examples *presuppose* ultimate conceptual commensurability by assuming that all true descriptions are true of an accessible objective reality regardless of the diversity of concepts employed.

Those moved to embrace relativism first consider the role of conceptualization in the determination of awareness. Their problem is that since experience is shaped and conditioned by conceptualization, neutral conflict-resolving access to objective reality looks unachievable. Once it is concluded that conflict-resolving access to objective reality is problematic, there is no recourse to an external standard that allows discriminatory assessment of conceptualizations, so all must be countenanced. Against this, Searle *begins* with the external standard: accessible objective reality. He therefore can construe diverse conceptualizations as only differing in the way his examples about furniture and weight illustrate or because of demonstrable error.

But examples having to do with counting furniture or measuring weight are not of the right order to rebut relativism.

The relevant relativism-prompting sort of example of conceptual diversity is quite different. One example of genuine conceptual diversity is precisely the disagreement between Searle and relativists. Searle conceptualizes our experience as constituting direct access to the objective world and so fails to understand why anyone should opt for relativism; the relativist conceptualizes experience as too aspectual and conditioned by one's conceptual framework to allow neutral access to reality. Another example of conceptual diversity of the right order and one closer to our concerns is where an individual conceptualizes the world as God-created and every event in it as manifesting divine guidance, while another individual conceptualizes the world and every event in it as effects of purely physical forces. Still closer to our concern is a case where one individual conceptualizes suicide as doing the will of God, another conceptualizes it as the most grievous sin against God's commandments, and a third conceptualizes it as annihilation preferable to enduring pain in a godless universe. Later I consider a particular example in more detail, but here we need to recapitulate briefly what is at issue.

The core of the relativist's position is that there is no access to an external standard for assessing varying and possibly conflicting conceptualizations of experience. The conclusion drawn is that we must accept diverse conceptualizations as legitimately held by those who hold them. As we saw, the cognitive libertarian adds to this the problematically coherent moral imperative to accept those diverse conceptualizations as *true for* those holding them. However, it seems clearly counterintuitive to conclude that diverse conceptualizations are on a par simply because the very fact that they are conceptualizations precludes their being checkable against how things are. This counterintuitiveness is what makes Searle's position attractive. On the other hand, the weakness of Searle's arguments against the relativist is that he presupposes conflict-resolving access to reality, which is precisely what is at issue. It seems, then, that contrary to our intuitions we must conclude that Searle's arguments do not preclude relativism.

*   *   *

Much of the force of Searle's arguments has to do with resistance to the idea that conceptualization could render problematic our access to matters of fact like water's expanding when it freezes – and note that I am not saying that water expands at zero degrees Centigrade or the Fahrenheit equivalent to avoid raising the matter of conceptualizations differing only regarding measurement systems.

What is important here is that we *know* water expands when it freezes, and conceptualizing water as expanding when it freezes is clearly *right*. Conceptualizing water as contracting when it freezes, like most other liquids, is just as clearly wrong. It seems absurd, then, to argue that the two conceptualizations are both legitimate and worse to claim that water's contracting when it freezes is "true for" someone who believes that it does. If you put a sealed bottle full of water in your freezer, it will eventually burst, and that will happen regardless of your conceptualization. It is true that under special circumstances water may contract on freezing, but these would be laboratory circumstances or possibly extraplanetary ones. As far as we are concerned in our daily dealings with water on Earth, it expands on freezing. This is where Searle's position is strongest and most intuitively appealing and why many find his otherwise problematic examples persuasive.

What Searle sees as the basic error in taking relativism as inescapable because of the role of conceptualization is the assumption that "knowing reality directly as it is in itself requires that it be known from no point of view." He rejects this assumption, arguing as follows: "I directly see the chair in front of me, but of course I see it from a point of view." Despite seeing the chair from a particular point of view, Searle maintains that he knows it "directly from a perspective. Insofar as it is even intelligible to talk of knowing 'reality directly as it is in itself,' I know it directly as it is in itself when I know that there is a chair over there because I see it."[14]

Persuasive though this might be initially, there is equivocation in it. As in the case of the furniture and weight examples, Searle is shifting the focus of discussion. In acknowledging he sees the chair from a particular point of view, Searle is actually talking about a spatial relation: where he is vis-à-vis the chair. But he speaks of knowing the chair directly "from a perspective." The use of the term

[14] Searle 1999, 21.

"perspective" is fine so long as reference is to point of view in the sense of where he is located vis-à-vis the chair. But the context is discussion of conceptualization, so use of the term "perspective" suggests he is referring not just to his spatial position vis-à-vis the chair but also to his conceptualized awareness of the chair. The difference between seeing the chair while standing to the right of it as opposed to standing to the left of it is not what is at issue; no one is claiming that mere difference in spatial position occludes our access to reality. What is at issue is *how the chair is seen*, how the chair is conceptualized. We are taken back, then, to the irrelevance of the sorts of differences Searle considers in offering the examples he offers: use of different measurement systems as in the weight case and different inclusion criteria as in the furniture case. None of these touch on the issue of conceptualization in a significant way.

There are two conclusions to draw at this point. First, Searle's examples do not constitute counterexamples to the relativist's claim that conceptualization renders our access to objective reality problematic. The examples that supposedly demonstrate direct awareness of reality do not establish the commensurability of diverse but equally correct conceptualizations; they do not address the issue of whether conceptualization obstructively conditions our access to reality. Second, even if Searle were right and his examples were successful against relativistic claims about conceptual diversity and its insulating effects, the trouble for us is that conceptual differences causing conflicts in assessment of elective death rarely center on matters of fact of the sort the examples present. The kinds of differences that arise in cross-cultural assessment of elective death cannot be resolved by looking to see how things are, no matter how direct our access to how things are might be. This is because typically the differences are of the sort where one individual conceptualizes suicide as doing God's will or as honor-bound atonement for shaming one's family, while another conceptualizes it as the most heinous sin against God's will or as expedient self-annihilation to avoid pointless suffering. These are *attitudinal* perspectives or points of view, and conflicts between them are not resolvable by recourse to reality, however accessible it may be. Regardless of arguments presented by intelligent-design advocates, for instance, divine planning – or its lack, for that matter – is not evident in the physical world.

Admittedly, it is true that some culturally determined conceptual differences regarding elective-death reasoning and motivation are about factual matters such as diagnostic test results or presented symptoms. In some cases the differences may have to do with acceptance or rejection of something factual. For instance, there may be culturally determined mistrust of various medical procedures and hence rejection of the prognostic importance of such medical procedures as blood tests or x-rays. But the great majority of conceptual differences about factual components in elective-death reasoning or motivation are not about the facts but about the *weight* given the facts: how decisive they are taken to be with respect to commission of PS1, SS2, or AS3 or requesting of RE4. Even where the focuses of conceptual differences are factual matters, then, the differences are more like those between seeing elective death as violation of a divine covenant by a child of God and seeing it as a free choice by a sovereign entity.

To understand better the kind of conceptual differences that concern us, as well as how they relate to factual matters, we need to move away from more straightforward examples like Searle's and my own about water's expanding when it freezes. Consider the following example, which I have used before: Imagine Tycho Brahe and Johannes Kepler standing together at dawn and looking eastward. Both see the Sun at the horizon, but Brahe sees the moving Sun *rising* over the horizon while Kepler sees the horizon *dropping* to reveal the fixed Sun. The point here is that what is at issue is *how the fact of the dawn is conceived*; it is not the clearly observable fact of *dawning* about which Brahe and Kepler disagree.

The conceptual difference between Brahe and Kepler illustrates both the strength of Searle's point about access to reality and how his point fails to resolve the issue of conceptualization. It is true that access to reality can show that Kepler was right to see the horizon dropping because the Earth does revolve. Brahe was wrong to see the Sun rising above the horizon because the Sun is more or less fixed relative to the Earth. But recourse to objective reality was not possible until long after Brahe and Kepler's deaths. Until the advent of space flight and access to a different reference point – the Moon – from which the Earth's rotation could be witnessed, there was no conclusive way to establish that Brahe was misconceiving the dawn while Kepler was conceiving it correctly. We have, then, an example of a conceptual conflict about a factual matter that despite being ultimately resolvable by access to reality was at one time irresolvable. The import of this is not, as Searle might argue, that conceptual conflicts are *eventually* resolvable; the import is that all the relativist needs to postulate against Searle is the possibility that resolution will never be practically achievable.

Consider now the difference between two individuals who perceive elective death either as a violation of a divine covenant by a child of God or as a free choice by a sovereign entity. What development involving access to new facts, comparable to the advent of space flight, could resolve this conceptual difference? Certainly many believe that the former individual's belief will be proved true after death, but even if it were to be, that is not a state of affairs that could be *public*, one available to us as is physical reality. That belief, then, is about an event that is properly part of the conceptualization in question rather than a potentially confirming one.

The difference between conceptualizing human beings as children of God and conceptualizing them as autonomous beings is the sort of case that concerns us regarding cross-cultural assessment of elective-death reasoning. It is this sort of case that raises the basic question of whether the irresolvable nature of divergent conceptualizations means only that there must be *social respect* for different conceptualizations that cannot be shown erroneous or – literally – misconceived, or that as the cognitive libertarian insists, there must be *cognitive acceptance* of different conceptualizations as true for those who hold them. It is the latter that poses problems for us.

The main problem posed is that cognitive acceptance of divergent conceptualizations, as opposed to only respect for them, leads to cultural fragmentation. It does so because cognitive acceptance isolates groups of individuals who see the world in certain culturally determined ways from others who see it differently. The isolation is effected by cultural groups taking the beliefs and values of other cultural groups as "true for" their members and so as uncontestable. If beliefs and values are uncontestable, there can be no significant interaction where differences exist. Cognitive acceptance, then, allows individuals only three options: adherence to their own culture's beliefs and values, adoption of another culture's beliefs and values, or creation of *new* beliefs and values. There can be conversion, but not working out of compromise positions because doing so requires critical appraisal and qualification of both sets of beliefs and values. Cognitive acceptance's only productive attribute, then, is the multiplication of sets of inviolable beliefs and values. Unfortunately, the isolation effected by cognitive acceptance masquerades as open-mindedness and tolerance; few think hard enough about it to see that it actually is or becomes indifference to what is not agreed with but cannot be challenged.

The consequence of this cultural fragmentation with respect to elective death is that cross-cultural assessment of elective-death reasoning and motivation is rendered ineffective if not impossible. Given cognitive acceptance of conceptual diversity, all that such assessment can amount to is a kind of reflective exercise in which various culturally specific perspectives on elective death are articulated for the benefit of individuals contemplating PS_1, SS_2, AS_3, or RE_4.

Stating matters differently, cognitive acceptance of different conceptualizations means that cross-cultural assessments of elective-death reasoning or motivation will lack authority because they will be merely articulation of a number of different perspectives on the contemplated PS_1, SS_2, AS_3, or RE_4. Individuals deliberating elective death will not receive cogent guidance but only be presented with a smorgasbord of views, some of which will more or less coincide with their own, others of which will diverge to a greater extent. None of the different perspectives presented will carry authority in the sense of providing good reason to adjust or change reasoning or motivation regarding elective death. The perspectives will be just that: differing views on what is contemplated. If one or another of the presented perspectives does influence the deliberator's decision, it will not be because the perspective highlights miscalculations or evaluative or attitudinal issues in the deliberator's thinking or provides a more reasonable option. This is because cognitive acceptance of conceptual diversity means that none of the perspectives in question – including the deliberator's own – is any better or worse than any other.

One or another presented perspective may influence a deliberator's elective-death reasoning and motivation by effecting changes in the weight given one or another of the deliberated factors. For instance, individuals inclined to commit SS_2 or AS_3 because of their distress or imposition on family and friends may be moved to bear greater levels of suffering or dependency after reflecting on a more stoical cultural perspective or one that takes a more compassionate or generous view of reliance on family and friends than their own. But this sort of influence does not work by bettering deliberators' reasoning or motivation; what it does is *change* the reasoning or motivation by supplanting or superseding one priority with another.

The difficulty caused for us by this sort of influence on elective-death deliberation is that newly adopted perspectives can just as easily prompt unreasonable abandonment of life as its preservation. That is, the new perspective may prompt individuals to commit PS1, SS2, or AS3 or request RE4 for reasons or at times that violate the rationality criterion by unduly overriding interest in survival. For example, individuals considering commission of PS1 or even SS2 may be disproportionately influenced by a culturally determined conceptualization of abandonment of life in untoward circumstances as heroic. They may then precipitously resolve well-grounded reservations about the commission of PS1 or the timing of SS2 by reinterpreting those reservations as cowardice and so commit PS1 or time SS2 in violation of their interest in continued life.

*   *   *

Our concern in this chapter is how relativism affects elective-death issues. Our focus is the impact of cognitive libertarianism, or more specifically of cognitive acceptance, on assessment of elective-death reasoning and motivation. Cognitive acceptance, or the preclusion of critical disputation of individuals' beliefs and conceptualizations, effectively reduces cross-cultural assessments of elective-death deliberations to argumentatively ineffectual surveys of divergent perspectives. Unfortunately, Searle's antirelativist arguments, though appealing, fall short of defeating relativism; more importantly, they fall short in ways that strongly suggest relativism is more a loss of innocence regarding conceptualization than it is a debatable position regarding truth. Relativism, then, most likely is not defeasible by argument and so cognitive libertarianism's enabling conditions remain in place.

The consequence for us of not defeating cognitive libertarianism by defeating the relativism that enables it is that we must find another way to deal with it. As should be clear, the main problem posed by cognitive libertarianism is cognitive acceptance or the dubiously coherent claim that beliefs and conceptualizations are "true for" those who hold them. Regrettably, it is not enough to offer good arguments against this claim because it articulates less a debatable philosophical contention than a pervasive and engrained attitude. Our primary objective, therefore, is to find a way to achieve compromise where conflicts occur among individuals whose deeply held culturally determined beliefs, conceptualizations, and values are deemed unchallengeable.

We can begin by noting that reasoning about anything is aspectual in that it entails that someone is construing what is at issue from a given perspective, is making some assumptions about what is at issue, and is reasoning about what is at issue to achieve one or another end. With this in mind, we can say that the cognitive libertarian's claim that individuals' beliefs, conceptualizations, and values must be cognitively accepted as true for them essentially is assertion that reasoners' construals, assumptions, and ends cannot be challenged with a view to changing them.

As we have seen, the result of this proscription is that cross-cultural assessment of elective-death reasoning and motivation reduces to presentation of a string of competing construals of the objects of assessment. This is a result that we cannot accept if we are committed to PS1, SS2, AS3, or RE4's having to be a *rational* option and needing to be judged as meeting both clauses of the rationality criterion. Establishing that both the reasoning and motivation clauses are met requires cross-cultural assessment, not mere provision of culturally determined alternative construals of the contemplated act.

Consider as a case in point three individuals from different cultures assessing a fourth's deliberation of PS1, SS2, AS3, or RE4. Because of different cultural beliefs and values, the assessors may conceptualize elective death quite differently: one as cowardly avoidance of personal discomfiture, another as noble withdrawal from hopelessly blighted life, the third as an unpardonable sin. Given these different attitudinal starting points, the respective assessments of the soundness of the deliberator's reasoning and/or acceptability of his or her motivation will differ in irreconcilable ways. For the cognitive libertarian, all that can be done in this situation and others like it is for the deliberator to consider each of the assessors' perspectives on elective death as possible alternatives to her or his own. Proscription of mind-changing argument is attributed to our having no recourse to any external standard that would enable critical comparison of conflicting beliefs. *Contra* Searle, we have no neutral access to conflict-resolving objective reality. Moreover, we have no recourse to intersubjective standards because of multiculturalism: beliefs and values now vary too widely to allow establishment of such standards. Supposedly, then, all we can do is accept diverse beliefs and values. This is what reduces cross-cultural assessment of elective-death reasoning and motivation to *intra*cultural assessment, as considered previously. So if an individual decides to commit PS_1, SS_2, or AS_3 or request RE_4 on the basis of a culturally determined belief in an afterlife, and fails to examine that belief, thus violating the reasoning clause of the rationality criterion, cultural peers assessing the decision will find it sound. And since cognitive acceptance of conceptual diversity bars disputing the belief in question, members of other cultures who find the decision unsound are effectively excluded from assessment of the decision.

I believe we can circumvent this impasse by borrowing from political philosophy.[15] My point of departure was alluded to earlier with reference to the political reality of multiculturalism; it is that political philosophers now recognize that European and North American democratic societies can no longer rely on national solidarity based on a common heritage, language, ethnicity, and values to support compliance with and loyalty to democratic ideals and practices. There is a dual need to find new grounding for political legitimacy and political stability.

Briefly, given the impact of massive immigration and the resulting multicultural nature of contemporary North American and European societies, political philosophers are faced with the need to rethink the grounding of democracy to legitimate governance and ensure stability. A number of theoretical frameworks have been proposed to meet these demands. I mention three to convey the flavor of the debate before saying a little more about the one most relevant to our interests. One proposed framework is *consociationalism*, which minimizes individual-citizen political activity to lessen discordance and relies on coalitions of influential management institutions representative of the

---

[15] Munro, Daniel. "Deliberative Citizenship in Multicultural Democracies," forthcoming.

various culturally distinct components of society. This representa-
tionalist structure is intended to provide legitimacy and to foster loyalty and compliance and so political stability. The problem with
consociationalism is that despite devices like minority vetoes, its
"segmental authority" could further weaken less powerful minorities
and proportionately strengthen more powerful majorities or larger
minorities. An older but now less workable alternative framework is
communitarianism, which maximizes individual-citizen political activity
in democratic governance but relies heavily on now-problematic
shared values to provide legitimacy and to foster loyalty, compliance,
and stability.

The theoretical framework most relevant to our interests is *deliberative democracy*, which, like communitarianism, prioritizes individual-
citizen political activity but recognizes that legitimacy and stability-
ensuring political compliance can no longer be grounded on shared
values. What deliberative democracy offers to replace shared values
are *established principles*: principles agreed upon and formalized
through social deliberation – hence the name. The basic idea is that
valid "norms and normative institutional arrangements" may be
agreed on by members of a multicultural democratic society in "special
argumentation situations."[16] Such agreed-on norms and institutional
arrangements provide a ground for legitimated and stable democratic
governance without recourse to now-problematically common beliefs,
values, and practices. Jürgen Habermas captures this shift from reliance on common values to reliance on established principles by
describing the new loyalty as "constitutional patriotism."[17]

Reliance on established principles clearly requires that deliberative
democracy foster other-regarding, culture-transcending attitudes in
citizens. This is necessary to enable deliberatively established principles
to be given priority over culturally determined values and beliefs.
Members of the same society, but of different cultural groups within
that society, must be prepared to give priority to agreed-on principles,

---

[16] Benhabib, Seyla. 2004. *The Rights of Others*. Cambridge: Cambridge University
Press, 13.
[17] Habermas, Jürgen. 1998. "The European Nation-State: On The Past and Future of
Sovereignty and Citizenship." In Jürgen Habermas, Ciaran Cronin, and Pablo De
Greiff, eds., *The Inclusion of the Other: Studies in Political Theory*. Cambridge, Mass.:
MIT Press.

such as the "one person, one vote" principle basic to democracy, even though their cultural values may, for instance, bar allowing women to vote.

The expectation underlying deliberative democracy, then, is that despite cross-cultural ideological differences, understanding of the nature of democracy and appreciation of its benefits, as well as understanding of the realities of multicultural societies, will make possible agreement across cultural boundaries on the fundamentality of some principles and so enable compliance with those principles and ensure stable democratic governance.

Of course, deliberative democracy, like other theoretical frameworks, has its problems. Some worry that the very process of deliberatively establishing new principles and validating existing principles can counterproductively enhance the influence of dominant groups at the expense of more marginal ones. However, this is not the place to pursue issues in political philosophy; what I want to do now is propose how we can borrow from deliberative democracy to make possible genuine and effective cross-cultural assessment of elective-death reasoning and motivation.

In my view, there are two aspects to the basic idea of deliberative democracy: the *process* of deliberation and the *prioritizing* of deliberatively established principles over cultural values and practices. My proposal is in line with the views of some adherents of deliberative democracy who believe it applicable beyond political issues to contentious moral issues like abortion and euthanasia.[18] However, what I want to propose is not applying deliberative democracy to *resolve* cultural conflicts in assessment of elective death, but rather borrowing from deliberative democracy to *preempt* the sort of intractable cultural conflicts we have been considering.

The trouble with trying to apply deliberative democracy to cultural conflicts regarding elective death is that I believe it very unlikely that agreement could be reached on principles overriding deeply engrained cultural beliefs and values about life itself. I suspect

[18] Gutmann, Amy, and Dennis Thompson. 1996. *Democracy and Disagreement.* Cambridge, Mass.: Harvard University Press. My thanks to Daniel Munro. It was not until he referred me to this book that I learned there was a related precedent for my proposal.

attempts to establish such principles would turn out to be as inconclusive and never-ending as the debate on abortion and that any
agreements reached would be short-lived and spottily adhered to
while in effect. This is the sort of worry some have about the efficacy
of deliberative democracy in the real political world.[19] Additionally,
there is a practical limitation on application of deliberative democracy to cross-cultural assessment of elective death: the sort of deliberation required would be too time-consuming to facilitate effective
assessment of elective-death deliberations. What, then, can we take
from deliberative democracy to facilitate genuine and effective cross-
cultural assessment of elective death?

Consider again the case mentioned where three individuals from
different cultures assess a fourth's deliberation of PS_1, SS_2, AS_3, or
RE_4. One of the assessors sees elective death as cowardly avoidance
of personal discomfiture, another as noble withdrawal from hopelessly blighted life, the third as unforgivable defiance of God. The
result, as we saw, is that the supposed cross-cultural assessment of the
contemplated elective death would be no more than articulation of –
in this case three – divergent perspectives on the contemplated act,
one or more of which might or might not coincide with that of the
individual deliberating elective death.

What I propose to deal with this sort of situation is related to my
earlier proposal to use proxy premises to circumvent difficulties with
metaphysical or religious beliefs operating as factual premises. The
point of the proxy premise proposal was to make explicit that some
elements of elective-death reasoning are actually choices, in the sense
that they are expressions of faith, and not facts as usually presented.
The allegedly factual premise "God does not want me to suffer
needlessly," then, is replaced by something like "I believe in God and
believe that God does not want me to suffer needlessly." What bears on
the present proposal is that where proposed proxy premises are
rejected and the nonfactual premises continue to be used as if factual,
there is no option but to forgo application of the rationality criterion.
Religious or metaphysical beliefs cannot be shown to be true, so if they
operate as factual premises in deliberation of elective death they

---

[19] Macedo, Stephen, ed. 1999. *Deliberative Politics: Essays on Democracy and Disagreement*. New York: Oxford University Press.

preclude satisfaction of the reasoning clause of the rationality criterion. Individuals refusing to accept proxy premises for articles of faith
functioning as premises, then, exclude themselves from assessment of
their elective-death deliberation for rationality and permissibility. The
consequences of this must be considered in terms of specific cases.
Sometimes it will be incumbent on others involved to prevent commission of PS1, SS2, AS3 or to ignore requests for RE4; sometimes
others involved may have to accept the choice to die.

My proposal deriving from deliberative democracy is somewhat
similar to the proxy premise proposal and is quite simple: if assessors
of elective-death reasoning cannot accept the priority of deliberatively established cross-cultural principles over their own culturally
determined beliefs and values, they exclude themselves from participation in cross-cultural assessment of elective-death deliberations. Unwillingness to accept the priority of deliberative principles
amounts to self-disqualification from assessment of elective-death
deliberation because it is refusal to qualify or overrule culturally
determined beliefs and values that proscribe elective death. It is
clearly unacceptable for individuals to function as assessors of elective-death deliberations and decisions if they are previously committed to finding elective death impermissible and/or irrational.

As for the deliberative principles that would facilitate cross-cultural
assessment of elective death, I propose that the rationality criterion be
restated to serve as the key deliberative principle regarding assessment
of elective-death deliberation. Recall that the criterion runs as follows:

> Autonomous self-killing as release from terminal illness is
> rational if the decision follows validly from true premises that
> include the pertinent facts and enacting it is judged in cross-
> cultural dialogue not to override interest in survival unduly.

By changing just one word, the criterion can be restated in the form
of a *principle* that can be cross-culturally deliberated and adopted to
override particular cultural values and beliefs proscribing elective
death:

> *Autonomous self-killing as release from terminal illness is permissible if
> the decision follows validly from true premises that include the pertinent*

facts and enacting it is judged in cross-cultural dialogue not to override interest in survival unduly.

It is important that individuals whose cultural beliefs and values proscribe elective death could accept this principle after due deliberation. The reasons for doing so might be such reasons as humanitarian inclinations prevailing over doctrinal tenets or reevaluation of religious or moral strictures in light of better appreciation of the pointlessness of great suffering in some terminal situations.

It is equally important to appreciate that the point of my proposal is not simply to exclude individuals whose cultural beliefs and values prohibit elective death from its cross-cultural assessment. Rather the point is to make clear – as proxy premises make clear that some premises are choices and not facts – that those individuals whose beliefs or values preclude elective death's permissibility and/or rationality are *opponents* of PS1, SS2, AS3, and RE4 and so cannot function as assessors of the rationality and permissibility of PS1, SS2, AS3, and RE4. There is something of a parallel here to how physicians and nurses strongly opposed to abortion refuse – and are not expected – to participate in abortive medical procedures.

Cross-cultural assessors of elective-death deliberation, as opposed to committed opponents of it, must be prepared to give priority to existing or deliberatively established or revalidated principles accepted in other cultures that allow elective death as a possibly rational and permissible option in some cases of terminal illness.

To close this chapter, I need to make two further points. First, what I say here about cultural beliefs and values that proscribe elective death applies also to culturally determined views on truth and rationality that might conflict with those of other assessors. If the conflict has to do with conceptions of rationality or truth, as opposed to, say, the sanctity of human life, the mechanics are the same: if individuals insist on giving priority to their own culturally determined conceptions, they also disqualify themselves as cross-cultural assessors of elective death, though they may, of course, participate in the debate as opponents.

Secondly, it must not be thought that disqualification of some potential assessors unwilling to yield the priority of their own cultural beliefs and values is tantamount to reducing cross-cultural assessment of elective death to intracultural assessment, as happens with cognitive acceptance. For one thing, the expectation is that enough assessors from diverse cultures will conduct themselves as deliberative democracy requires of its citizens in order to make assessment of elective-death deliberation genuinely cross-cultural. But more important is that cognitive acceptance reduces cross-cultural assessment of elective death to mere listing of diverse perspectives by giving *all* judgments equal weight, on the grounds that operant beliefs and values cannot be disputed. The disqualification of some potential assessors on the basis of their own refusal to prioritize other cultures' principles is quite different because what it does is simply exclude those whose minds are already made up about the unacceptability of elective death.

7

The Role of Religion

As must be evident from the foregoing chapters, as well as from what we all know about elective-death issues, the influences of generally secular cultural beliefs and values tend to be less significant than those of religious ones in most cases where culturally determined factors affect judgments and decisions. Actually, it is a good question how far we can go in separating out defining secular cultural values, beliefs, and practices from religious ones in most cultures, so religious influences likely are that much more significant. Language and ethnicity, geographic location, and survival methods are fundamental in determining a people's culture, but the ideological objectification and consequent influences of these basic cultural components are invariably shaped by religious beliefs and practices. There are few cultures with purely secular defining principles and traditions.

Whether or not separable from secular ones, religious values and beliefs have a role in elective-death deliberation and the assessment of that deliberation that is enormously important and, in perhaps the majority of cases, decisive. That this is so is of great concern to us; the exercise of sound reasoning in choosing to die, the articulation and acceptance of proper motives in enacting the decision to die, and the assessment of the reasoning and motivation often can be skewed, if not misdirected, by religious beliefs and commitments.

What may be surprising is that unlike what many might assume, religion's role with respect to PS1, SS2, AS3, and RE4 is not universally proscriptive. This is to a significant extent why the motives clause of the rationality criterion is formulated as it is, since in some cases religious beliefs or doctrines are the main impetus to the surrender of life. If religions did universally proscribe elective death, the issue of religion's role in elective death would be different but much less worrying. That is, our problem would be mainly one of attempting to circumvent religious proscription where elective death is in the best interests of terminal patients. But this is not the case; though numerically small, there are cases where religious beliefs and doctrines prompt suicide although the individuals concerned have a greater interest in remaining alive than in dying. The examples of religious motives prompting individuals to surrender their lives unjustifiably that now come most readily to mind revolve around aspired-to martyrdom driven by militant extremism regarding political issues. There are, however, examples that bear much more directly on our concern with the rationality of choosing to die in terminal illness.

To proceed, I need to make a number of points about elective death and religion. As with cultural beliefs and values, it is not my intention to delve into specifics. For my purposes, discussion of the various aspects of multiculturalism, including its religious components, must be kept at an abstract level to enable the order of generalizations required to deal effectively with issues about the rationality of elective death. Nonetheless, in this chapter it will prove necessary to name particular religions because of an important difference among the world's major faiths that bears importantly on deliberation of elective death and assessment of such deliberation.

The reason for the need to refer to particular religions has to do with what I think is religion's greatest single influence on the deliberation of elective death and on its assessment. That influence is a function of whether deliberators' and assessors' respective religious faiths promise a *personal* afterlife.

What I mean by a personal afterlife is one that offers what I will describe as *continuity of consciousness* or absence of major changes in self-awareness or identity in the transition from life to afterlife. The alternative is some kind of *impersonal* survival of death in the sense that, for instance, one's life force rejoins a universal soul, or some essence that defines one while alive continues and is capable of rebirth, or one becomes again an undifferentiated part of a pantheistically conceived God, or something of the sort.

I think it incontestable that the more individuals believe that they will survive death *as themselves*, the more prepared they will be to choose to die in various circumstances. Moreover, and this is the key point here, the extent to which assessors of elective-death reasoning and motivation believe in a personal afterlife is of great consequence to their estimation of the soundness of deliberators' reasoning and the acceptability of their motivation. This is especially so if the belief in a personal afterlife is shared by deliberators and assessors. The more assessors believe that elective-death deliberators will survive death as themselves, the likelier it is those assessors will find deliberators' reasoning about choosing to die sound and their motivation acceptable.

The basic reason for this attitudinal inclination is simple enough: if one believes in a personal afterlife, choosing to die is not perceived as choosing to annihilate oneself. It is perceived as embarking on a transition to another form of existence. Belief in a personal afterlife, then, alters perception of what is at stake in deliberating elective death; it ameliorates a frightening decision – especially in the cases that concern us, choosing to die to avoid or escape hopeless suffering, where the stakes in continued earthly life are significantly reduced. However, what belief in a personal afterlife then makes crucial, in deliberation and assessment of elective death, is that at least with the major faiths religion's promise of personal survival of death is invariably tied to proscription of suicide.

In order to assess properly the soundness of their reasoning and the acceptability of their motivation, it is crucial to determine whether individuals deliberating elective death believe that they will survive death as themselves, only in some more amorphous manner, or not at all. But it is not only a matter of ensuring that those assessing others' elective-death reasoning and motivation understand what it is deliberators believe or do not believe about an afterlife. It is just as crucial that the assessors reflect on their own beliefs about an afterlife and appreciate the possible effects their beliefs may have on the assessment they are conducting.

It is not hard to see the sorts of problems that arise if there is inadequate reflection on the beliefs about an afterlife held by both deliberators and assessors. Some assessors might not appreciate the extent to which those deliberating elective death see their choice to die as no more than a momentary – albeit frightening – transition to a happier state and so fail to appreciate adequately their interest in continued survival. Again, some assessors who believe in a personal afterlife might not be able to envisage anyone's rationally deliberating PS1, SS2, AS3, or RE4 while believing either in nebulous impersonal survival or no afterlife at all. Also, some deliberating PS1, SS2, AS3, or RE4 who believe in a personal afterlife, and who see dying as a way of being reunited with loved ones and gaining an eternity of bliss, might not heed properly the cautions offered by those with different beliefs who are assessing their deliberations. Yet again, deliberators who believe in an impersonal survival of death and assessors who believe in a personal afterlife might be irrevocably at odds about the rationality of surrendering life for what the assessors see as an empty or unintelligible promise of continued existence as part of some indefinable eternality. And where it is deliberators who believe in a personal afterlife, some assessors who believe in impersonal survival or no survival at all might fail to understand how anyone can rationally deliberate surrendering life while believing a simplistic fairytale.

Deliberators' and assessors' beliefs about what ensues after death – if anything – clearly introduce troublesome complexity to cross-cultural assessment of elective-death reasoning and motivation. Just as belief in a personal afterlife influences deliberation of elective death, disparity of belief on the matter among assessors will influence their assessment of both the reasoning and the motivation of those choosing to die. And matters are made even more complex by the role of religious doctrines regarding an afterlife because the promise of personal survival invariably is closely tied to what happens in that afterlife, which in turn is tied to the consequences of deliberately choosing to die.

Simply put, my point has two parts: the first part is that belief in a personal afterlife eases the choice to die – to an extent – by promising survival of death as oneself. The complication is that belief in a personal afterlife may lead to undue diminishment of the interest in survival. Moreover, belief in a personal afterlife also may influence assessment of the choice to die. If the belief in a personal afterlife is shared by elective-death deliberators and assessors, assessors may be unduly lenient because sympathetic; if the belief is not shared, assessors may be unduly severe because unsympathetic. The second part of my point is that religions promising a personal afterlife usually deter elective death by threatening dire consequences to suicidists' surviving souls or spirits. This further complicates matters because to whatever extent belief in a personal afterlife eases the choice to die, that choice is impeded by doctrinal proscription of suicide. This proscription may disproportionately impede choosing to die as well as negatively influence assessment of the choice to die. We now need to look a little more closely at how religions give with one hand and take with the other regarding elective death.

* * *

Our starting point is that the world's major religions differ on their doctrines about what follows earthly death as they differ on their conceptions of God. The difference that most concerns us is whether religions promise a personal afterlife or some other sort of survival of death. Generally speaking, Christianity, Islam, and Judaism promise an afterlife in which individuals survive death as the persons they were in life – perhaps with enhanced capacities, but essentially as *themselves*. That is, these faiths hold that individuals survive death continuing to be conscious of themselves as themselves. The doctrinal basis for this promise has to do, first, with conception of the nature of the soul. In Christianity, Islam, and Judaism, the soul *is* the person. This is in contrast to faiths that conceive of the soul more as an animating infusion or transient embodiment of a universal spirit or life force. Secondly, the doctrinal basis has to do with continuity of consciousness's being necessary to allow responsibility when the soul is judged and rewarded or punished for its conduct during earthly life. Without continuity of self-consciousness, assignation of merit or blame in an afterlife would be arbitrary or capricious. It is persons themselves who are saved or dammed and either enjoy eternal bliss or suffer eternal anguish.

Hinduism is more ambiguous on the matter of continued consciousness after death and Buddhism is more ambiguous still – enough so that it depends on particular sects as to whether there is any kind of afterlife at all. However, doctrinal specifics are not what matters for our purposes; what matters is that there *are* doctrinal differences regarding what follows earthly death. The important point, then, is that *ex hypothesi*, cross-cultural assessment of elective-death reasoning and motivation will involve participants with different religious backgrounds and therefore with different beliefs about whether there is an afterlife and whether it is of a personal or impersonal sort. Moreover, only some of the assessors will share particular beliefs about an afterlife – or lack thereof – with deliberators whose elective-death reasoning and motivation they are assessing.

The significance of this disparity is that, as suggested, the nature of beliefs held about an afterlife bears appreciably on the degree to which elective death is deemed acceptable or unacceptable by both deliberators and assessors. Nor is this necessarily a doctrinal issue; it mainly has to do with what we can describe as the credibility of elective death as a rational option. Choosing to die may well look more *reasonable*, if not precisely more rational, to those who believe in a personal afterlife because they will not see the loss in elective death as loss of *oneself*. However, as noted, proscription of suicide is likely strongest where there is doctrinal promise of personal survival after death, and such proscription introduces a deterrent different from but at least as powerful as the threat of personal annihilation: eternal damnation. The consequence is that, for deliberators, if belief in a personal afterlife serves to make choosing to die look more reasonable and achievable, the threat of damnation consequent on commission of suicide serves to make choosing to die irrational and all but impossible. As for assessors, belief in an afterlife together with acceptance of the doctrinal threat of damnation resulting from suicide certainly will impede, if not preclude, finding elective-death deliberators' reasoning sound and their motivation acceptable.

Buddhism provides an example of a religion – in the broad sense of the term – that accommodates two views on suicide, an accommodation that assuredly is at least partly a function of its doctrinal diversity and ambiguity regarding survival of death, if any. On the one hand, Buddhism incorporates a fundamental commitment to the preservation of all life; on the other hand, it condones suicide done as other-regarding self-sacrifice for religious or political ideals. Self-immolation has been used by Buddhists for this purpose, most recently to protest human-rights violations against Tibetans.

Hinduism also seems to accommodate two views on suicide. On the one hand, it holds suicide on a par with the killing of another and self-killing as resulting in suicidists' remaining in a kind of limbo, becoming ghostlike, and not proceeding to the next stage after earthly life. On the other hand, Hinduism condones fasting oneself to death and apparently attaches no punishment to doing so.

Christianity, of course, honors martyrdom, but it does not condone suicide. Martyrdom is the willing surrender of life for principle, but at someone else's hand; martyrdom is not *self*-killing. Suicide by a Christian is heinously sinful and supposedly guarantees damnation. Though some early Christians understood self-killing to be, indeed, martyrdom and to guarantee entrance into heaven, by Augustine's time suicide was categorically condemned and those who took their own lives were regarded as damned and their burial in consecrated soil was forbidden.

The Christian view of suicide essentially is the idea mentioned earlier, namely, that life is a gift of God and simply not ours to dispose of at will. Taking one's own life is first and foremost disobedience of divine law – the Fifth Commandment, Thou shalt not kill, prohibits taking one's own life as much as taking the life of another. But taking one's own life is also defiance of God in that it is to spurn the divine gift of life. Among Christian sects, Catholicism seems to be the least amenable to tolerating suicide. With respect to what interests us, choosing to die in terminal illness, the furthest that the official Catholic position goes is to allow that there is no obligation to pursue extreme measures to keep oneself alive.

As does Christianity, Islam proscribes suicide. However, unlike with Catholicism and some other Christian sects, suicide is not the unforgivable sin in being total rejection of God's goodness and ultimate defiance of God's will. Islam holds unbelief or lack of faith the unforgivable sin. Suicide, though generally proscribed, is forgivable if done with acceptable intentions. There is some reflection in this of Buddhist tolerance of suicide done for other-regarding reasons in ideological protest. Judaism considers life sacred and sees suicide as grievous defiance of God and so proscribes self-killing as categorically as does Catholicism.

With respect to Christianity, Islam, and Judaism, then, given the shared promise of a personal afterlife and the common proscription of suicide, the most pressing question about elective death – at least for our purposes – is what happens to those who choose to die rather than bear the suffering of terminal illness. Differently put, what potential suicidists who adhere to Christian, Muslim, or Judaic doctrine must consider are the consequences of committing PS1, SS2, or AS3 to avoid or escape the suffering of terminal illness. (The requesting of RE4, while it raises similar issues, is not of immediate relevance since euthanasia, whether requested or not, is an act performed by another person.) Similarly, the question of what happens to suicidists' souls is a pressing one with respect to the beliefs held by those assessing potential suicidists' reasoning and motivation.

We can recapitulate as follows: In the context of deliberating elective death to avoid or escape needless suffering in terminal illness, belief in a personal afterlife tends to assuage the difficulty of choosing to die because death is not seen as personal annihilation. As for assessors of elective-death deliberation, belief in a personal afterlife, whether or not shared with the deliberator, tends to make choosing to die seem a more reasonable option than it might appear in the absence of the belief. However, where the belief in a personal afterlife is based on religious doctrine, the promise of personal survival almost invariably goes hand in hand with prohibition of suicide. This means that whatever alleviation religious promise of a personal afterlife affords regarding choosing to die is countered by religious proscription of self-killing – and especially the threatened penalties for taking one's own life.

The way that this predicament affects the issue of elective death in terminal illness has less to do with how particular individuals, whether elective-death deliberators or assessors of deliberators' reasoning and motivation, actually deal with the predicament. Instead it has to do with the fact that deliberators and cross-cultural assessors will usually, if not invariably, differ in what they believe about both the nature of an afterlife and the justifiability or unjustifiability of suicide in light of its possible consequences. Just as we can expect the sorts of problems outlined in the last section regarding variance in belief about the personal or impersonal nature of an afterlife, then, we can expect more problems centering on whether elective-death deliberators and assessors see proscription of suicide as absolute or as defeasible by special circumstances.

As in the examples at the end of the last section, it is not difficult to imagine the following sorts of conflicts: Elective-death deliberators might believe that there is a personal afterlife, and they might believe, as does Ms. A, that a merciful God forgives suicide in some circumstances so that those committing PS1, SS2, or AS3 to avoid or escape the suffering of terminal illness will not be automatically damning themselves. However, some cross-cultural assessors of deliberators' reasoning and motivation, who also believe in a personal afterlife, might understand proscription of suicide as categorical and allowing no exceptions. These assessors are not likely to see the deliberators' reasoning as sound because they will take those deliberators as not appreciating the dire consequences of their contemplated acts of self-killing. Of course, there will be some individuals who believe in a personal afterlife and believe that proscription of suicide is categorical, but they are not likely to contemplate ending their lives.

Another worrying scenario is where elective-death deliberators believe in a personal afterlife and believe that a merciful God will forgive their taking their own lives, but where some assessors do not believe in a personal afterlife or any afterlife at all. These assessors are likely not to find the deliberators' reasoning sound because they will see those deliberators as underestimating the value of continued survival when weighed against what the assessors will see as a naively accepted promise of an ingenuous happy-ever-after daydream. It is possible, too, that deliberators who do not believe in an afterlife might have their reasoning or motivation rejected by assessors who believe in a personal afterlife and see the deliberators as acting out of despair and lack of faith and so likely damning themselves by committing PS1, SS2, or AS3.

* * *

Is there anything that can be done to allow productive cross-cultural assessment of elective-death reasoning and motivation, anything that can alleviate the difficulties bound to arise when deliberators and assessors hold diverse beliefs about an afterlife? For instance, is there a device comparable to proxy premises that might be used to avoid or overcome the problems discussed in the previous two sections?

To begin with, we can summarize the root of the difficulties as follows: most religions promise either a personal afterlife or some form of impersonal survival after death, most cultures are significantly shaped by religion, and most members of a given culture hold religious beliefs. Admittedly, in a few cases, one or another religion or particular sect may not promise any kind of survival after death, but these cases are not significant in number and influence with respect to our concerns. It also is possible to hold wholly secular beliefs about survival after death, for instance, a religious belief that we survive death as physical energy, but these cases are numerically insignificant. The point here is that assembling even a small number of people and charging them with assessing the elective-death deliberations of a given individual is bound to involve people holding diverse beliefs about an afterlife or its lack. When we factor in the need to have representatives of different cultures in the assembled group, diversity of belief about an afterlife will be inescapable.

The consequences of diversity of belief, then, are the sorts of problems reviewed and alluded to in the last section. How can assessment of reasoning and motivation for choosing to die be conducted effectively? In short, how can we prevent such assessment from either being skewed by the interplay of different beliefs or simply bogging down in irresolvable conflicts?

I think the answer is actually rather straightforward, though admittedly its practical application will prove decidedly less so. Consider that belief in a personal afterlife, especially when connected to doctrinal proscription of elective death, raises what we can describe as a *practical* concern about the consequences of choosing to die. This concern is the factor that likely will weigh most heavily both in deliberation of elective death and in assessment of that deliberation. Belief in some form of impersonal survival, again especially when connected to proscription of elective death, raises what is best described as a *metaphysical* question about the propriety of choosing to die in light of whatever beliefs or doctrines may apply regarding the grand scheme of things. However, as in the case of belief in a personal afterlife, the practical concern is about the consequences of choosing to die.

To simplify, it seems fair to say that in both believing in a personal afterlife and believing in impersonal survival, the pressing question is "What will happen *to me* if I end my life?" The difference between the two cases is basically that in the former, where there is belief in a personal afterlife, the question has to do with what the individual may experience or suffer after death; in the latter case, the question concerns eventual rebirth, assimilation into the world soul, or the like. The key point, though, is that in both cases the pressing question about what happens to the individual on dying differs totally from that which arises for those who do not believe in any sort of survival and accept that death is annihilation. In this latter case, the pressing question is not about the *consequences* of choosing to die, but about one's *preparedness* to die; the question is "Am I ready to cease to exist?"

What I want to propose relates to a point made in Chapter 3 about the need for deliberators of elective death to understand that death is at least possibly, if not certainly, personal annihilation. In brief, for choosing to die to be rational, elective-death deliberators must allow that regardless of their beliefs, death may well be their final and irretrievable obliteration. Belief in a personal afterlife or in some other form of survival of death is *a matter of faith*; it is not knowledge and therefore cannot be assumed in deliberating choosing to die; nor can that belief function in elective-death reasoning or motivation as a matter of fact.

The proposal I make here is based on the same point about the finality of death, and it can be most succinctly put in terms of the requirement that the question "Am I ready to cease to exist?" be most seriously considered by anyone deliberating PS1, SS2, AS3, or RE4 whether or not he or she believes in an afterlife. In other words, regardless of their beliefs, those contemplating elective death must allow that their death may be their annihilation. Only if they consider this possibility earnestly and with an open mind can their choice to die be a rational one. Belief in survival of death, of whatever sort, cannot be allowed to occlude the possibility that that there is no such survival – on pain of jeopardizing or ruling out the rationality of choosing to die.

Once the need to allow that death at least may be personal annihilation is recognized and acknowledged, it becomes clear that the question "Am I ready to cease to exist?" underlies rational deliberation of elective death. Because belief in some form of survival of death is just that, belief, the question about preparedness to cease to exist is fundamental and takes priority over any other about the possible consequences of choosing to die.

The proposal, then, is that it be made explicit in the criterion for rational suicide that the question about personal annihilation is basic to sound reasoning about PS1, SS2, AS3, and RE4 and must be applied to motivation for choosing to die. It seems, therefore, that we need to revise the criterion yet again.

It is important to be clear on what we are doing in revising the rationality criterion. First, we are conceding that cultural and particularly religious factors directly affect reasoning about elective death as well as motivation for choosing to die. What makes this concession noteworthy is that we are not here attempting to prevent *errors* in reasoning or motivation. That is, the revision is not like adding elements to the criterion designed to exclude logical mistakes, invalidity, relevant ignorance, and the like. Nor are we attempting to exclude certain sorts of motives. What we are doing is acknowledging that reasoning and motives regarding choosing to die will, in the overwhelming number of cases, presuppose and be shaped by beliefs about an afterlife of one sort or another. Differently put, we cannot assume that individuals deliberating elective death will, without exception, appreciate that their religious or cultural – or for that matter personal – beliefs about surviving death in some way must be given a lower priority than the possibility that death is total and permanent annihilation of oneself in deliberating PS1, SS2, AS3, or RE4.

The second thing we are doing in revising the rationality criterion is requiring assessors of elective-death deliberation to respect deliberators' beliefs – or lack of beliefs – about a personal afterlife or impersonal survival of death and not allow their own beliefs, or lack thereof, to condition their assessment of deliberators' reasoning and motivation. The question is how to achieve these ends as efficiently as possible and without rendering the criterion for rational elective death in effect impossible to apply by making it too complex.

Recall that the criterion runs as follows:

Autonomous self-killing as release from terminal illness is rational if the decision follows validly from true premises that include the pertinent facts and enacting it is judged in cross-cultural dialogue not to override interest in survival unduly.

The trouble is that including reference to belief in an afterlife seems to open the door to a long series of qualifications. However, religious belief in one or another form of survival after death is so prevalent across most cultures that it constitutes a special case and including reference to it in the criterion is justified. The hard fact is that belief in some sort of afterlife will be virtually inescapable among elective-death deliberators and assessors of their deliberations, even if all are members of a single culture. Actually, what multiculturalism adds to this fact has less to do with the sheer presence of such belief than with the strength of the influence it has on both elective-death deliberation and its assessment.

I believe that the following minimal revision of the rationality criterion will suffice:

> Autonomous self-killing as release from terminal illness is rational if the decision follows validly from true premises that include the pertinent facts and recognition that death may be personal annihilation, and enacting the decision is judged in cross-cultural dialogue not to override interest in survival unduly.

The revision, however, makes the criterion even more stilted than before, so we can take this opportunity to improve how the criterion is stated while changing nothing essential. For instance, the phrase "as release from" adds little to the criterion's formulation and tends to exclude PS1. Again, on reflection it seems unnecessary to use the phrase "follows validly from true premises" to refer to sound reasoning on the assumption that the phrase "sound reasoning" may be too liberally understood. Moreover, using the phrase "follows validly from true premises" may actually obscure the reference because of its rather technical air. "Sound reasoning" probably suffices, especially given that its objects are referred to as the "pertinent *facts*." While we are at it, we can also restate the motives clause to make its deliberative nature explicit. The revised version of the criterion, then, reads as follows:

> Autonomous self-killing in terminal illness is rational if choosing
> to die follows on sound reasoning about pertinent facts,
> including that death may be annihilation, and cross-cultural
> deliberative dialogue finds it best serves the agent's interests.

*   *   *

As alluded to in the last section, practical application of the revised rationality criterion will not be as straightforward as its revision. The main reason has to do with how the requirement that there be acknowledgment that death may be personal annihilation will prove difficult for individuals who believe in survival of death in some form. There are, of course, obvious personal and psychological reasons for this, but the main obstacle is doctrinal.

Individuals who believe their religion's promises of survival of death, especially of a personal afterlife, no doubt will find it difficult to reflect on their beliefs and to recognize that in considering elective death, they must take into account the possibility that death is annihilation in order for their choosing to die to be rational. Some of the difficulties will center on their own convictions and expectations, as we would expect. However, some of the difficulties will be due to doctrinal requirements or, differently put, canonical demands of dutiful compliance with doctrine. Along with proscribing PS1, SS2, and AS3, most religions promising some form of afterlife interpret consideration of the possibility that death is annihilation as profanation of a central element of faith and so as essentially heretical.

The consequence of individuals' complying with the rationality criterion's required acknowledgment that death may be annihilation, then, is that they will be judged by their religious prelates and peers as repudiating divine covenant and committing the sin of despair. This means that the sacrilegiousness of their contemplated or intended commission of suicide will be greatly worsened by what will be judged to be rejection of faith. As we saw previously, Catholicism and especially Islam consider suicide committed in this spirit of denial to be unforgivable and therefore as self-damnation.

The problem is that without recognition that death may be annihilation, the choice to die cannot be considered rational. The reason is not that belief in some sort of afterlife is false; rather it is that the belief cannot be known to be true and hence cannot function as a factual premise or as a decisive motivational element in deliberation and decision about choosing to die. This is not to say that belief in an afterlife cannot play a part in elective-death deliberation and decision; it is to say that it must be recognized as a *belief* and not taken as something known. People choosing to die must acknowledge that what they believe on the strength of doctrine and tradition may actually not be so, and that therefore their commission of PS1, SS2, or AS3 may be self-annihilation. For individuals to consider and to commit suicide while convinced that to cause their own death is to initiate some sort of transition and not – possibly, if not probably – to cause cessation of their existence is for those individuals to act irrationally. It is to act irrationally because it is to consider doing something with momentous and irrevocable consequences for their interests on the basis of an unsubstantiated article of faith.

And that is, of course, the heart of the problem: belief in an afterlife *is* an article of faith. Therefore, the acknowledgment required by the rationality criterion, if made, constitutes a qualification of faith. Precisely because the acknowledgment that death possibly is annihilation must be genuine recognition of the possibility and cannot be merely perfunctory, the acknowledgment is, in effect, a partial but serious suspension of religious belief. As such, the acknowledgment contravenes devoutness. Elective-death deliberators, then, may be unwilling or unable to make the acknowledgment because of fear that doing so will jeopardize their state of grace or meritorious standing vis-à-vis their God.

The required acknowledgment, of course, does not apply only to elective-death deliberators; it also applies to those assessing their deliberations. In applying the rationality criterion, assessors must evaluate whether deliberators' reasoning and motivation take into account the possibility that death is annihilation, but the other side of the coin is that the assessors also must themselves take that possibility seriously in forming their judgments. In the most obvious case, if individuals choosing to die fail to acknowledge the possibility that death is annihilation, the assessors have to acknowledge that possibility in finding deliberators' reasoning unsound or motives unacceptable. Otherwise, we end up with exactly the problems posed by intracultural assessment of elective-death deliberation, namely, too

strong a likelihood that cultural peers will find deliberators' reasoning sound and motivation acceptable largely because of shared
beliefs and values.

Does religious belief in an afterlife therefore preclude rational
suicide? And does it also preclude impartial assessment of suicidal
reasoning and motivation? The first point that must be taken into
account in trying to answer these questions is that there is significant
diversity among religions and among religious believers regarding
how strictly doctrines are held to and applied. In some cases, there
may be enough latitude so that acknowledging death possibly is
annihilation would be doctrinally acceptable. However, whether or
not the acknowledgment is at least tolerated by doctrine is not the
primary issue here. What is primary is how individual potential suicidists and assessors of their reasoning and motivation deal with the
required acknowledgment. The concern is that doctrine aside,
potential suicidists and assessors may not succeed in genuinely
acknowledging the possibility, thus jeopardizing or precluding satisfaction of the rationality criterion.

As discussed in Chapter 3, Freud claimed that human beings at
some deep level think themselves immortal. As I put it in Chapter 3,
human beings cannot imagine themselves ceasing to exist. I also
agreed with Battin's view that human beings' inclination to believe
themselves immortal is a psychological issue, and so not a conceptual
bar to rational deliberation and commission of suicide. To expand
the point, we need to distinguish between *imagining* oneself as ceasing to exist, which is impossible, and *conceiving* of oneself as ceasing
to exist. The latter requires only that we understand the concept of
annihilation and that it may apply to us when we die. Conceiving of
death as (possibly) annihilation is what is necessary to rationally
deliberate and commit PS1, SS2, or AS3.

As argued in Chapter 3, the crux of the matter is not whether
illusions about an afterlife persist at the back of one's mind. Rather,
the crux of the matter is whether one's own death can be thoughtfully
considered as at least possibly personal annihilation, and there is no
conceptual bar to such consideration. If there were, then human
beings as a class would be incapable of deliberating or committing
rational suicide. However, this point about conceptual possibility
does not preclude that particular individuals may be incapable of

deliberating or committing rational suicide because of beliefs they hold about survival of death. It is this latter point that most concerns us in this chapter, and it concerns us because religion introduces a consideration having to do with the import of overwhelming *numbers*.

Recurrent surveys have shown that the prevalence of religious faith among people worldwide is somewhere in the high-80th to low-90th percentile. This near-universality of faith, together with the fact that religious faith nearly always involves belief in some form of afterlife, gives real force to the question asked in the Preface about how many Socrateses die. That question brings out that the capacity to end one's own life in a rational manner, which requires acknowledging that death may be annihilation, may be limited to a relative handful of individuals. It may be that whatever is the case at the conceptual or abstract level, rational suicide is *practically* impossible for most people because they believe that they will survive death in some manner and so are unable to acknowledge genuinely that death may be annihilation as is required by the rationality criterion.

The import of the number of people holding religious belief in some form of afterlife, then, is that it would seem there is little point in widely deploying a criterion for rational suicide that can be satisfied by only 10 or so percent of those to whose deliberations and actions it might be applied. In the end, so to speak, we may have to concede that only a very few Socrateses die. It may be that only a handful of us are capable of rationally deliberating and committing PS1, SS2, or AS3.

It will be clear that the foregoing applies equally to the rationality of deliberating and requesting RE4. However, since requested euthanasia involves the agency of others, the matter is more complex. In the case of euthanasia, it would seem that it is not only the person requesting euthanasia who must acknowledge the possibility that death is annihilation. Unless the persons performing euthanasia are considered mere instruments of the requestors' will, it seems logical that those acting as agents also must acknowledge that death may be annihilation in order for their own actions to be rational. However, application of the rationality criterion to the deliberations and actions of individuals performing euthanasia – or, for that matter, assisting in suicide – is not something that we can properly pursue here.

The problem of numbers, then, is a serious obstacle to deployment of the rationality criterion. Admittedly, religious beliefs in an after-life need not be preclusive of rationally choosing to die. Religious individuals' capacity to acknowledge that death may be annihilation despite doctrinal promises and personal attitudes regarding an after-life will range from their finding the acknowledgment unthinkable to finding it quite compatible with an expectation of survival that is more a hope than a belief. But for the most part, the majority of religious individuals will be somewhere between these two extremes, and that means the numbers problem is not much lessened by some religious individuals' being capable of making the required acknowledgment. Those who find the acknowledgment unthinkable, and those for whom surviving death is only a hope, represent the clear cases, but they also represent a minority. Most religious individuals will fall somewhere between the extremes, and in doing so they raise difficult questions about the seriousness or adequacy of the required acknowledgment.

Acknowledgment of what is or may be undertaken in choosing to die naturally will be in part a function of how deeply the relevant beliefs about survival of death are held. It will also be in part a function of individuals' perspicacity or insightfulness into their own thinking, their motives, and the autonomy of their decisions. Many, if not most, religious individuals no doubt will think themselves capable of making the required acknowledgment that death may be annihilation, but it may prove impossible for them or those assessing their deliberations to be sure that the required acknowledgment is in fact adequately made in being well reflected on and resolute.

In sum, the presence of religious beliefs in one or another personal or impersonal form of afterlife may prevent those deliberating elective death from seriously enough acknowledging that death possibly is annihilation. If the acknowledgment is inadequate – if it is unthinking or irresolute – the rationality criterion will not be satisfied because the deliberators would be choosing to die while convinced of something for which they have no decisive evidence.

*   *   *

Consideration of the role of religious belief in the deliberation and assessment of choosing to die strongly suggests that the class of people capable of rationally deliberating and committing PS1, SS2, or AS3 may be a small – perhaps a very small – subset of those who might want to die to escape the hopeless ruin of terminal illness. We seem to be rather forcibly taken back, then, to the question asked in the Preface about how many Socrateses die.

What considering the role of religion does is show that limitations on how many people can achieve rational elective death are not limitations arising only from the disrupting effect of the special pressures and trying circumstances of terminal illness. These exceptional influences are undeniably powerful and usually disruptive of clear thought and perceptive understanding of motives, but they are not the sole considerations regarding impediment of rational elective death.

The thought processes of terminal patients obviously are seriously hampered by their physical conditions. As obvious is that thought is also hampered by the psychological effects of concerns about those patients' situations, the effects of medication, varying levels of depression, constant or recurring pain, and conflicting advice and demands from family members and close friends. These physical and psychological factors alone are quite sufficient to prevent the level of balanced and lucid thought necessary to satisfy the rationality criterion. It is little wonder, then, that the conference participants referred to in the Preface were impatient with discussion of the intellectual requirements for rational elective death.

But as just suggested, there is considerably more possibly obstructing rational elective death than the physical and psychological hindrances generated by terminal illness. Consideration of religious belief brings out sharply that deliberators of elective death are, after all, individuals partly defined by a number of held beliefs, beliefs whose content in many ways may skew or impede the kind of systematic thought that is exemplified in valid syllogisms and that the rationality criterion seems to require for elective-death deliberation to be sound.

The beliefs that in part define the persons who individuals are, and so how they deal with terminal illness, are preexisting elements of individuals' cognitive makeups. As such, they may intensify aspects of individuals' perspectives on their situations and prospects, they may reinforce problematic priorities, they may detrimentally slant how problems and issues are thought through, and they may weaken resolve by introducing or worsening uncertainty.

And matters are still more complex. Along with the possibly troublesome actuality of individuals' preexisting beliefs and their influence on thought, there is the undeniable fact that people differ in their ability perspicaciously to think their way through their options and to reflect effectively on their own motivation. They also differ in their resolve regarding decisions they may make regarding what they deliberate.

We have, then, potential if not probable hindrances to clear, logically coherent thought that are due to the physical and psychological particular circumstances of specific medical conditions; potential if not probable hindrances due to preexisting, person-defining cognitive factors; and potential if not probable hindrances due to varying levels of cognitive aptitude and capability. All of this shows that the question about how many Socrateses die has real force and does suggest that formulating and deploying a criterion for rational elective death may be a waste of time: those capable of satisfying the criterion do not need it, and it should not be applied to those who are not capable of satisfying it.

However, matters are not as hopeless as they might seem, and the importance of formulating and deploying a criterion for rational elective death is not lessened by the problems we face in applying it. There are two important points that need to be considered. In the next chapter I consider one of these, which is whether there can be some latitude in application and satisfaction of the rationality criterion. To close this chapter, I consider the other point, which is how the possibility of latitude arises in the first place. Doing so takes us back to RE4 or requested euthanasia.

I have not said much about RE4 in this chapter because the involvement of others as agents in elective death complicates the role of religion in elective-death deliberation and assessment tremendously. Religious beliefs and doctrines not only affect the deliberations and decisions of those requesting euthanasia, they very seriously affect – where they do not preclude – the deliberations, decisions, and especially actions of those whose place it might be to perform euthanasia. When we factor in the matter of multiculturalism, the topic grows well beyond what is manageable in only one or two chapters among others. Nonetheless, RE4 provides important illumination regarding the question of latitude in applying the rationality criterion.

The way consideration of RE4 illuminates the grounds for introducing some latitude to application and judged satisfaction of the rationality criterion has to do with the way that what mainly distinguishes deliberation of and requests for RE4 from deliberation and commission of PS1, SS2, and AS3 is that where RE4 is the appropriate option for terminal patients, their situations generally are quite hopeless, and, most importantly, the hopelessness is evident to all concerned. The significance of this evidency is that in such cases the *reasonableness* of choosing to die – in these cases by having one's life ended for one – usually is obvious both to the terminal patients concerned and to those caring for them and assessing their treatment decisions.

Stating the point differently, assessment of someone's choice to die is a much more straightforward matter when the only option open is euthanasia – though I am here excluding cases where individuals choose to die, are capable of taking their own lives, but simply are unwilling to do so themselves. Euthanasia is not justified in such cases.

How assessment of RE4 is more straightforward than of PS1, SS2, and AS3 is that if individuals are beyond even AS3, their reasoning and motives for electing death over agony-ridden survival or heroic efforts to keep them alive will be transparent to assessors. What interests us about this transparency is that it inevitably influences assessment of elective-death deliberations and decisions by making assessment more compassionate and therefore less demanding than in situations where assessors must work harder to understand reasoning and motivation.

Of course, compassion may be misplaced or at least too narrowly focused on elective-death deliberators' physical circumstances. Requesting euthanasia could appear reasonable to assessors and still not be rational in even a generous sense. For instance, euthanasia might be requested by someone under the unquestioned conviction that death is only a transition to reunion with a deceased spouse, but the request might be assessed as rational purely on the basis of the requestor's dire medical condition. In such cases it would be a hard call as to whether euthanasia might be performed in response to a request judged reasonable enough if not fully rational, or whether euthanasia would be performed on purely compassionate grounds, in which case it would not be a case of RE4.

But what is important at this juncture is that in the hopeless circumstances in which euthanasia is normally requested, the central factors involved in terminal patients' elective-death deliberations and decisions mostly are apparent to assessors, and so it is easier for those assessors to understand the reasoning and motivation behind the requests for RE4. While there may be possible assessment errors due to overemphasis of terminal-patients' calamitous situations, the readily grasped desperateness of those situations does reduce the importance of reasoning and motivational lapses.

The point here, then, is that elective-death deliberations become essentially more public as deliberators' conditions deteriorate. As terminal patients' conditions worsen, reasoning and motivation recede in importance in contrast to the increasing magnitude of obvious suffering and hopelessness. This process continues until the point at which deterioration reaches a level where RE4 is no longer appropriate. If euthanasia is performed at that point, it must be done on purely compassionate grounds; at that point it is no longer a case of *elective* death.

What we need to draw from this consideration of requested euthanasia is that as elective-death deliberators' plights become more obviously unsustainable to assessors, deliberators' reasoning is much easier to follow and their motivation is more readily grasped. But it is not only a matter of accessibility; it also is that the factors involved in deliberators' reasoning and motivation are pared down to essentials. This means that assessors not only better follow deliberators' reasoning and better appreciate their motives; they have fewer factors to balance in their assessments.

For example, individuals deliberating PS1 may need to consider in their reasoning their obligations to friends and family, whereas individuals deliberating RE4 will be well past having such obligations. Again, individuals deliberating SS2 need to focus on the timing of their suicide, weighing whether they might bear more suffering in order to live a bit longer. Those deliberating RE4 will not be concerned with eking out a little more life.

Of course, the danger is that assessors of deliberations and requests for RE4 may be *too* disposed to judge those deliberations and requests acceptable because of deliberators' medical conditions and bleak prospects. This danger is similar to that of wholly intra-cultural assessment of elective-death deliberations and decisions. In the next chapter I return to this point in considering how the accessibility of individuals' deliberations increases as their circum-stances deteriorate and how this accessibility introduces some latitude to application and satisfaction of the rationality criterion.

8

Assessment Latitude

Formulation, deployment, and application of the rationality principle look pointless to many medical ethicists and physicians who daily work with terminal patients. Immersed in the medical, practical, and emotional complexities and vicissitudes that characterize situations in which patients are dying in a protracted and punishing manner, these practitioners see the criterion as an inapplicable abstraction. This perception effectively precludes clinical application of the rationality criterion. Additionally, many medical ethicists and most physicians dismiss the criterion because they see the important question as being whether elective death is ethically permissible, not whether it is rational in a conceptual sense.

But as I have argued, it is a mistake to see the rationality criterion as an inapplicable abstraction or as an unnecessary element because ethical permissibility of elective death *presupposes* the rationality of the choice to die. It is true, though, that the criterion fosters practitioners' perception of it as inapplicable in practice because its requirements appear too demanding to be applied in actual cases. In this chapter I need to show how the rationality criterion's requirements are tempered by elective-death deliberators' deteriorating circumstances and hence how a measure of latitude is introduced to assessment of their choices to die.

Physicians' and medical ethicists' focus on the ethical permissibility of elective death in terminal illness is not determined only by the nature of the day-to-day decisions they have to make regarding terminal patients' choosing to die. It is mainly determined by present legal and professional constraints on enactment of those patients' choices. These constraints ensure that at present, dealing with patients who choose to die to escape their hopeless situations is a matter of practitioners' complying with those choices by *not* acting, rather than by allowing or assisting suicide, much less performing requested euthanasia. The decisions practitioners face regarding patients' wanting to die are about whether to administer indicated treatments and whether to resort to heroic efforts to keep patients alive. This means that medical ethicists and physicians assessing terminal patients' choices to die rarely need to assess intended positive actions to be taken by patients or by them. Instead they need to assess whether given terminal patients' expressed choices to die, their own professional ethics allow them to forgo administering indicated life-sustaining medication or procedures.

That complying with patients' choices to die now calls for inactivity rather than positive action allows practitioners a good deal of latitude in dealing with patients' problematic beliefs and dubious motives that impede satisfaction of the rationality criterion's requirements. It also strongly inclines them to dismiss the rationality criterion's importance and practical applicability. But this is a shortsighted view. Not only may practitioners soon need to assess the permissibility of positive action regarding elective death, and so need the rationality criterion, the criterion is in fact practically applicable in actual cases. This is because a steadily increasing measure of latitude is allowed in judging its requirement to be met as elective-death deliberators' circumstances worsen – a fact that belies the view some have of the criterion as an inapplicable abstraction.

To illustrate, recall from the last chapter that the rationality criterion requires acknowledgment that death may be annihilation because of the impact on reasoning and motivation of beliefs about an afterlife. If the acknowledgment is not made, the criterion will not be satisfied because elective-death deliberations then incorporate unproven beliefs functioning as factual premises in reasoning or as part or the whole of motivation for choosing to die. However, the problem posed by failure to make the acknowledgment clearly becomes less pressing as elective-death deliberators' conditions worsen. The reason is the obvious one that as deliberators' conditions worsen, their interest in survival reduces, and the criterion's point in determining that elective death is rational precisely is to protect the interest in survival.

Unfortunately, while this is an important point regarding the allowance of latitude in applying the criterion, the point actually works against practitioners' taking the criterion seriously. This is because they tend to generalize from the most desperate cases, and those are cases where the criterion may be practically inapplicable or even redundant. Practitioners then see allowing latitude because of circumstances as simply manifesting the criterion's redundancy. But the criterion is most certainly not redundant. There must be principles guiding the treatment of elective-death decisions; such decisions cannot be dealt with purely in a case-by-case manner and solely on the basis of the desperateness of patients' circumstances. If nothing else, there are and will continue to be cases where terminal patients choose to die before their condition becomes desperate.

What we have, then, is that the rationality criterion's requirements may be tempered by two different factors. The first factor has to do with how assessment of some choices to die does not involve assessing positive actions but rather involves assessing only negative actions in the sense that indicated treatments or procedures or even food and water are forgone. The tempering impact of this factor on assessment of elective-death deliberation is due to the way the choice to forgo treatment, procedures, or nourishment is not itself *decisive* in causing death. That is, forgoing a particular treatment, a given procedure, or simply water and nourishment is the *proximate* cause of death, not its *immediate* cause. Even in those few cases where the forgoing of an immediately necessary treatment or procedure is deemed to be decisive regarding death, the forgoing of the procedure or treatment remains the proximate cause of death. The immediate or direct cause of death is the condition that the treatment or procedure would alleviate. Assessment of the reasonableness of choices to forgo treatments, procedures, or nourishment, therefore, is intrinsically less demanding than assessment of the rationality of choices to end one's life directly and positively.

This first factor is not of primary concern in the present context. For one thing, it is one that will diminish in importance as legislation about elective death is liberalized. The second assessment-tempering factor, the gravity of terminal patients' circumstances, is usually taken for granted. However, it is the one most pertinent to the introduction of latitude in assessment of elective-death deliberation and so is the tempering factor on which we need to focus.

*   *   *

The measure of latitude allowable in assessment of choices to die runs through a range whose terminal points are defined by two different sorts of cases. At one end of the range are cases that allow little or no latitude in application of the rationality criterion. These are cases where elective-death deliberators have the greatest interest in survival. The relevant forms of elective death in these cases are all instances of PS1 or preemptive suicide and many instances of SS2 or surcease suicide. In these cases, rigorous application of the criterion is required to ensure that choosing to die is strictly rational in not unduly contravening the interest in continuing to live for a significant period. And the force of "significant" here is not only that the time in question is more than a few hours or days, but that it is time in which important value may be attained, such as completing a project or living to see a grandchild. It is also time in which medical circumstances could change for the better, such as by remission of one or another kind. What the use of "significant" excludes is sheer physical survival in a vegetative or comparable state.

At the other end of the range are cases that allow a good deal of latitude in applying the criterion and judging it adequately satisfied. These are cases where the criterion's requirements reduce to ensuring that the choice to die is the most reasonable option open to terminal patients. The relevant forms of elective death in these cases are most instances of AS3 or assisted suicide, all instances of RE4 or requested euthanasia, and some instances of SS2. In these cases, elective-death deliberators' interest in survival has become vanishingly small because of the amount of time left to them as well as the suffering that time will entail. As the interest in survival decreases as a result of the severity of elective-death deliberators' circumstances and the hopelessness of their prospects, the rationality criterion's requirements grow less demanding. But it is important to see that this is not because the assessment requirements for rational elective death *change*. Reasoning must be sound and motivation acceptable. What happens is that the requirements are applied more leniently because what they are intended to protect – the interest in survival – has decreased markedly in significance and sustainability. Eventually, of course, application of the criterion is made redundant by the imminence of death and evaporation of the interest in survival, but in those cases the possibility of *elective* death disappears, as does the need to assess its rationality.

With respect to just how latitude may be introduced into assessment of elective-death deliberations, allowing some latitude in assessing problematic reasoning and/or motivation mainly has to do with accommodating *uncertain* and *unprovable* beliefs that qualify or determine premises or motives or function as premises or motives. Elective-death deliberators may reason about choosing to die or be motivated to choose to die on the basis of ideas they believe to be true but that have not been established as true. They also may reason about choosing to die or be motivated to choose to die on the basis of ideas they believe to be true but that cannot be established as true. The former beliefs generally have to do with diagnoses and prognoses; the latter with personal, religious, and cultural convictions and values. For easier reference, I will call the former "factual beliefs," in that they are establishable as true or false; I will call the latter "evaluative beliefs," in that they are not establishable as true or false.

The basic question about allowing latitude in applying the rationality criterion is whether factual and evaluative beliefs that jeopardize reasoning soundness and acceptability of motives may be overlooked because deliberators' circumstances have deteriorated to a point where their interest in survival is significantly diminished.

We can think graphically of the allowing of latitude by picturing two lines converging. In this image or visual metaphor, a descending line tracks the deterioration of terminal patients' conditions and prospects while an ascending line represents the amount of latitude allowable in assessing whether the criterion's requirements are met. The point at which the lines finally meet is where application of the rationality criterion becomes redundant because patients' circumstances have deteriorated to a point where elective death is no longer an option. The narrowing gap between the converging lines illustrates how as terminal patients' conditions deteriorate, their interest in survival reduces, and as their interest in survival reduces, the criterion's application increasingly allows compassion to override strict compliance.

At a point early in individuals' terminal illnesses, when their conditions are serious but not desperate, and when there may even be hope of remission of one or another kind, the criterion's applicability must be rigorous because at that point elective-death deliberators have a somewhat reduced but still significant interest in survival. At a later time, as elective-death deliberators' circumstances worsen and their prospects grow increasingly bleak, satisfaction of the criterion becomes less demanding and admits more lenient assessment because of deliberators' diminishing interest in survival. Briefly put, the greater the interest in survival, the stricter must be assessment of satisfaction of the rationality criterion's requirements.

Consider the case of an elective-death deliberator's refusal or psychological or emotional inability to question or suspend an evaluative belief in an afterlife by acknowledging that death may be annihilation. A lenient assessment of reasoning soundness in this case might allow the refusal or accommodate the inability by accepting simple affirmation of the evaluative belief in an afterlife as a deeply held one instead of demanding the more negative affirmation that death may be annihilation. That is, given the deliberator's circumstances, expression of the problematic belief as a belief may be deemed adequate to satisfy the requirement for acknowledgment that annihilation likely is the consequence of dying. This is a significant concession in that the deliberator need only state the belief rather than voice it in a way that accentuates its unprovable nature. Admittedly, the concession does allow that some deliberators may not appreciate that in affirming their beliefs *as* beliefs they are only affirming what they hold to be true rather than what they *know* to be true. But toleration of this possibility precisely is part of allowing latitude in applying the criterion.

Unfortunately, there is a major risk posed by letting deterioration in elective-death deliberators' circumstances govern the rationality criterion's application. The risk is that just as wholly intracultural assessment of elective-death deliberation may be too *value*-indulgent to protect deliberators' interest in survival properly from undue depreciation, circumstance-responsive assessment of elective-death deliberation may be too *empathy*-indulgent to protect their interest in survival properly. Compassionate assessment could be excessively accommodating because of subtle and not-so-subtle shifting of the focus of assessment from the soundness of individuals' reasoning and the acceptability of their motivation to their medical conditions. More needs to be said about how allowing latitude in applying the rationality criterion is not simply a matter of responding to deterioration in medical conditions.

* * *

It must be appreciated at this point that there is a conceptual basis for applying the rationality criterion more leniently to terminal patients' elective-death deliberation when those patients' circumstances are or are growing desperate. The underlying rationale for allowing latitude in assessing elective-death reasoning or motivation that incorporates unproven factual beliefs and unprovable evaluative beliefs is what lies at the core of *decision theory*. This is the fact that rational decisions *can* be made despite inherent uncertainties.

To begin with, we need to marshal two points relevant to allowing latitude in applying the rationality criterion. The first is the point already made, which is that there is reduction of interest in survival as elective-death deliberators' conditions deteriorate. The second is that the factors involved in their deliberations and in assessment of those deliberations reduce in number. For instance, questions about obligations to family members and friends recede in importance or cease to be relevant considerations. Again, the central question of the timing of elective death decreases in importance as a function of the lessening of significant time left to elective-death deliberators and the growing threat of what that time holds.

As a result of the reduction of factors in elective-death deliberations and their assessment, the role of evaluative beliefs in those deliberations gains prominence, and it emerges that allowing latitude in applying the rationality criterion largely is a matter of accommodating evaluative beliefs. This is because allowing latitude in applying the rationality criterion largely amounts to accommodating *ineliminable* uncertainties in elective-death deliberators' reasoning and motivation and forgoing insistence on those deliberators' accepting proxy premises or making various acknowledgments.

The ineliminable uncertainties are of two sorts. The first sort are unproven factual beliefs. In elective-death deliberations, a number of unproven factual beliefs are ineliminable because the overwhelming majority of patients lack the expertise and resources to establish independently what they are told by their physicians. Seeking second medical opinions is the only practical option open to them but is one that rarely produces decisive results. The second sort are unprovable evaluative beliefs that deliberators are either cognitively unwilling or emotionally unable to qualify or question by accepting proxy premises or making called-for acknowledgments. Assessors, too, are in very much the same position. Few can independently establish the accuracy of deliberators' diagnoses and prognoses, and beyond offering clarifications and advice, they can do little to force changes of mind on deliberators' holding troublesome evaluative beliefs.

This is where decision theory enters because it is concerned with making the best and most productive – the most rational – choices in situations where there are ineliminable uncertainties and where it is necessary to make estimations and conjectures about various elements pertinent to those choices.

Decision theory basically is prescriptive or normative and has to do with maximizing value in the making of decisions. In being prescriptive, decision theory assumes that, ideally, decision makers are fully rational and fully informed about the various factors relevant to the decisions they must make. The rationality criterion is prescriptive in just this way: it aims to ensure that the best decision about choosing to die is made and – again ideally – assumes that decision makers are fully rational and fully informed about matters relevant to elective-death decisions. The trouble is that the assumptions made in both cases are seldom met: very few decision makers are fully rational and fully informed, and in the case of elective death, very few Socrateses choose to die.

Decision theory focuses on a number of types of decisions where there is ineliminable uncertainty. One type has to do with choosing between incommensurable options: that is, decisions where maximization of value is impeded by having to choose among options that are not comparable one to another. Another type of problematic decision has to do with choosing between options that are not temporally synchronous. In these cases, a choice must be made between a present or imminent alternative and one more distantly future. This is the sort of decision that corporations and governments are regularly forced to make regarding policy alternatives having either long- or short-term implications. The focus of our interest, though, is the classic model often referred to in decision theory, namely, *Pascal's wager*.[1]

The decision Blaise Pascal addresses is whether or not to accept that God exists. The problem is that there is no conclusive evidence for God's existence or nonexistence, but once the question of God's existence arises, a decision needs to be made whether to affirm or deny God's existence because of the stakes raised by the question. On the one hand, if God *does* exist, what is gained by affirming God's existence on the basis of unsubstantiated faith is of infinite value: eternal heavenly life. However, if God does exist, the cost of denying God's existence also is infinite: eternal damnation. On the other hand, if God does *not* exist, what is gained by denying God's existence is comparatively trivial, namely, avoidance of worship, and the cost of wrongly affirming God's existence is also comparatively trivial: the need to engage in worship. Pascal's conclusion is that given the ineliminable uncertainty of God's existence, the value of affirming God's existence far outweighs the risk of denying it. Therefore, the rational decision is to affirm the existence of God.

What interests us is that Pascal's wager shows rational choices can be made despite ineliminable uncertainties, and so also shows that the reasoning determining those choices may be sound even if it incorporates uncertainties. Admittedly, the reasoning in question is not sound in the strict syllogistic sense requiring that conclusions follow from premises *known* to be true. Nonetheless, Pascal's wager does illustrate that some decisions involving uncertainties can be soundly reasoned and therefore rational to a satisfactory degree.

With respect to elective-death deliberation, ineliminable uncertainties basically are of two sorts: unproven factual beliefs and unprovable evaluative beliefs. Unproven factual beliefs mostly have to do with the accuracy of estimations physicians must make in framing their diagnoses and prognoses and what elective-death deliberators accept regarding those diagnoses and prognoses. Unprovable

---

[1] Pascal, Blaise. 1941. *Pensées*. Trans. W. F. Trotter. New York: Modern Library.

evaluative beliefs mostly have to do with deliberators' cultural and religious beliefs. What Pascal's wager allows us to conclude here is that the presence of either or both types of uncertainty – factual and/or evaluative beliefs – does not *of itself* preclude elective-death reasoning being sound and motivation being acceptable.

*   *   *

As outlined in Chapter 4, proxy premises can be used to accommodate some ineliminable uncertainties by replacing premises incorporating evaluative beliefs and identifying those beliefs as preferences or choices. Acceptance by elective-death deliberators of proxy premises is essentially the same cognitive move as their acknowledging that death may be annihilation. In both cases evaluative beliefs are recognized *as* beliefs. The problem is that as mentioned previously, some elective-death deliberators are unwilling or unable to accept proposed proxy premises or to acknowledge the possibly annihilatory nature of death. The reasons for the unwillingness or inability will vary among deliberators, but typical ones are the feeling that accepting a proxy premise or making the required acknowledgment is a breach of faith or an emotional powerlessness to question or qualify deep-seated beliefs.

What forces allowance of latitude in assessing elective-death deliberations incorporating evaluative beliefs is *necessity*: the decisions have to be made. In the case of Pascal's wager, the mere posing of the question of God's existence necessitates deciding whether or not to affirm God's existence because not doing so is tantamount to answering the question negatively or denying God's existence by default. In the case of elective death, two conditions necessitate that decisions be made. The first is that circumstances have arisen that prompt the question whether to curtail the prolonged, hopeless, and devastating process of dying of terminal illness or to let it run its course with all that entails. The second is that once this question arises, a decision is compelled by temporal constraints. If a decision is not made within a certain time, the possibility of elective death evaporates and a negative decision is made, again by default, not to commit PS1, SS2, or AS3 or to request RE4.

Given the necessity of making decisions about elective death in light of terminal diagnoses and bleak prognoses – and given the paucity of fully rational Socrateses – cross-cultural assessors of elective-death deliberations inevitably face having to deal with deliberators' evaluative beliefs affecting motives and functioning as premises in reasoning. Allowing latitude in applying the rationality criterion, then, is virtually unavoidable if the choice to die is not to be the privilege of the rare terminally ill Socrates.

However, the formulation of the rationality criterion cannot be qualified to accommodate the uncertainties that characterize the realities of elective-death deliberations. To attempt to introduce exceptions and qualifications would be to elaborate the criterion well beyond what is practical and effectively to make it the hopeless abstraction some already think it is. This is why our concern must focus on the more viable alternative of accommodating problematic factors in reasoning and motivation by introducing latitude in assessment of individual cases. The point must be to judge whether in relatively extreme circumstances the criterion's requirements are *adequately* met.

As should be clear from what has been said, the basic idea regarding latitude in applying of the rationality criterion is that the better deliberators' circumstances and prospects, the more strictly the criterion must be applied; the poorer deliberators' circumstances and prospects, the more lenient and compassionate the criterion's application.

To understand better the allowing of latitude regarding evaluative beliefs, we can return to the case of Ms. A. Her case can be used to illustrate a basic point about latitude and *timing*. Recall that in Chapter 4 Ms. A chooses to die to avoid the ravages of ALS and that part of her reasoning is that merciful God does not want her to suffer needlessly. This is an evaluative belief, and as noted in Chapter 4 it entails three tacit premises: that there is a God, that God is merciful, and that God, being merciful, does not want Ms. A to suffer needlessly. The proposal made in the same chapter was that there is a more attractive option to Ms. A's deliberation assessors' trying to induce Ms. A to acknowledge that her evaluative belief about a merciful God is not an established fact but rather is her acceptance as true of what she believes about God's existence, nature, and will. My proposal was that an effective way of dealing with Ms. A's evaluative belief is to propose a proxy for the problematic premise the belief affects – a proxy premise that allows the original conclusion to follow validly. The proxy premise suggested was

> I *choose* not to bear the dreadful debilitation of ALS because I *believe* merciful God does not want me to.

But Ms. A needs to accept the proxy premise, and she may be unwilling or unable to do so. One possibility is that she may be cognitively unwilling to accept a proxy she sees as dangerously irreverent because it qualifies her belief in God precisely by making it explicit that it is a belief. Another possibility is that she may find herself emotionally unable to accept the proxy because of her life-long devotion. A third possibility is that Ms. A may be drawing strength from her religious beliefs and is psychologically incapable of making matters worse for herself by impugning those beliefs even by implication. A fourth possibility, perhaps the likeliest one, is that she feels all of these things to some degree and so cannot accept the proxy.

However troublesome one or more of these possibilities may prove in the early stages of Ms. A's terminal illness, as her condition and prospects become more desperate, she almost certainly will find it increasingly difficult to accept the suggested proxy or others like it. As her circumstances deteriorate, the reasons for her unwillingness or inability to qualify her beliefs directly or indirectly will grow stronger. The result is that just as it grows more important for her to be able to choose to die, and as temporal constraints tighten, the strictures on Ms. A's reasoning and motivation in effect grow more demanding. This is not because the rationality criterion's require-ments escalate; it is precisely because they do not change while Ms. A becomes less and less able to meet them. Unless latitude is allowed, therefore, the worsening of terminal patients' conditions will in most cases make it progressively less likely that their choices to die are judged rational and so permissible. If the rationality criterion is to be of practical use, some latitude must be allowed in applying it to elective-death deliberations performed in the middle and later stages of terminal illness.

* * *

In day-to-day practice, the medical circumstances of terminal patients deliberating elective death are the main determinants for allowing latitude in judging that their reasoning and motives are acceptable, whether their deliberations are assessed by applying the rationality criterion or by more conventional methods. Whatever other factors may need to be considered, medical circumstances normally are given priority and the worse those circumstances, the more latitude will usually be allowed. But it is just here that we most directly face the issue of how allowance of latitude is to be used and governed.

Given the practical impossibility of formulating rules and principles to cover the variety of eventualities involved in elective-death cases, our only recourse is to Choron's basic point about the permissibility of elective death's turning on assessors' *understanding* why someone chooses to die. But what is not sufficiently stressed in Choron's work is the crucial role of dialogue. This is largely because Choron focuses on the understanding of *peers*, and that would include culture. However, our concern is with *cross*-cultural assessment of elective-death deliberation.

It is only through dialogic comparison and consequent reflection that cross-cultural assessors' individual understandings of elective-death deliberators' choices to die can be appreciated by the other assessors and modified in light of others' views. Only in that way can a consensus having legitimate authority be reached about overlooking elective-death deliberators' reasoning and motivational shortfalls in light of their deteriorating medical circumstances. Unfortunately, matters are still more complicated. It is not only deteriorating medical circumstances that call for allowing latitude in assessment of elective-death deliberations.

To make explicit what has been implicit in earlier references to very few Socrateses' dying, there is more than problematic factual or evaluative beliefs that impedes sound reasoning and acceptable motivation. It is an undeniable fact that terminal patients who choose elective death present a wide spectrum of intellectual capacities, levels of resoluteness, and capabilities to understand both their own motivation and the realities of their situations. Elective-death deliberations may be flawed by more than questionable premises and dubious motives; they may be flawed by underperformance in the process of reasoning itself, by insufficiencies in understanding of motives and personal circumstances, and by irresoluteness.

To one degree or another, some elective-death deliberators will be capable of thinking more clearly than others about what is in their best interests; some will be more objective about their circumstances and prospects, while others will be unrealistically hopeful or despairing about both; some will make their own decisions, while others will be too easily influenced; and some will be resolute, while others will vacillate. These differences pose assessment problems that have to do with the individual characters of elective-death deliberators and – barring pathological extremes – there is little that can be done about them. But they do need to be factored into assessment of elective-death deliberations, and that they do increases the need for governance of the use of latitude in assessment.

The main danger posed by allowing latitude in deeming the rationality criterion's requirements met is that compassion may unduly override more detached assessments. There is a decided risk that letting severity of medical circumstances or individuals' limitations justify latitude in assessing elective-death deliberations may prove too empathy-indulgent adequately to protect deliberators' interests in survival. This risk is similar to the way wholly intracultural application of the criterion may prove too value-indulgent to protect interests in survival.

At present, the only institutionalized or systemic protection against overly empathetic assessments of choices to die is the participation in elective-death deliberations of medical practitioners who are bound by codes of professional ethics. As the Morrison case considered in Chapter 1 amply illustrates, regardless of how desperate terminal patients' circumstances or unresponsive their pain to medication, professional ethics severely restrict practitioners from engaging in positive death-inducing actions. By extension, this restriction provides some protection against assessments of elective-death deliberations that are too forgiving of lapses in reasoning and questionable motives. The restriction provides protection by being preclusive in that participating code-bound practitioners are barred from supporting choices to commit PS1, SS2, or AS3. Code-bound practitioners are limited to considering only patients' choices to forgo treatment – choices protected by law in most jurisdictions.

The participation of code-bound practitioners in assessment of elective-death deliberations, then, is of itself insufficient.

There is another aspect to the insufficiency of relying on professional-ethics codes to guard against overly empathetic assessments of elective-death deliberations. Again as the Morrison case illustrates, application of professional ethics by some in particular circumstances can be unrealistically rigid. This exacting application may be prompted by overly literal interpretation of the codes or by the influence on that interpretation of deeply held religious beliefs or cultural values about the sanctity of life. Additionally, rigid application of professional ethics may well be prompted more by concerns about liability than by concerns about protecting patients' interests in survival.

What emerges is that we must rely on the good judgments of assessors more than on available institutional rules. And to appreciate better the basis for good judgments, consider again the point made in the Preface that what the criterion does is provide standards for choosing to die by delineating what conditions must be met for elective death to be rational. By setting those standards, the criterion in effect provides a rationale for choosing to die. It does so because when its standards are met, it is not only rational but *sensible* to choose to die. That is, given the devastation of terminal illness, if it is rational to die and therefore doing so does not contravene the interest in survival, then dying likely is the best option available in the circumstances.

The import of this to assessment of elective-death deliberations returns us to the key point about understanding. First, once the rationale for elective death is fully grasped by assessors of elective-death deliberations, they will better comprehend the rationality of individuals' choices to die in their particular desperate circumstances. Second, assessors' knowledge of individuals' circumstances will enable them to appreciate better the diminished nature of what the rationality criterion protects: the interest in survival. It will then be clear to assessors that basically what needs to be established in applying the rationality criterion in actual cases is that its requirements are met in a manner commensurate with individual deliberators' capacities and circumstances. This understanding allows judicious use of latitude in applying the criterion when combined with dialogue. Dialogue enhances assessors' understanding by enabling them to check their individual estimations regarding latitude against those of other assessors. A balanced consensus can then be achieved with respect to how leniently some or all of the rationality criterion's requirements may be applied in particular cases.

Nor is it the case that the criterion's requirements may be applied less strictly only when patients' circumstances are desperate or their capabilities limited. The very idea of circumstances' being desperate raises the point that people vary widely in what they are willing or able to tolerate. One person's unbearable anguish may be another's endurable pain. This variation is especially notable when we compare individuals who can no longer bear what is happening to them in terminal illness with those who may be willing to tolerate more distress to attain something of special value to them, like witnessing the birth of a grandchild or completing a career-defining work.

Individuals' tolerance levels must be taken into account when applying the rationality criterion. The point of doing so is to allow for some elective-death deliberators' lower tolerances for distress. It also is important for assessors to be sensitive to timing issues when dealing with individuals whose tolerance levels are higher or who are prepared to endure more than they might for the purpose of realizing some goal.

Consideration of tolerance levels raises another point about assessment of elective-death deliberations and especially about timing. There are what we can think of as aesthetic factors importantly operant in elective-death deliberations that may warrant allowance of latitude independently of desperateness of circumstances, capability issues, and tolerance considerations. People's attitudes toward death vary a good deal. Some may see dying at a certain time as *fitting*, given that their lives are blighted and ending anyway, given what they have achieved, and given that they disdain survival gained at great cost purely for its own sake. Aesthetic factors are not as clear-cut as elective-death deliberators' medical conditions and prospects, but nonetheless they are integral to their choices to die and must be taken into account in assessing their reasoning and motivation. These factors are most significant in deliberation of SP1 and some cases of SS2 where assessors may feel that those choosing to die are being precipitous.

The matter of latitude ultimately centers on how choosing to die to avoid futile suffering and degradation should not be the perquisite of a tiny elite capable of strict syllogistic reasoning and of acting on entirely objective motives. Terminal illness does not discriminate; anyone can face horrendously destructive prospects, and barring incompetence or similar impediments, most terminal patients should be able to opt to avoid those prospects by surrendering their blighted lives.

*　*　*

As has been indicated, the most probable difficulties with elective-death deliberations are those caused by deliberators' cultural and religious evaluative beliefs' hampering their reasoning or skewing their motivation. When this occurs and assessors factor in terminal patients' bleak circumstances, they may empathize excessively with patients and overlook reasoning flaws and motivational issues in judging those patients' choices to die as rational and therefore permissible. The likely result is that some patients may not be discouraged or impeded regarding less-than-rational commission of PS1 or SS2. A less likely but still possible result is that on the basis of overly empathetic assessments some patients may be assisted in commission of AS3 or even be provided with RE4. In either case, when assessors unduly empathize with elective-death deliberators and unwarrantedly overlook reasoning flaws or motivational issues, those assessors allow or inadvertently encourage contravention of the deliberators' interests in survival.

Further complicating overly empathetic assessment of elective-death deliberations is that the interaction between reasoning and motivation is complicated. For example, in the case of Ms. A, her belief that merciful God does not want her to suffer needlessly, a belief incorrectly functioning as a matter of fact in her elective-death reasoning, may disproportionately strengthen her motivation. She may unwarrantedly perceive the suffering she faces as unbearable, whereas lacking the belief in question, she would be prepared to endure the suffering for a significant period.

The other side of the coin is that patients may reason soundly but in ways that serve unacceptable motives. Fortunately, this is a less likely scenario. The reason is that in cases of elective-death choices, motivation tends to take precedence. This is most evident as patients' circumstances worsen. While at some time patients' motives for choosing to die might have to do with a desire to rejoin a deceased partner or with what they take to be God's will, most eventually reduce simply to wanting to die to avoid further suffering and degradation.

This practical narrowing of the variety of motives for choosing to die simplifies assessment by making elective-death deliberations more intelligible to assessors. That intelligibility in turn facilitates determining which evaluative beliefs may be tolerated in assessing reasoning soundness and acceptability of motives. For instance, assessors could well find rational, and so permissible, a terminal patient's choosing to die primarily to end her hopeless suffering despite her also believing that by dying she will rejoin her dead spouse.

The key point here is that when terminal patients' circumstances are bad enough, elective-death deliberation is essentially a matter of patients' recognizing that the time left to them promises only more and likely worse physical and emotional pain and their deciding whether to sacrifice a little time for reprieve from hopeless torment. Sound reasoning and acceptable motivation for choosing to die are most important earlier, while there is a real issue about patients' interest in survival. That is, scrupulous assessment of elective-death reasoning and motivation is most called for when survival still offers some compensation for the suffering and degradation patients must bear to continue living. By the time patients' conditions deteriorate to a point where survival promises only more physical and psychological anguish, the reality of patients' circumstances reduces the priority of the soundness and acceptability of their elective-death reasoning and motives because there is little at stake. At that point the issue is a relatively straightforward choice between terminating the process of painful death and allowing it to run its course.

When deliberation of elective death becomes mostly a matter of deciding whether or not to curtail the process of dying, deliberators' evaluative beliefs recede in significance and tend to become something like metaphors for the cessation of senseless misery. Whether they continue to condition reasoning or motives becomes decidedly less important than when there is still some interest in surviving. By this point, elective-death options no longer include PS1 or some sorts of SS2, and as those options are largely narrowed to AS3 and RE4, decisions to abandon life are no longer entirely patients' own to make. This is because both AS3 and RE4 involve the participation of others. Patients' own deliberations, then, become more or less continuous with the deliberations of those others who may choose to assist in suicide or even to administer requested euthanasia.

The last point, of course, raises the question of application of the rationality criterion to elective-death assessors themselves and to others participating in elective death by assisting in suicide or providing requested euthanasia. Fortunately, that is a topic beyond the scope of this book. Suffice it to say that the criterion decidedly is applicable to elective-death assessors' own reasoning and motivation and to the reasoning and motivation of those assisting suicide or administering euthanasia.

The various points made in this chapter about using latitude in applying the rationality criterion may be summed up by saying that rather than soundness of reasoning and acceptability of motivation, what becomes all-important at a certain point in terminal illness is the genuineness of patients' desires to surrender time left to them for escape from their anguished circumstances. What assessors then must focus on are signs of vacillation or lack of resolve. The central point to appreciate regarding the allowance of latitude in applying the rationality criterion is that the criterion is a *tool*. It is a tool used to protect the interest in survival. Allowing latitude as elective-death deliberators' circumstances worsen is, therefore, less a matter of applying the criterion more leniently than it is of recognizing the criterion's diminishing utility.

What consideration of allowance of latitude in applying the rationality criterion reveals is that the criterion's utility diminishes as elective-death deliberators' circumstances worsen because as their circumstances worsen, their interests in survival lessen markedly. This point may seem obvious now, but it can be neither assumed nor introduced too early on because doing so jeopardizes appreciation of the criterion's importance by shifting the focus of attention from elective-death deliberators' reasoning and motivation to their medical conditions.

The rationality criterion's main task is to protect elective-death deliberators' interests in survival against unsound reasoning and flawed motives for choosing to die. But as has become clear, as the interest in survival declines in importance, the criterion's applicability declines in efficacy. Applicability of the criterion, then, is in effect scaled by practical considerations. The various forms of elective death – PS1, SS2, AS3, and RE4 – constitute a range running from a point at which deliberators' interests in survival are greatest and call for rigorous application of the criterion, to a point where those interests are virtually nonexistent and the criterion may be applied much less strictly – if at all.

The way that this range relates to forms of elective death is that early in terminal illness, or even before its diagnosis, while elective-death deliberators have a significant interest in survival, they may consider PS1 to avoid what they see as inevitable degradation and suffering. At that point the rationality criterion must be applied to their deliberations with little or no allowance of latitude regarding reasoning soundness and motivational acceptability. Later in terminal illness deliberators may consider SS2. At that point their interests in survival will be reduced and application of the criterion may allow some latitude. Still later in terminal illness deliberators may consider SS2 or AS3. At that point their interests in survival will be quite reduced and the measure of latitude allowed in applying the criterion may be extensive. Finally, in the last stages of terminal illness deliberators may consider AS3 or RE4. At that point their interests in survival will have all but vanished and the measure of latitude allowed in applying the criterion may be comprehensive. Alternatively, application of the criterion may be deemed futile except, as noted previously, to monitor resoluteness.

As considered earlier, other factors must be taken into account regarding allowance of latitude, such as individuals' tolerance levels and capabilities. These factors, however, will usually be secondary to physical deterioration in importance. Most of them are essentially background factors: that is, they have to do with the characters of deliberators and will largely antedate terminal illness and its effects. Assessors, then, will deal with these factors in the process of coming to know elective-death deliberators as persons deciding whether to relinquish life for the sake of release. In the final analysis, we must rely on deliberators' and assessors' good sense and on consensus-building dialogue among them to establish reasonable allowance of latitude in applying the criterion.

Unfortunately, however clear the foregoing may be when stated in general terms, it remains true that in the actual making of elective-death decisions, and in the assessing of those decisions, numerous factors are prone to color and condition deliberators' and assessors' perceptions and judgments. Evaluative beliefs cannot be eliminated from human reasoning and motivation. Even Socrates, in choosing to drink the hemlock, reasoned that it was the course of action most conducive to respecting Athenian law and was motivated by respect for that law.

Within a given culture, evaluative beliefs tend to be transparent because shared. Those who counseled Socrates to avail himself of the help offered to him to flee Athens disagreed with his decision to drink the hemlock, but they *understood* it; they appreciated his reasoning and motivation. Because of multiculturalism we now face a situation in which some individuals' elective-death reasoning and motivation are incomprehensible to other individuals who may share their citizenship but not the evaluative beliefs that define them. In the next chapter we need to look again at the matter of multiculturalism.

9

The Realities of Cross-Cultural Assessment

In the last chapter we considered the need for allowance of latitude in applying the rationality criterion's clauses in order to deal with the realities of actual cases. We now have to consider another aspect of the realities of actual cases: an aspect that is in some ways even more difficult to deal with than limitations on the soundness of individuals' reasoning and issues with their motives. What we have to consider here essentially is an unanticipated effect of multiculturalism, one that complicates fulfillment of the rationality criterion's requirement that elective-death reasoning and motivation be cross-culturally assessed for soundness and acceptability.

The problem arises from the very fact that multicultural societies are precisely that: *multi*cultural. This fact poses difficulties with identifying the values that have the greatest determining influences on individuals' perceptions and judgments regarding elective-death deliberations. As will emerge, identification of fundamental values that elective-death assessors actually hold has been complicated by how multiculturalism's pluralities have made elusive the values individual members of traditional cultures can be expected to hold. Multiculturalism has produced this elusiveness by fostering a proliferation of the sets of values that characterize cohesive social groups.

In too many cases, identifying assessors as, say, European Christians or Asian Buddhists no longer suffices to provide any surety that the individuals so identified hold the values that define those particular cultures. As I explain later, we now have to deal not only with diverse cultures and their respective subcultures, but also with groupings or communities that constitute something less than subcultures but whose members hold values that significantly influence their perceptions and judgments. Note, too, that while our focus in this chapter is cross-cultural assessment of elective-death deliberations, and so our concern is with the values held by assessors, the ambiguities introduced by multiculturalism apply equally to understanding elective-death deliberators' perception- and judgment-influencing values.

* * *

Unfortunately, when most people consider multiculturalism, they think in terms of historically traditional or what can be described as *iconic* cultures. For instance, they think in terms of their own culture as, say, Western European and Christian, and contrast it with historically prominent Asian Buddhist or Islamic cultures. This focus tends to obscure important aspects of cultural groups, but the obscuration is made worse by how the contrasts drawn usually are limited to language, ethnicity, religious-observance practices, and dress. In short, most people focus on the more obvious characteristics that mark cultures off from one another. This narrow focus ignores subtler differences among and within cultural groups, and it especially ignores historically recent differences among delineable communities that, though they do not constitute formal cultures or subcultures, do constitute cohesive, value-defined groupings.

As outlined in Chapter 1, my concern in this book is not with the specifics of the various different cultures included in contemporary North American multicultural society. Unlike its actual application, the introduction, formulation, and discussion of the rationality criterion – the test of whether choosing to die is rational and permissible – must be conducted at an abstract level. The criterion's applicability cannot be compromised by consideration of particular cultural beliefs and values that might inadvertently tie the criterion too closely to one or another archetypal culture. I realize that some readers will have expected more detailed discussion of cultural specifics in the foregoing chapters, but this book is, after all, a *philosophical* treatment of the rationality of elective death, not an anthropological or sociological study.

My concern, then, is with the role that diverse cultural values *generally* play in the deliberation of elective death and in the assessment of that deliberation. What is of greatest importance here regarding elective death is *the fact* of cultural diversity, not the particular diverse contents of the component cultures in our multicultural society. The fact of cultural diversity means that in our multicultural society we cannot allow assessment of individuals' choices to die to be purely *intra*cultural because of possible value-affected diminishment of the interest in survival. It also means that to ensure assessment *is* cross-cultural, we must be able to determine *who counts* as a legitimate cross-cultural assessor.

Aside from their cultural values and beliefs, individuals naturally have personal values peculiar to them and their histories that bear on their own elective-death deliberations and their assessments of others' deliberations. But aside from cases of extreme or unacceptably idiosyncratic views, little can be done about assessors' personal values. This is why the values that are of primary interest in the present context are those shared among members of cohesive groups. Cultural values are integral to the norm-establishing symbolic structures that define cohesive, identifiable groups, so they are *systemic* in a way that personal ideas are not. What is crucial about values' being systemic is that the roles they play in assessment of elective-death deliberations, as well as in those deliberations, are generally *predictable*. That is, if the shared values are known, it is possible to anticipate with some assurance how those holding them will perceive and judge the choice to die on the basis of how restrictive or permissive the operant values are regarding elective death.

This predictability is precisely why assessment of elective-death deliberation needs to be cross-cultural. It is crucial that assessment of the reasoning and motivation for choosing to die be conducted in a manner that guards against unduly lenient or preclusive biasing of the assessment by systemic values. It is necessary, then, to identify potential assessors as members of particular groups holding preclusive or lenient views of elective death. But as indicated, we can no longer rely on membership in iconic cultures to facilitate this identification. Many will see this as a good thing, interpreting it as an end to cultural stereotyping. However, the issue here is not stereotyping; the point is not to prejudge individuals' thinking and decisions about choosing to die, but rather to have a basis on which to understand their thinking and decisions.

As should now be clear, the purpose of cross-cultural assessment of elective-death deliberations is to guard against intracultural bias by involving assessors from different cultures who give different perspectives to the assessment in order to prompt *reflection* on the values influencing the choice to die and its assessment. The expectation is that the introduction of different values will induce participants to reexamine their own and to understand better how their own values and beliefs are influencing their thinking.

Of course, the requirement of cross-cultural assessment is not the unworkable one of involving representatives from all or even the predominant component cultures of a multicultural society. To require that level of involvement would not only be unfeasible, it would generate bureaucratic nightmares if even attempted. Contrary to this hopeless sort of comprehensive cross-cultural assessment, the requirement is that assessors of the reasoning and motivation behind someone's choice to die include at least one member of that individual's own culture and at least one member of another culture. The aim is to introduce perspectival *difference*; it is not to canvass all available perspectives.

Note that contrary to likely expectations, it is not required that cross-cultural assessors necessarily belong to cultures with positions on elective death *opposed* to the deliberator's own. Consider that an individual whose values sanction elective death may choose to die in large part because of cultural values having to do with family obligations: the deliberator may be loath to burden family members with the emotional and financial consequences of terminal illness. A cross-cultural assessor's values may proscribe elective death and may emphasize family love and willingness to care for one of their own. However, another cross-cultural assessor's values may also sanction elective death but be considerably more tolerant with respect to what constitutes unacceptable burdening of family. In either case, the different perspective introduced should prompt the deliberator and other assessors to reflect productively on their positions.

Unfortunately, because of the consequences of multiculturalism, it is no longer possible to assume anything about individuals' likely perceptions and judgments on the basis of identifying their membership in one or another iconic culture. This means that medical ethicists and others counseling those choosing to die can no longer rely on common knowledge about iconic cultures to structure their own efforts to understand elective-death deliberators' thinking and motives, or to determine who might usefully serve as assessors of their deliberations.

* * *

The developments that have made cross-cultural assessment necessary and that now threaten its practicality, if not its effective possibility, have to do with the cumulative effect on North American society of historically recent immigration and related internal social changes. The latter changes have to do with a polarization fostered by the social and individual adjustments imposed by the rise of multiculturalism.

What I am describing as polarization needs some explanation. A key point is that culturally diverse immigration to North America in the past several decades has been predominantly from Asian countries – including significant numbers from what used to be called "the Middle East." Because of greater linguistic and cultural differences this immigration has resulted in less cultural integration than did earlier immigration from Western and Central Europe. The result has been cohesive immigrant groups' establishing themselves in certain regions and maintaining their languages and cultural practices to a greater degree than previous immigrant groups. This lack of integration has led to issues exploited by the media about conflicts involving dress, language, and religious observances. Political scientists, sociologists, government officials, and others have tended to cast these issues in terms of minority rights, and official policy has been to accommodate differences in keeping with commitment to "the politics of difference" and "political plurality." As a result of this policy, there has been even less cultural integration than might have occurred.

The polarization in question shows how multicultural society no longer conforms to the old American notion of the host nation as a *melting pot* with respect to its immigrants. That notion focused on integration and was apt enough at a time when most immigrants were European and cultural differences among them were relatively minor in comparison to present-day ones. That notion also arose at a time when there were economic and political incentives to integrate. In the twentieth and twenty-first centuries multicultural society conforms more to the Canadian notion of the host nation as a *mosaic* in which immigrant and indigenous cultural and linguistic differences are preserved.[1] Cultural integration, then, has receded both as an actual phenomenon and as a desirable objective.

But matters are still more complicated. Immigrants belonging to iconic cultures that historically were relatively homogeneous have encountered pressures and opportunities to emphasize or deemphasize aspects of their traditional cultures. While integration may no longer be a priority, immigrants do find they need to make some integrative accommodations to achieve success in commercial, educational, and social spheres. Adjustments in dress are the most obvious of these but are by no means the only ones. And where there is readiness to accommodate, there is also resistance. The result is the growth of subcultures in which fundamental cultural values are either adjusted to new situations or embraced more fervently in refusal to make what are perceived as erosive adjustments.

Subcultures complicate matters considerably, but there are other groupings that make them still more complex. Added to immigrant cultures and subcultures are groupings that arise as results of various sustained practices and relationships. Many of these groupings are familiar and their activities evident and are describable as "single-interest" or simply "interest groups." For instance, one such grouping is the homeless; others are the advocates or opponents of abortion. These groups with shared values and objectives are active politically, lobbying individuals and parties to achieve their ends.

---

[1] Canada, already bilingual in English and French, now has a significant enough Chinese population that official recognition of the language seems likely. The United States, officially unilingual, may have to accommodate its large and growing Hispanic population by recognizing Spanish as an official language. Corporations are well ahead of governments in this respect. A new ATM let me choose among English, French, Chinese, Italian, and Portuguese, even though my town's population provides the barest justification for including three of the five languages.

The connection between these groups and iconic cultures and their subcultures is that the groups are value-defined in very much the way cultural groups are. Membership in these groups involves espousal of the values, aspirations, and objectives that characterize the groups, as well as adoption of the symbolism that partly defines them. Moreover, members of these groups establish continuing relationships with one another and jointly engage in practices that both define participation and sustain the group.

However, cultures, subcultures, and interest groups are not the only value-defined groupings we need to consider. Less easily identified than these are groupings that are essentially the creation of marketing and the media. Most of these are defined by what many think to be superficial differences, but superficial differences lose their superficiality when – rightly or wrongly – they become highly significant to people. The groupings in question are real enough and the values individuals adopt and exhibit in being members may play a significant role in their own elective-death deliberations or in their assessments of others' deliberations.

The largely created groupings I have in mind are a result of how in the past three or four decades the media and the advertising and entertainment industries have manufactured and made much of "life-styles" and the preferences and aspirations that define them. Persistent emphasis on life-styles, effected by portrayal of individuals engaged in certain activities and favoring certain products, has Balkanized North American consumer society by stressing and sometimes creating differences among people having to do with age, income, interests, acquisitive desires, career aspirations, and recreational preferences. While cultures, subcultures, and interest groups are not new, life-style groups are new. It is difficult to imagine their creation in the absence of the now-omnipresent influences from marketing, entertainment, and media concerns that are delivered through these concerns' own products: television, movies, magazines, newspapers, popular music, and celebrity role models. What matters here, though, is that these life-style groupings effectively are as value-defined as cultures, subcultures, and interest groups, and their acquired values decidedly condition their members' perceptions and judgments.

We have, then, cultures, subcultures, interest groups, and life-style groups. All of these are value-defined, and the values that define the groups influence their members' behavior. Moreover, all of these are practice-sustained. In the final analysis, the main differences between iconic cultures and interest or life-style groups are matters of degree: the length of their histories, the formality of their precepts, the extent and solemnity of their rituals, the extent of their control over individual members, the complexity of their hierarchies. However, there is still another type of value-defined group that we need to consider.

*   *   *

To proceed and to clarify the foregoing, I distinguish between *foundational* and *coincidental* cultures. I apologize for introducing two more relatively technical terms, but as will become clear, it is necessary to mark differences that are too often neglected to the detriment of productive consideration of multiculturalism and its implications.

What I mean by a "foundational" culture is one having its roots in historically significant social, religious, regional, and political events and developments, and one that is defined by orally or textually articulated touchstone beliefs, values, norms, and inclusion criteria. Foundational cultures also are at least initially unilingual and ethnically singular. Foundational cultures are what I called "iconic" cultures earlier. In what follows I will include subcultures in references to foundational cultures, because subcultures are permutations on foundational ones, usually being the products of internal disputes or schisms over interpretation of fundamental values and doctrines.

What I mean by a "coincidental" culture is a grouping of individuals arising from concurrence of interests, objectives, and aspirations. Coincidental cultures include interest groups and life-style groups. Though value-defined as are foundational cultures, coincidental cultures lack the formal symbolism and articulated tenets that characterize foundational cultures. Again, coincidental cultures are not tied to ethnicity, language, or region. Coincidental cultures may also be the products of deliberate efforts such as marketing campaigns. It is important that coincidental cultures are not regional because some exemplary instances are *virtual* communities or groupings whose members' contact with one another is not by physical proximity but by online access.

The type of value-defined or coincidental culture I referred to in the last section as still to be considered is the coincidental culture of the *institution*. The paradigm of institutional coincidental cultures is that of the workplace. Institutional coincidental cultures have many of the trappings of foundational cultures, and their defining values can have as great an influence on individuals' perceptions and judgments as any foundational culture. But to clarify coincidental cultures, I need to say more about how coincidental cultures are acquired.

Becoming a member of a coincidental culture can be clarified by drawing a parallel with *language*. In the parallel, foundational cultures are like natural languages, which are acquired as children learn to speak. Coincidental cultures are like vernaculars or colloquial dialects or jargons. They are learned in particular contexts and in the company of particular people. My model for distinguishing between foundational and coincidental cultures is Donald Davidson's distinction between *prior* and *passing theories* in language use. I apologize again for introducing more technicalities and ameliorate doing so by limiting my exposition of Davidson to a couple of perilously brief paragraphs.[2]

Davidson's concern is with linguistic understanding, and he introduces the concepts of a prior and a passing theory to explain how we manage to speak and understand language at two levels: a general level and a context-specific level. Natural languages are "prior theories": they are the linguistic capacities that precede all refinement of interpretive practices. "Passing theories" are context-determined interpretive practices. A paradigm of how a passing theory is acquired is individuals in new jobs learning the vernacular of the workplace. The individuals share a natural language – their prior theory – with their new coworkers but have to learn the

---

[2] I most strongly urge readers to read what I believe to be the most accessible exposition of Davidson I know of, namely, Bjørn Ramberg's *Donald Davidson's Philosophy of Language: An Introduction*, 1989, Oxford: Blackwell's. To supplement the sketch I offer, the following is a key passage from Davidson: "For the hearer, the prior theory expresses how he is prepared in advance to interpret an utterance of the speaker, while the passing theory is how he *does* interpret the utterance. For the speaker, the prior theory is what he *believes* the interpreter's prior theory to be, while his passing theory is the theory he *intends* the interpreter to use." Davidson, Donald. 1986. "A Nice Derangement of Epitaphs." In Ernest LePore, ed., *Truth and Interpretation*. Oxford: Blackwell's, 442.

vernacular of their new workplace. Our society is rife with these vernaculars and the media and corporations seem bent on multiplying them, forever introducing new expressions and acronyms. The point is, though, that while an institution's language may be, say, English, how English actually is used on a daily basis within the actual and virtual confines of that institution differs significantly from how English is used beyond those boundaries. The same is true of the home, the school, favored places of recreation, and particular sets of friends.

As a speaker of two natural languages, English and Spanish, I have two prior theories. On being addressed by a stranger in either English or Spanish – but not in Hungarian or Chinese – I automatically marshal a host of basic interpretive practices to understand what is said to me. I do the same if I am reading a set of instructions or an encyclopedia entry. This is to apply one or other of my prior theories. But if I am addressed in either Spanish or English by someone close to me, someone I work with, or a fellow wine enthusiast, I marshal a host of secondary interpretive practices peculiar to specific contexts and specific relationships. This is to apply one of my passing theories, which I acquired as I established relationships with fellow workers, others who share my interests, and my peers in various activities. My passing theories are needed to deal with how any number of ordinary English or Spanish words, phrases, and expressions work differently and convey different senses in particular contexts than they would in more neutral circumstances. My passing theories also allow understanding of allusions, indirect references, deliberate exaggerations, hyperbole, implications, understatements, private jokes, and insinuations.

The point of the parallel between prior and passing theories, on the one hand, and foundational and coincidental cultures, on the other, is to show how individuals become members of several coincidental cultures as well as being members of their respective foundational cultures, just as they learn several passing theories as well as having one or more prior theories. The parallel clarifies the notion of acquiring a coincidental culture by comparing it with learning a vernacular. The strength of the comparison is that acquiring a coincidental culture *is* in large part learning a vernacular, though of course there are various practices also involved.

For present purposes, the importance of coincidental cultures is that it is not only the values that define foundational cultures that shape and condition individuals' perceptions and judgments. The values that define their coincidental cultures do so as well; in fact, in some cases they may supersede foundational-culture values. Elective-death deliberations and their assessment, then, are as much affected by coincidental-culture values as by foundational-culture ones. This fact greatly complicates cross-cultural assessment of elective-death deliberations because it is no longer possible to assume that because individuals are members of particular foundational cultures, those cultures' values are the ones primarily influencing individuals' assessments of elective-death deliberations or, for that matter, individuals' choices to die.

* * *

In practical terms, it is medical ethicists who bear the burden of understanding elective-death deliberators' reasoning and motives and of determining whom to include as cross-cultural assessors of their deliberations. It is medical ethicists who on notice from attending physicians consult with terminal patients deliberating forgoing treatment or – more rarely and allowing for present ethical and legal constraints – committing SS2 or AS3. What the proliferation of cultures means for medical ethicists is that they cannot rely on elective-death deliberators' and assessors' foundational-culture affiliations to indicate dependably the values that influence deliberators' choices or assessors' judgments.

Of course, the point is not to stereotype elective-death deliberators and assessors on the basis of their foundational cultures. Rather the point is that knowing those affiliations used to provide relatively dependable grounds for dialogue about deliberators' choices and useful indications regarding the suitability of potential assessors. Those grounds and indications have grown uncertain because of divergences regarding values and priorities among foundational cultures, their respective subcultures, and coincidental cultures.

At one time, knowing the foundational cultures deliberators and assessors belonged to, together with basic knowledge of the relevant cultures' defining values and beliefs, facilitated understanding of individuals' positions and inclinations. But foundational cultures have come to encompass numerous subcultures, including ones with more and less liberal attitudes. This increase in value- and doctrine-divergent subcultures is partly due to the evolution of doctrines, but it is also a consequence of how multiculturalism has legitimized difference. Views and positions that would once have been seen as heretical by most members of a foundational culture are now seen as new perspectives by many of those members; what was once seen as deviancy is now seen as productive change and growth. The other side of the coin is that what was once seen as principled defense of orthodoxy is now seen as tenacious dogmatism.

But the complications introduced by the increase in foundational subcultures are more than matched by those due to coincidental cultures. While many have more or less formally adopted liberal subcultural positions on matters like elective death, as many or more have liberalized their views, not on the basis of debate but on the basis of their day-to-day experiences in the workplace and other venues in which institutionalized behavior promotes the formation of coincidental cultures. Sometimes the coincidental-culture adoption of more or of less liberal views is reflective, sometimes not, but regardless of how acquired, coincidental-culture values influence perceptions and judgments.

It seems, then, that what is needed is for medical ethicists and others counseling terminal patients to take nothing for granted. They should enter into consultations without anticipations and make every effort to determine individual elective-death deliberators' and assessors' own particular views. In ideal circumstances, this would be the best way to proceed, but this approach is seriously hampered in two ways: First, without reasonably reliable prior general knowledge of individuals' cultural values, counselors lack grounds on which to interpret deliberators' and assessors' statements and responses and likely would miss much that is determined by deliberators' and assessors' held values but that they might be taking for granted, might themselves not be fully aware of, or might be misconstruing. Second, without prior general knowledge of values held by patients, counselors would be unprepared to deal with the influences of deliberators' and assessors' cultural values on their statements and behavior. For instance, cultural beliefs about gender and gender roles might cause deliberators' and assessors' responses to male and to female counselors to differ significantly both in content and in candor.

To close this section, it merits mention that much of the foregoing may appear to some readers as if I am using the concept of a culture too broadly. But this is an appearance due less to my use of the concept than to the proliferation of self-identifying and cohesive value-defined and norm-establishing groupings in contemporary society. It is a proliferation that has stretched the notions of a culture, a subculture, and a community well beyond the senses those terms had when talk about culture was mainly about iconic cultures and talk about communities was largely about regional groups. Perhaps most important is that it is a proliferation in which self-identification of groups *as* groups has elevated assemblages of people sharing interests and practices to the status of cultures: specifically, to what I am calling coincidental cultures.

The practical problem posed by the proliferation of cultures is that the more foundational and coincidental cultures are encompassed by a multicultural society, the harder it is to infer individuals' judgment- and behavior-governing values. It can no longer be assumed that individuals who on the basis of ethnicity, language, and geographic location are identified as, say, European Christians or Asian Hindus are most influenced by their foundational cultures' traditional values. It is now necessary to explore in some detail what foundational subcultures and coincidental cultures individuals consider themselves to be members of, and the specific respective values they hold because of those memberships.

Of greatest concern to issues about elective death is the contemporary reality that the primary influences on individuals' elective-death deliberations or assessments of such deliberations can no longer be reliably anticipated on the basis of foundational-culture affiliation, even if only in general terms. Therefore, it has become much more difficult to understand what values most significantly shape elective-death deliberators' and assessors' reasoning and motivation, perceptions, and judgments. Some no doubt will see this new reality positively: they will see it as liberating, as strengthening individuality and weakening stereotyping – invariably seen as discriminatory or debasing. In practical terms, though, the new reality means that counseling those choosing to die is now immensely demanding to the extent that counselors must start from scratch with every terminal patient deliberating elective death.

*   *   *

The purpose of my introducing the notion of a coincidental culture is to show how *interest-* and *practice*-defined groupings come to function and to be construed as *value*-defined and norm-determining groupings on the model of value-defined and norm-determining iconic cultures. The phenomenon is an interesting turnabout in which the practices and interests that unite a group of people, and that then generate values and norms, are reconceived as *preceding* the relevant interests and practices and so underlying and supporting them. Individual members of an interest- and practice-defined group then see themselves as affiliating first with the underlying values and as a consequence having the interests they do and engaging in the practices they engage in. In brief, membership in the group is reconceived as *being* something along with others, rather than as *doing* something along with others.[3] The practical significance of this turnabout is that individuals engaged in institutional activities – in the workplace, the academy, the corporation, the hospital, the school, the military – knowingly or inadvertently form groups whose interests and practices in effect function as perception- and judgment-influencing values.[4]

   How the turnabout happens, how practice- and interest-defined groups turn into coincidental cultures, is an unanticipated result of multiculturalism – but it is one that on reflection is not surprising. The way it works has two aspects, one having to do with principle and one having to do with practice. The aspect having to do with principle is that multiculturalism commits societies to recognizing and

---

[3] I recall a colleague's once saying, "I am a feminist, a philosopher, and a mother, in that order." While another colleague took exception to the "in that order" comment, I was struck at how an ideological position, a professional activity, and a social and biological reality were being ranked as of a kind.

[4] It will be obvious to some readers how Michel Foucault's genealogical analytics have influenced my thinking. See my *Starting with Foucault: An Introduction to Genealogy*, 2nd edition, 2000, Boulder, Colo., and New York: Westview Press (Perseus Books).

respecting all cohesive social groupings as valid components of themselves.[5] This is what multiculturalism and "the politics of difference" are all about. Once a society deems itself to be multicultural, it cannot limit its component cultures to previously recognized iconic cultures without showing prejudice against new or marginal cultures. Iconic or what I am calling foundational cultures may continue to serve as models of social, ethnic, religious, regional, and ideological groupings, and of attendant norms, practices, and symbolisms. But it is of the essence to multiculturalism that history, prominence, and number of members do not justify exclusive legitimacy.

The practical aspect of the transformation of practice- and interest-defined groups into coincidental cultures is that when people are taught to respect others' cultures as being as valid as their own, and to accept the legitimacy of culture-defining values they do not themselves hold, they are in effect taught to acknowledge the validity of *all* value-defined groups.[6] Value-defined groups are seen as valid in themselves because of having worth for their members, and as meriting acceptance and respect by others. It is then but a short and nearly inevitable step for individuals to perceive their own practice- and interest-defined groups as value-defined and hence as valid components of multicultural society. This is the turnabout that produces what I am calling coincidental cultures.

Consider now an example that illustrates how coincidental cultures may play a significant role in elective-death deliberations and in assessments of those deliberations. A terminal patient deliberating declining necessary treatment or commission of SS2 or AS3 belongs to a particular foundational culture. One assessor of the patient's deliberation and decision belongs to a different foundational culture,

---

[5] One is inclined to add "legitimate" to the phrase "all social groupings," but doing so is disallowed because illiberal, since "legitimate" social groupings would only be those judged so from the perspective of one or another given culture – most likely a dominant one. On the other hand, it is clear that a multicultural society will not tolerate just *any* social grouping as one of its sanctioned components – for instance, pedophiles constitute a grouping. But it is unclear what the precise arguments for exclusion might look like.

[6] As mentioned in the previous note, it is obvious that no society will tolerate every value-defined group that may arise, but beyond pragmatic considerations, such as endangering the very survival of the society, it remains unclear what arguments might be marshaled to exclude particular value-defined groups.

and whereas the deliberator's foundational culture takes a relatively permissive stand on elective death, the assessor's foundational culture proscribes elective death of any sort – other than martyrdom in the service of the culture's values and doctrines. In the example, this cultural opposition on elective death is deemed sufficient to satisfy the rationality criterion's cross-cultural requirement by prompting productive reflection by the deliberator and one other assessor who is the deliberator's cultural peer.

The complication in the example is that the deliberator and the extracultural assessor are both members of the same *coincidental* culture, and it is a coincidental culture that puts a high priority on autonomy and independence and assigns a low priority to blighted survival. It is likely, then, that the deliberator and extracultural assessor's common coincidental cultural values will supersede or at least weaken the influence of the extracultural assessor's foundational cultural values. The result is that the reflection that cross-cultural assessment is intended to prompt may be inadequately prompted or not prompted at all. As a consequence, what appears to be cross-cultural assessment of the deliberator's reasoning and motivation is in effect *intra*cultural assessment. This means the deliberator's interest in survival may be underestimated, and that is exactly what the rationality criterion's requirement of cross-cultural assessment is designed to prevent.

The point of cross-cultural assessment, as stressed earlier, is to ensure that there is representation of diverse culturally determined perspectives on elective death. The objective is to prompt reflection on the values those perspectives presuppose to deter undue diminishment of elective-death deliberators' interests in survival. The concern, then, is that the new mix of foundational and coincidental cultures may obscure the degree of value-driven concurrence that can occur among assessors despite their being members of different foundational cultures. It seems clear, then, that the importance of coincidental cultures must not be underestimated.

Consider that educated and affluent North American Muslims, say, have more in common with educated and affluent North American Christians as *coincidental* cultural peers than either of them have with their respective but less fortunate *foundational* cultural peers. Affluent Christians and Muslims may share coincidental-culture values rooted in their common professions, up-scale neighborhoods, and expensive forms of recreation. These values in numerous ways and on numerous occasions may eclipse their foundational values rooted in their respective ethnicities, native languages, family structures, rearing, and religions. As a consequence, their assessments of someone's choice to die may coincide in ways at odds with their different foundational cultures' proscriptive or permissive positions on elective death.

The foundational and coincidental cultural mix may, of course, also result in unexpected *disagreement* as much as in unforeseen concurrence. Just as assessors from different foundational cultures but similar coincidental cultures may be unexpectedly in accord in their judgments, members of the same foundational culture but different coincidental cultures may be unexpectedly at odds in theirs.

$$* \quad * \quad *$$

It is of some importance that when agreements or disagreements occur between elective-death deliberators and assessors, as well as among assessors, they are likelier to be about motivation than about reasoning. Most individuals are more concerned with *why* someone intends to do something than with that person's reasoning about doing it. This is because the reasons why people do things more immediately involve values than does reasoning about doing those things, and so more directly coincide or conflict with others' values. Reasoning about anything presupposes motivation, and so operant values. As David Hume assured us, reason is neither autonomous nor primary; reason serves "the passions" or our desires.[7] Even when we solve puzzles purely for amusement, we reason to achieve something we want to do. Without desires we are not moved to reason. It is not surprising, then, that individuals' *reasons for* choosing to die are likelier to raise intra- and intercultural issues than is their *reasoning about* choosing to die.

The priority of motivation affects assessment of elective-death deliberation in a crucial way because assessment begins with how assessors of others' choices to die perceive those choices. For example,

---

[7] Hume, David. 1967. *A Treatise of Human Nature*. Ed. L. Selby-Bigge. Oxford: Clarendon Press, 415.

an assessor from one foundational or coincidental culture may see someone's choice to die as motivated by cowardice and desire to avoid a trial sent by God; another assessor from another culture and with different values may see the choice as motivated by heroic self-assertion in the face of devastating misfortune; a third assessor may see it as a precipitous move motivated by depression and lack of familial support; and a fourth may see it as the most advisable decision motivated by pragmatic recognition of the hopelessness of medical circumstances and prospects.

These different perceptions may impede the reflection that is supposed to be prompted by cross-cultural assessment of elective-death deliberation, both of assessors and of deliberators. The reason is that the differences among assessors from diverse foundational and/or coincidental cultures, in how they see someone's choice to die, may prompt retrenchment and defensiveness regarding values rather than reflection on those values.[8] Conflicts about the permissibility of elective death may be construed by some assessors as *challenges* to their values, and so as occasions for reaffirmation of allegiance to those values rather than occasions for reflective reconsideration of them.

This response to encounters with opposed views on elective death may affect individuals both accepting and rejecting the permissibility of elective death. As a result, their reaffirmation of their cultural values may be seen as dogmatic, narrow-minded, or intransigent, and those holding opposing values may become just as set in their positions. All of this hampers and may even prevent the called-for reflection on values influencing judgments in the assessment of someone's choice to die, and it may also hamper or prevent reflection by deliberators who may see their choices to die as simply dismissed by assessors committed to positions proscribing elective death.

Impediment of the reflection on values called for by the rationality criterion is worsened by the fact that at present the great majority of those called on to assess others' deliberations about elective death strongly incline to opposing any form of self-killing. The reality is that with few exceptions involving martyrdom, the preponderance of cultures and their organized religions proscribe elective death.

---

[8] My thanks to Mel Wiebe for his suggestion regarding this point.

Reasons for proscription run the gamut from doctrinal ones, such as the belief that life is God-given and so not ours to take; through attitudinal ones, such as perception of self-killing as cowardly; to more technical ones, such as construal of self-killing as psychologically pathological.

There is growing acceptance of elective death, perhaps especially among younger medical practitioners. Nonetheless, this change is proceeding slowly in the population as a whole and is mainly limited to progressive coincidental cultures and some liberal foundational subcultures. Most important, though, is that acceptance of elective death very much tends to be restricted to self-killing in extremis. That is, individuals' medical conditions have to be desperate and their projected survival time short before many find elective death permissible. This means that in many cases, particularly those involving slowly destructive terminal illnesses like ALS, by the time commission of SS2 or AS3 is deemed acceptable, it is too late from the perspective of patients wanting to die to avoid the personal devastation and degradation they are then forced to endure.

Admittedly, since what is at issue are people's lives, it is, on balance, better to err on the side of caution. Therefore, the fact that most judgments about the acceptability of elective death tend to be negative is a good thing to the extent that it protects individuals' interests in survival. It is, though, a bad thing to the extent that it causes prolongation of needless suffering for terminal patients. But the trouble is that even if we are willing to pay the cost of needless suffering for some patients to ensure the protection of all patients' interest in survival, we are not dealing with a stable situation. As populations grow and their members age, attitudes change and the tendency for judgments about elective death to be negative could change radically. This is Caplan's worry that too many people will begin to think that the old and sick should do "the responsible thing."[9]

Impediments to the required reflection on values influencing perceptions and judgments about elective death, and the ambiguities about operant values introduced by proliferation of foundational subcultures and coincidental cultures, are problems that no criterion for rationally choosing to die can resolve because no criterion can be

[9] Caplan 1996.

formulated in a way that anticipates them. These are problems that arise in the *application* of the criterion to individuals' choices to die; they are problems to do with the construal or interpretation of the criterion's requirements by those deliberating elective death and those assessing their deliberations. All that can be done is to provide the criterion – and thereby a rationale – for rationally choosing to die. The hopeful expectation is that as application of the criterion becomes established as a routine procedure, the impediments and ambiguities just discussed will be reduced to manageable proportions. Use of the criterion then will become a workable method for dealing with choices that more people are going to need to make as medicine's ability to sustain life increases and the personal, social, and financial costs of doing so escalate.

*   *   *

In conclusion, there is little doubt that given certain prospects and alternatives, choosing to die can be rational and actually advisable. Some situations are not to be borne even if at the cost of dying. This has been understood for as long as there have been living beings capable of anticipating their futures, but what is relatively new is the priority now given to rewarding life over mere survival: a priority that has lowered the threshold of what is deemed bearable for the sake of continued existence. Central to this change is that modern medicine's increasing ability to keep people alive often keeps them alive for far longer than is meaningful or even bearable for many. To some, this ability is a great boon; to others, it is a great burden. Certainly the ability has great promise to the extent that *worthwhile* life can be extended, but there will always be a point at which the benefits of survival will be overridden by its personal and other costs. The reality is that medicine's ability to sustain life has made it necessary for terminally ill patients – or in some cases their caretakers – to make *decisions* about how long to do so.

That patients are making decisions about how long to survive means that medical ethicists have been reluctantly pushed into the role of arbiters with respect to those decisions. Their work has expanded from dealing with issues about the ethics of *administering* treatment to dealing with issues about the ethics of *forgoing* treatment. More difficult still, their work has expanded from guarding against decisions that *endanger* life to evaluating decisions to *terminate* life.

There is a pressing need, then, for an articulated rationale for choosing to die and for a systematically applicable standard to assess the rationality and potential permissibility of elective death. Medical ethicists need a systematic method for dealing with patients' choices to die; they also need a systematic method for dealing with physicians and others involved with terminal patients who choose between meaningful *self*-determined death and meaningless and often degrading *other*-determined survival.

Of course, medical ethicists have dealt with patients choosing to die for as long as their profession has been in existence, as have chaplains, physicians, and others, so there are practices in place to deal with elective-death choices.[10] The trouble is that these practices are heterogeneous at least insofar as they are institution-related. Cultural and especially religious affiliations produce significant variations in how elective death is dealt with in different institutions. There is need for a basis on which to rationalize diverse practices. Provision of the rationality criterion is not intended necessarily to *replace* some present practices; it is intended to regularize how elective death is dealt with in the various hospitals, clinics, and hospices where terminal patients are treated and may choose to forgo treatment or more proactively end their lives.

---

[10] For the most part, the most common cases medical ethicists have had to and do deal with are not the focus of interest here; these are cases where patients have little or no say in decisions to terminate treatment, such as when physicians routinely make unofficially consulted or unilateral decisions about ceasing treatment for patients in hopeless circumstances. Mercifully or conveniently hastened death certainly is not new in medicine; "passive" euthanasia, in which the death of patients is effected by reducing, delaying, or omitting indicated treatment, is more common than most want to admit or believe. A high percentage of deaths in intensive care units (ICUs) are instances of passive euthanasia. The common procedure is to use medication that keeps patients "comfortable" but does not treat their afflictions or associated conditions, such as pneumonia. In my own experience I was told by a physician treating a close relative, who had broken a hip and suffered from Alzheimer's, that she would almost certainly contract pneumonia after the hip operation and that her doing so was "an opportunity" to refrain from treating the pneumonia, which he then described to me as "the old person's friend." Sometimes the main consideration is not the patient's situation; an ICU nurse admitted to me that treatment options sometimes are manipulated to ensure that patients do not die at particular times, say on Christmas Day, for the sake of family members.

Much of the point of the preceding chapters and the framing of the rationality criterion, then, is to systematize practices engaged in at present by medical ethicists by providing a foundational rationale and a universally applicable criterion for dealing with choices to die. Whatever may have been the case in the past, medical ethicists now need to deal effectively with patients who share few of their values, beliefs, attitudes, and perceptions regarding human life. It is no longer possible to rely on traditional case-centered training and experience because cases now vary too much. Nor is it viable to rely on institutional or personal cultural or religious principles because too many of those patients choosing to die have different cultural and religious values and beliefs.

What I offer medical ethicists to facilitate dealing with the new complexities is the rationality criterion with its reasoning and motivation clauses. As indicated, the criterion has two aspects: First, it effectively articulates the rationale for elective death by saying when PS1, SS2, AS3, and RE4 are rational and hence possibly permissible – barring particular moral or other proscriptions. Second, the criterion affords a cross-culturally applicable standard to assess choices to die because it *utilizes* cultural diversity to establish the rationality of elective death.

Admittedly, the criterion initially looks dauntingly demanding as a standard for rational elective death. That is why I have tried to show the ways in which some measure of latitude may be allowed in applying its two clauses in actual cases. To facilitate application of the criterion further, I have introduced the device of a *proxy premise* to deal with otherwise intractable value-determined beliefs held by those choosing to die, beliefs that jeopardize reasoning soundness or acceptability of motivation. Finally, I distinguish between *foundational* and *coincidental* cultures to help medical ethicists determine just what values most significantly influence elective-death deliberators' reasoning and motivation, as well as what values most condition assessors' perceptions and judgments regarding elective-death deliberations.

I close with a half-admonition, half-plea regarding appreciation of the importance of a theoretical basis for dealing with elective death. Recalling the points made earlier about coincidental cultures and Davidson's notion of a passing theory of interpretation, the importance of a theoretical basis can be illustrated by briefly considering potentially dangerous misunderstandings in assessments of terminal patients' choices to continue or forgo vital treatment.

There are two aspects to these misunderstandings: lack of concurrence on the nature and scope of operant *concepts* and lack of concurrence on the meaning and use of operant *terms*. Though distinguishable, these aspects are inseparable because lack of concurrence on the use of terms invariably reflects the application of either different or only partially comprehended concepts. With respect to terms, it cannot be assumed that standard dictionary definitions of key terms are being agreed with or are even known by all those participating in the assessments, and if terms are being used differently, it is virtually certain that dissimilar concepts are being applied.

Consider an example that recapitulates points made earlier: many think that the terms "rational" and "reasonable" have the same meaning and can be used interchangeably. Those who think this have an unclear idea of what the concepts of reasonableness and rationality encompass. In assessment of a terminal patient's choice to forgo further life-sustaining treatment, one assessor may believe that the patient's choice's being *reasonable* is the same as its being *rational*. But another assessor will understand that the two terms are not equivalent, despite common usage, because they apply to different concepts. The second assessor appreciates that while the patient's choice may be reasonable, given his or her circumstances, it may not be a rational choice.

For instance, the patient may firmly believe in an afterlife and be prepared to forgo treatment mainly because he or she is sure that dying guarantees not only escape from intolerable circumstances, but immediate entry into heaven. As considered in Chapter 4, beliefs of this sort undermine the soundness of elective-death decisions because they function as factual premises when they actually are unprovable beliefs. As considered in Chapter 8, there may be reason to allow latitude in applying the rationality criterion and to make allowances for soundness-jeopardizing beliefs. But if latitude is to be allowed, it is essential that those assessing the patient's decision to forgo life-sustaining treatment understand that what is at issue is easing the *rationality* requirements in light of the circumstantial *reasonableness* of the patient's choice.

If this example seems too abstract, consider another case in which a patient chooses to continue life-sustaining treatment against the advice of physicians and counselors. In this case there may be lack of concurrence among assessors on the meaning of the term "competent," and so on the use of the concept of *competence* – specifically competence to make decisions about treatment options.

The notion of "psychological deafness" is used by those counseling terminal patients.[11] Psychological deafness is an unwillingness to accept bad news, a rationalizing away of what one does not want to hear. Denial of this kind seriously impedes patients' making sound decisions about treatment options. In this second example, the patient is given a dire prognosis and told that to continue life-sustaining treatment will serve only to extend a quickly worsening and increasingly punishing level of survival. But the prognosis and advice fall on psychologically deaf ears and the patient chooses to continue treatment.

One assessor of the patient's decision may have a strict understanding of the concept of competence and take it that as long as the patient is *compos mentis* and is informed of her or his prognosis, the patient's decision to continue treatment must be accepted. A second assessor may understand the concept of competence more inclusively, despite using the term in a way not obviously different from the first assessor's use. The second assessor may not judge the patient competent to choose continuation of treatment because of recognition that the patient refuses to accept his or her prognosis and the frightful nature of ensuing survival. The second assessor, then, is prepared to override the patient's decision. This lack of concurrence on the concept of competence hampers assessors' reaching a cogent conclusion about whether to accept or override the patient's decision.

The trouble is that it is highly inefficient, if not practically impossible, to establish concurrence on key terms and operant concepts as particular cases arise.[12] A theoretical basis will not of itself resolve concurrence issues, but it does two things that are vital

---

[11] My thanks to Sandy Taylor for making this point.
[12] My thanks to Jonathan Wouk for making this point.

to assessment of elective-death decisions. First, it facilitates alertness to how terms are being used and what concepts are being applied by providing a common standard and thereby enables establishment of concurrence. Second, and most importantly, a theoretical basis ensures *consistency* in assessment of elective-death decisions.

Works Cited

Audi, Robert, ed. 1995. *The Cambridge Dictionary of Philosophy*. Cambridge: Cambridge University Press.

Barry, Brian. 2001. *Culture and Equality*. Cambridge, Mass.: Harvard University Press.

Battin, Margaret Pabst. 1982. *Ethical Issues in Suicide*. Englewood Cliffs, N.J.: Prentice-Hall

1984. "The Concept of Rational Suicide." In Edwin Shneidman, ed., *Death: Current Perspectives*, 3rd edition. Mountain View, Calif.: Mayfield, 297–320. (Note: Battin's article does not appear in the 1995 4th edition.).

1990. *Ethics in the Sanctuary: Examining the Practices of Organized Religion*. New Haven, Conn.: Yale University Press.

Beauchamp, Tom L. 1980. "Suicide." In Tom Regan, ed., *Matters of Life and Death*. Philadelphia: Temple University Press.

Benhabib, Seyla. 2004. *The Rights of Others*. Cambridge: Cambridge University Press.

Bergman, Brian. 1998. "The Final Hours: Does a Doctor Have a Right to End a Patient's Life?" *Maclean's*, March 9.

Brock, Dan. 1989. "Death and Dying." In *Life and Death: Philosophical Essays in Biomedical Ethics*. Cambridge: Cambridge University Press, 144–183.

Bullock A., O. Stallybrass, and S. Trombley, eds. 1988. *The Fontana Dictionary of Modern Thought*. London: Fontana.

Caplan, Arthur. 1996. Interview on "The Kevorkian Verdict"; includes interview with Timothy Quill, courtroom coverage, and film of Kevorkian and individuals he assisted in committing suicide. *Frontline*, Public Broadcasting System (WGBH, Boston), May 14.

Choron, Jacques. 1972. *Suicide*. New York: Scribner's.

Davidson, Donald. 1986. "A Nice Derangement of Epitaphs." In Ernest LePore, ed., *Truth and Interpretation*. Oxford: Blackwell's.

Derrida, Jacques. 1976. *Of Grammatology*. Trans. G. C. Spivak. Baltimore: Johns Hopkins University Press.

Donnelly, John. 1978. *Language, Metaphysics, and Death*. New York: Fordham University Press.

Foucault, Michel. 1988. "Critical Theory/Intellectual History." In Lawrence D. Kritzman, ed., *Michel Foucault: Politics, Philosophy, Culture: Interviews and Other Writings, 1977–1984*. New York and London: Routledge, 17–46.

Gutmann, Amy, and Dennis Thompson. 1996. *Democracy and Disagreement*. Cambridge, Mass.: Harvard University Press.

Habermas, Jürgen. 1998. "The European Nation-State: On the Past and Future of Sovereignty and Citizenship." In Jürgen Habermas, Ciaran Cronin, and Pablo De Greiff, eds., *The Inclusion of the Other: Studies in Political Theory*. Cambridge, Mass.: MIT Press.

Honderich, Ted, ed. 1995. *The Oxford Companion to Philosophy*. Oxford: Oxford University Press.

Hume, David. 1967. *A Treatise of Human Nature*. Ed. L. Selby-Bigge. Oxford: Clarendon Press.

Humphry, Derek. 1992a. *Final Exit: The Practicalities of Self-Deliverance and Assisted Suicide for the Dying*. New York: Dell

1992b. "The Last Choice." *Hemlock Quarterly*, October.

Krausz, Michael. 1989. *Relativism: Interpretation and Confrontation*. Notre Dame, Ind.: Notre Dame University Press.

Macedo, Stephen, ed. 1999. *Deliberative Politics: Essays on Democracy and Disagreement*. New York: Oxford University Press.

Mautner, Thomas, ed. 2005. *Dictionary of Philosophy*, 2nd edition. London: Penguin Books.

Mullens, Anne. 1996. *Timely Death: Considering Our Last Rights*. New York: Alfred A Knopf.

Munro, Daniel. "Deliberative Citizenship in Multicultural Democracies," forthcoming.

Nehamas, Alexander. 1985. *Nietzsche: Life as Literature*. Cambridge, Mass.: Harvard University Press.

Nietzsche, Friedrich Wilhelm. 1968. *The Will to Power*. Ed. Walter Kaufman and trans. W. Kaufman and R. J. Hollingdale. New York: Vintage Books.

Pascal, Blaise. 1941. *Pensées*. Trans. W. F. Trotter. New York: Modern Library.

Prado C. G. 1990. *The Last Choice: Preemptive Suicide in Advanced Age*. New York and Westport, Conn.: Greenwood Group.

1998. *The Last Choice: Preemptive Suicide in Advanced Age*, 2nd edition. New York and Westport, Conn.: Greenwood and Praeger Presses.

2000a. "Ambiguity and Synergism in 'Assisted Suicide.'" In Prado 2000b.

2000b, ed. *Assisted Suicide: Canadian Perspectives*. Ottawa: University of Ottawa Press, 43–66.

2000c. *Starting with Foucault: An Introduction to Genealogy*, 2nd edition. Boulder, Colo., and New York: Westview Press (Perseus Books).

2003. "Foucauldian Ethics and Elective Death." *Journal of Medical Humanities*, 24(3/4): 203–211.

2006. *Searle and Foucault on Truth*. Cambridge: Cambridge University Press.

Prado, C. G., and Lawrie McFarlane. 2002. *The Best Laid Plans: Health Care's Problems and Prospects*. Montreal: McGill-Queen's University Press.

Prado, C. G., and S. J. Taylor. 1999. *Assisted Suicide: Theory and Practice in Elective Death*. Amherst, N.Y.: Humanity Books (Prometheus Press).

Purdum, Todd. 1997. "Tapes Left by 39 in Cult Suicide Suggest Comet Was Sign to Die." *New York Times*, March 28.

Quill, Timothy. 1996. *A Midwife Through the Dying Process: Stories of Healing and Hard Choices at the End of Life*. Baltimore and London: Johns Hopkins University Press.

2001. *Caring for Patients at the End of Life: Facing an Uncertain Future Together*. New York: Oxford University Press.

Ramberg, Bjørn. 1989. *Donald Davidson's Philosophy of Language: An Introduction*. Oxford: Blackwell's.

Rhem, James. 2006. "Responding to 'Student Relativism.'" *The National Teaching and Learning Forum*, 15 (May 4): 1, 2, 4.

Rorty, Richard. 1992. "A Pragmatist View of Rationality and Cultural Difference." *Philosophy East and West*, 42(4): 581–596.

Searle, John. 1992. *The Rediscovery of the Mind*. Cambridge, Mass.: A Bradford Book, MIT Press.

1995. *The Construction of Social Reality*. New York: The Free Press.

1999. *Mind, Language and Society*. London: Phoenix.

Williams, Bernard. 1998. "The End of Explanation." Review of Thomas Nagel, 1997, *The Last Word*, New York: Oxford University Press. *The New York Review of Books*, 45(18): 40–44.

Index